WILLIE MAYS

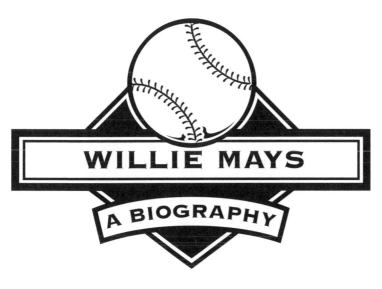

WILLIE MAYS
A BIOGRAPHY

MARY KAY LINGE

BASEBALL'S ALL-TIME GREATEST HITTERS

GREENWOOD PRESS
WESTPORT, CONNECTICUT • LONDON

Library of Congress Cataloging-in-Publication Data

Linge, Mary Kay.
   Willie Mays : a biography / Mary Kay Linge.
       p.   cm.—(Baseball's all-time greatest hitters)
   Includes bibliographical references and index.
   ISBN 0–313–33401–3 (alk. paper)
   1. Mays, Willie, 1931– 2. Baseball players—United States—Biography. I. Title.
II. Series.
   GV865.M38L47 2005
   796.357′092—dc22   2005017408

British Library Cataloguing in Publication Data is available.

Library of Congress Catalog Card Number: 2005017408
ISBN: 0–313–33401–3

First published in 2005

Greenwood Press, 88 Post Road West, Westport, CT 06881
An imprint of Greenwood Publishing Group, Inc.
www.greenwood.com

Printed in the United States of America

The paper used in this book complies with the
Permanent Paper Standard issued by the National
Information Standards Organization (Z39.48–1984).

10 9 8 7 6 5 4 3 2 1

FOR TOM, WHO, ALWAYS, HAS GOTTA BELIEVE

CONTENTS

Contents

SERIES FOREWORD

The volumes in Greenwood's "Baseball's All-Time Greatest Hitters" series present the life stories of the players who, through their abilities to hit for average, for power, or for both, most helped their teams at the plate. Much thought was given to the players selected for inclusion in this series. In some cases, the selection of certain players was a given. **Ty Cobb**, **Rogers Hornsby**, and **Joe Jackson** hold the three highest career averages in baseball history: .367, .358, and .356, respectively. **Babe Ruth**, who single-handedly brought the sport out of its "dead ball" era and transformed baseball into a home-run hitters game, hit 714 home runs (a record that stood until 1974) while also hitting .342 over his career. **Lou Gehrig**, now known primarily as the man whose consecutive-games record Cal Ripken Jr. broke in 1995, hit .340 and knocked in more than 100 runs eleven seasons in a row, totaling 1,995 before his career was cut short by ALS. **Ted Williams**, the last man in either league to hit .400 or better in a season (.406 in 1941), is widely regarded as possibly the best hitter ever, a man whose fanatical dedication raised hitting to the level of both science and art.

Two players set career records that, for many, define the art of hitting. **Hank Aaron** set career records for home runs (755) and RBIs (2,297). He also maintained a .305 career average over twenty-three seasons, a remarkable feat for someone primarily known as a home-run hitter. **Pete Rose** had ten seasons with 200 or more hits and won three batting titles on his way to establishing his famous record of 4,256 career hits. Some critics have claimed that both players' records rest more on longevity than excellence. To that I would say there is something to be said about longevity and, in both cases, the player's excellence was the reason why he had the opportunity to keep playing, to keep tallying hits for his team. A base hit is the mark of a successful plate appearance; a home run is the apex of an at-bat. Accordingly, we could hardly have a series titled "Baseball's All-Time Greatest Hitters" without including the two men who set the career records in these categories.

Joe DiMaggio holds another famous mark: fifty-six consecutive games in which he obtained a base hit. Many have called this baseball's most unbreakable record. (The player who most closely approached that mark was Pete Rose, who hit safely in forty-four consecutive games in 1978.) In his thirteen seasons, DiMaggio hit .325 with 361 home runs and 1,537 RBIs. This means he *averaged* 28 home runs and 118 RBIs per season. MVPs have been awarded to sluggers in various years with lesser stats than what DiMaggio achieved in an "average" season.

Because **Stan Musial** played his entire career with the Cardinals in St. Louis— once considered the western frontier of the baseball world in the days before baseball came to California—he did not receive the press of a DiMaggio. But Musial compiled a career average of .331, with 3,630 hits (ranking fourth all time) and 1,951 RBIs (fifth all time). His hitting prowess was so respected around the league that Brooklyn Dodgers fans once dubbed him "The Man," a nickname he still carries today.

Willie Mays was a player who made his fame in New York City and then helped usher baseball into the modern era when he moved with the Giants to San Francisco. Mays did everything well and with flair. His over-the-shoulder catch in the 1954 World Series was perhaps his most famous moment, but his hitting was how Mays most tormented his opponents. Over twenty-two seasons the "Say Hey Kid" hit .302 and belted 660 home runs.

Only four players have reached the 600-home-run milestone: Mays, Aaron, Ruth, and **Barry Bonds**, who achieved that feat in 2002. Bonds, the only active player included in this series, broke the single-season home-run record when he smashed 73 for the San Francisco Giants in 2001. In the 2002 National League Championship Series, St. Louis Cardinals pitchers were so leery of pitching to him that they walked him ten times in twenty-one plate appearances. In the World Series, the Anaheim Angels walked him thirteen times in thirty appearances. He finished the Series with a .471 batting average, an on-base percentage of .700, and a slugging percentage of 1.294.

As with most rankings, this series omits some great names. Jimmie Foxx, Tris Speaker, and Tony Gwynn would have battled for a hypothetical thirteenth volume. And it should be noted that this series focuses on players and their performance within Major League Baseball; otherwise, sluggers such as Josh Gibson from the Negro Leagues and Japan's Sadaharu Oh would have merited consideration.

There are names such as Cap Anson, Ed Delahanty, and Billy Hamilton who appear high up on the list of career batting average. However, a number of these players played during the late 1800s, when the rules of baseball were drastically different. For example, pitchers were not allowed to throw overhand until 1883, and foul balls weren't counted as strikes until 1901 (1903 in the American League). Such players as Anson and company undeniably were the stars of their day, but baseball has evolved greatly since then, into a game in which hitters must now cope with night games, relief pitchers, and split-fingered fastballs.

Ultimately, a list of the "greatest" anything is somewhat subjective, but Greenwood offers these players as twelve of the finest examples of hitters throughout history. Each volume focuses primarily on the playing career of the subject: his early years in school, his years in semi-pro and/or minor league baseball, his entrance into the majors, and his ascension to the status of a legendary hitter. But even with the greatest of players, baseball is only part of the story, so the player's life before and after baseball is given significant consideration. And because no one can exist in a vacuum, the authors often take care to recreate the cultural and historical contexts of the time—an approach that is especially relevant to the multidisciplinary ways in which sports are studied today.

Batter up.

ROB KIRKPATRICK
GREENWOOD PUBLISHING

ACKNOWLEDGMENTS

This book would not have been possible without the boundless resources of the New York Public Library. I am especially grateful for the patient assistance of the staff of the Stapleton Branch, the St. George Branch, and the Periodicals Room. Laura Caldwell Anderson of the Birmingham Civil Rights Institute and Ann Hobbs of the *Birmingham News* helped uncover key facts about Mays' family history. Thanks also to Patricia M. LaPointe of the Memphis/Shelby County Public Library, Claus Guglberger of the *New York Daily News* Archive, and Bill Burdick of the National Baseball Hall of Fame Library for their help in gathering images. Kevin Ohe of Greenwood Press got the ball rolling; the guidance and support of Steven Vetrano and John Wagner were instrumental. Finally, thanks to Xavier, who was there for every word.

Chronology

1931   Willie Mays is born in Westfield, Alabama, on May 6.

1946–   The teenage Mays plays occasionally for the local industrial league
1947   team and for the semipro Fairfield Gray Sox.

1948   Mays joins the Birmingham Black Barons while attending high school. He plays center field in the last-ever Negro Leagues World Series, which Birmingham loses to the Homestead Grays.

1950   Mays signs a contract with the New York Giants. He plays a season of B-level minor league ball with the Trenton Giants, integrating the Interstate League.

1951   Mays begins the season with the AAA Minneapolis Millers, hitting .477. Called up to the New York Giants in May, he sparks the team in a pennant drive that ends with Bobby Thomson's "Shot Heard 'Round the World" and a dramatic playoff win against the Brooklyn Dodgers. The Giants lose the World Series to the Yankees. Mays is named Rookie of the Year.

1952–   Drafted, Mays serves stateside in the U.S. Army.
1953

1954   Mays returns to the Giants and leads the team to a dominant season; his .345 average wins him the batting title on the last day of the season. The Giants sweep the Cleveland Indians in the World Series, which is highlighted by Mays's spectacular catch in Game 1. Mays is named the National League MVP.

1955   Mays leads the league with 51 home runs.

1956   A week before spring training begins, Mays marries Marghuerite Wendell Kennedy Chapman. He leads the league with 40 stolen bases; with 36 homers on the season, he establishes the "30–30 Club."

1958   The Giants move to San Francisco; Mays hits .347, the highest average of his career, finishing second in the league.

1959   Willie and Marghuerite Mays adopt a baby boy, Michael.

1960   The Giants play their first season at Candlestick Park.

1961   Mays hits four home runs in one game and leads the league with 129 runs scored.

1962   Willie and Marghuerite Mays divorce. Mays hits 49 home runs to lead the league, but is hospitalized for exhaustion. A tied season forces the Giants into another pennant playoff with the Dodgers; San Francisco wins, but loses the World Series to the Yankees in seven games.

1963   Mays hits his 400th career homer.

1964   Mays is named team captain of the Giants. He leads the league with 47 home runs.

1965   With 17 home runs in August, Mays sets the National League record for most homers in a single month; his 52 home runs on the season are Mays's career high and lead the league. Mays hits his 500th career home run and is voted National League MVP.

1966   Mays hits 37 home runs on the season, surpassing Mel Ott, Ted Williams, and Jimmie Foxx on the all-time leader list. He is now second only to Babe Ruth.

1968   Mays wins the last of 12 consecutive Gold Glove awards and is named MVP of the All-Star Game.

1969   Mays hits his 600th career home run.

1970   Mays is named Player of the Decade for the 1960s by *The Sporting News*, following Stan Musial and Ted Williams.

1971   Mays marries Mae Louise Allen.

1972 The Giants trade Mays to the New York Mets. Hank Aaron betters Mays' lifetime home run total, placing Mays third on the all-time list.

1973 Mays announces his retirement, then remains with the Mets as they improbably win the National League pennant; the team loses a seven-game World Series to the Oakland A's.

1979 In his first year of eligibility, Mays is elected to the Baseball Hall of Fame with 94.6 percent of the vote. Shortly thereafter, he takes a public relations job with a casino and is banned from baseball.

1985 Mays is reinstated by a new baseball commissioner and rejoins the Giants organization as an instructor and club representative.

1993 Mays' godson Barry Bonds signs with the Giants as a free agent; Mays mentors Bonds as he pursues a successful—and controversial—career.

2004 Bonds passes Mays on the lifetime home run list; Mays is now in fourth place.

INTRODUCTION

It's the top of the eighth in the big game, the score is tied, and the visiting team has two men on base with only one out. At second, a runner is poised to bring the go-ahead run home. At the plate stands a slugger of fearsome reputation.

The pitcher winds up and releases the ball, and the home crowd holds its breath. The batter swings, connects. The ball rockets out to the deepest reaches of center field—extra bases for sure. The visiting fans in attendance, and there are many of them, roar their approval—their team is about to pull ahead.

But far out in center, a fielder streaks to the wall. He shows no hesitation as the barrier looms. Back he goes—back still farther—sprinting all out. Still in motion, still facing the wall, as if he can sense the ball's trajectory without having to see it, he reaches his left hand just above shoulder height. Neatly, he snatches the ball out of the air and into baseball history.

The batter is out, but the fielder's work is not done. The runners can still score on a fly so deeply hit. He whirls about—was he still in midair? The spectators cannot tell, the move is so quick. Corkscrewing, he hurls the ball back to the infield, with an unerring sense of the runners' movements. His cap flies off as he twists right down to the ground with the force of his action. But the throw is true, a 400-foot strike to second base. The runners are forced to hold at first and third. No one scores.

The home team survives the inning unscathed; the visitors go on to lose the game—and the World Series, too.

"I don't see how Willie did it, but he's been doing it all year," the play-by-play announcer tells the audience watching at home.

They call it "The Catch," the signature play of the 1954 World Series, and baseball fans to this day revere it. But the man at the center of it all downplayed the achievement. "It's not my best play," he has always insisted.

Willie Mays is a Baseball Hall of Famer par excellence. The quintessential "five-tool player," he came to the major leagues in 1951 with the ability to do it all—run, throw, field, hit, and hit for power. That he did it with such exuberant athleticism was easy for fans to see. He got less credit for his intense knowledge of the game, or for his keen understanding of its hidden patterns. Later analysts saw racism at work in the popular image of Mays as a "natural talent," and no doubt the racial attitudes prevalent in the 1950s shaped those early perceptions. Mays himself, though, believed that it was his youth, not his race, that gave rise to his image as a stickball-playing overgrown kid. He was, after all, only 20 when he came to the majors. And he *did* play stickball. (Good for the hand-eye coordination, he would say.)

Mays' career bridged several eras in baseball history. He was one of the earliest of the game's African American superstars, and one of the last major leaguers to have played in the segregated Negro Leagues. He was a pioneer of baseball's cross-country expansion, moving with his New York Giants to San Francisco in 1958. And, in his final seasons before retirement, his quiet support of his fellow players in the strike of 1972 had a part in ending the reserve clause and bringing free agency to the game.

Through his 22 seasons in baseball, Mays played with a dramatic flair that made it difficult for fans to tear their eyes away from him—at any moment he might do some new remarkable thing. He was a study in perpetual motion. In the outfield, he'd often break on a ball before it was hit, just based on the pitch that was coming and his knowledge of the batter's tendencies. At the plate, he bobbed and weaved out of the way of inside pitches, often sprawling theatrically into the dirt, but rarely being drilled or losing his composure. On the bases, he teased and distracted the opposition. When he turned up the speed for a steal or to gain an extra base on a play, his cap would whip off his head as if he had run right out from under it.

Mays and his flying cap are so paired in the popular memory that physics discussions have centered on the phenomenon (velocity + wind resistance = flying cap). Mays himself has sometimes claimed that it was a deliberate strategy. In one of his memoirs, he said, "I started thinking about what I could do to give the fans a show, generate a little more excitement. So I came up with a gimmick: I started wearing a cap that was too big for me." There was a strategic benefit, too; when Mays lost the cap after stealing a base, he'd have to take a little time to dust himself off, walk back, and retrieve his headgear. "The moment's delay would keep the fans worked up and make the opposing pitcher think a bit more about the spot I'd got him in, which was fine by me."[1] His other dramatic trademark, the basket catch, had a similar dual purpose; its daring gave the fans some extra thrills, and its positioning put Mays' hands where they needed to be so he could get off an extra-quick throw.

It was the thought he gave to details like these, combined with his great abilities, that made Mays a player for the ages. He'd strike out on purpose early in the game to trick the pitcher into feeding him the same pitch later, when it mattered. He'd get on base and in minutes nail the other team's signs. "You would see games where he would win it for us and he wouldn't even get a hit," Giants teammate Willie McCovey has said. "He did things that nobody else does."[2]

The stats don't tell the full story of Willie Mays, but they are telling: 660 home runs, .302 lifetime batting average, .557 slugging average, the first 30–30 man in baseball history, with more than 30 homers and 30 stolen bases in a single season. The awards don't tell the full story either, but they indicate the opinion of his contemporaries: Rookie of the Year, two Most Valuable Player awards, 12 Gold Gloves.

It's often been posited that Mays' lifetime statistics would have been even more impressive if his home field had been anywhere but San Francisco's Candlestick Park, where right-handed batters had to hit into a vicious headwind. In fact, the numbers point to another of Mays' hidden skills. Even with 12 of his 22 years in Candlestick, his home runs are almost evenly divided between home and away games, like most other sluggers on the lifetime leader list. After struggling with Candlestick's conditions in the first year the Giants played there, Mays used his great adaptability to excel there anyway. At home, he altered his swing, inside-outing the ball into the right-field stands. On the road, he'd pull the ball to left. Mays' ability to adjust to changing conditions (unlike, for example, Joe DiMaggio, who never learned to take advantage of Yankee Stadium's short right-field porch) is more significant, in terms of his all-around skill, than any speculative homer total.

Mays' single World Series ring is no indicator of his talent, or even of the talent of his teams; his San Francisco Giants won more games than any other ballclub in the 1960s, but they had only one pennant to show for it. To Mays, that was a source of constant frustration. None of his individual achievements mattered to him as much as winning did.

To Mays, passing that desire along to the next generation became paramount in the final years of his career and in his retirement. Mentors and role models had had a critical place in his life, from his ballplayer father to his managers Piper Davis and Leo Durocher. When he was traded to the New York Mets in 1972, Mays was shocked and saddened to have to leave the Giants after two decades with the team, but he took solace in the way the young players on his new team looked to him as an icon. "He had instincts and insights into the game that far out-stripped anybody we had on the ballclub," remembered Mets pitcher Jon Matlack, who was 22 at the time. "I was thrilled to call him a team-mate."[3] After retirement, some coaching jobs gave him more opportunities to teach.

But it was his mentorship of Barry Bonds, Mays' godson, that finally fulfilled his longing to hand on a baseball legacy. Mays and Bonds had a relationship reaching all the way back to the late 1960s, when Bonds was four or five years old. When the younger man came to the San Francisco Giants in 1993, he and Mays grew closer. Mays cheered Bonds on as he caught up with, then surpassed, Mays' home-run records. He was a stalwart supporter as Bonds was accused of steroid use, telling reporters that Bonds' achievements were not diminished even if the accusations were true.

If nothing else, the Bonds controversy served to remind baseball fans of Mays' own career. Without weight rooms or training programs, without supplements or injections, Mays brought power, speed, smarts, and his own brand of energy to the game. Whatever numbers they may put up, those who come after him will still be following Willie Mays.

NOTES

1. Willie Mays, with Lou Sahadi, *Say Hey: The Autobiography of Willie Mays* (New York: Simon and Schuster, 1988), 5.
2. Mark Emmons, "In These Days of Bloated Stats, Mays's Greatness Still Stands Out," *San Jose Mercury News*, September 18, 2003.
3. Paul Post and Ed Lucas, "Turn Back the Clock," *Baseball Digest*, March 2003.

CHILDHOOD

Westfield, Alabama, a steel-mill town just outside Birmingham, was hard hit by the Great Depression in the early 1930s. Then again, so was every other town and city in the nation, as farms failed and unemployment rates rose. Work was erratic, and people grabbed what jobs they could. Families expanded as extended relatives, friends, and neighbors banded together to care for each other's children, share each other's food, and help each other through hardship.

Those hardships were many, and not only because of the poor economy. Here in the deepest of the Deep South, people lived under a racism that was so pervasive it was rarely challenged or even questioned. Blacks and whites lived side by side, but in parallel worlds: separate schools, separate businesses, separate churches, separate seating areas in public places, all the way down to separate water fountains.

This was the world into which Willie Mays was born on May 6, 1931.[1] His 18-year-old parents, Ann Satterwhite and William Howard Mays, were members of a black working-class community that, in this age of segregation, relied on one another to get by.

Race, class, and geography might have placed terrible constraints on his future, but Willie was born with a gift—an athleticism that came from both sides of his family. Ann had been a track star as a schoolgirl. Willie Sr. was a semi-professional baseball player, an outfielder with his steel mill's company team whose own father, Walter Mays, had been a well-known semi-pro pitcher.

Willie Sr.—known as "Cat" or "Kitty Kat" for the speed and grace with which he'd pounce on a baseball in the field—saw his son's potential early on. He began to develop the baby's baseball skills before he could walk. "Getting a base-ball was just about the first thing I was able to do," Mays remembered years later.[2] As soon as his baby son learned to stand, Cat Mays would show the child a baseball, place it on the seat of a chair, prop Willie up at another chair a few feet away, and encourage him to venture out the step or two to reach the ball. In later years, whenever he was asked where he first started playing baseball, Mays's stock response would be, "In the living room."[3]

Baseball was the thread that bound their relationship. In their early "batting lessons," Cat Mays would hand his son a rubber ball and a small stick, and the child would "play with the ball all day long, hitting it with the stick, then crawl-ing or toddling after it across the room."[4]

As he happily crawled, then walked, then ran after baseballs at home, the tod-dler Willie might not have been aware that his parents' marriage was failing. His father worked mainly as a railroad porter on the Birmingham-to-Detroit line, a job that kept him away from home for days at a time. The young couple began to drift apart. When police caught Ann selling the illegal alcohol known as moonshine, Willie Sr. took the fall for it. He spent a night in jail while his wife stayed home with their son.[5] As a man who disapproved of drinking, perhaps this was enough to end their marriage.

Soon after, Ann left her husband and son, although she remained nearby in Westfield and maintained a relationship with her eldest child. She bore a baby with her second husband, Frank McMorris, when Willie was no more than three.[6]

The loss of his mother could have been a shattering experience for Willie, but the strength of his extended family came to the little boy's aid. The Satterwhite's were in crisis too; the death of Ann's mother had left her younger sisters, Willie's aunts, orphans. Sarah and Ernestine Satterwhite were barely teenagers at that time. They needed a home; Willie needed care. "My father moved the girls in with us to help raise me," Mays related years later.[7] Aunt Sarah and Aunt Ernes-tine did raise the boy, providing a home for him and for a shifting array of sib-lings, half-siblings, cousins, and neighbors.

Money was tight all through Willie's childhood, but Aunt Sarah and Aunt Ernestine worked hard to keep him happy and well nourished. Their home gar-den was a mainstay of the household. The flowers they grew in front of the house were the pride of the neighborhood; out back they raised beans, squash, tomatoes, corn, and other fruits and vegetables that the family ate all year round, fresh or home-canned.[8] As Willie grew older, he would participate, too, in put-ting food on the family table. The aunts' home-baked bread was enjoyed with the fresh butter that Willie brought home as payment for his share in caring for a neighbor's cow.

2

Within a few years, Cat Mays gave up his railroad-porter job for other work closer to home, mainly in the local TC&I steel mill. One of his coworkers there became a permanent member of the household. "Uncle" Otis Brooks took on much of the heavy work of the house, from chopping wood for the stove to tidying the yard.

"I don't recall that we had any suffering," Mays said later. "As far as I remember, my dad always had work."[9] It was far from a privileged childhood, but Mays never believed it to be a hard or unhappy one.

The family lived in company-owned housing in Westfield for Willie's youngest years, but his father's dream was to own a home of his own. The steel mill paid its workers in company "scrip," credits that could be used to pay rent on a company house or to buy food and clothing at the company store. To buy his own house, Cat Mays had to earn money in other ways. He had put away some of his railroad-porter earnings already. The rest, he made playing baseball.

Birmingham's Industrial League was made up of teams from the various mills and factories in and around the city. Its games could draw up to six thousand fans at a time. Admission was free—a major attraction—but according to tradition, fans would "pass the hat" through the stands to collect money for the ballplayers. When the teams divided up the take, their members might bring home $10 or $12 for each game, and sometimes more if the fans had been numerous or enthusiastic enough.

When he was as young as five or six, Willie would sit on the players' bench at his father's games, soaking up baseball knowledge and lore. Like baseball men everywhere, they called the kid by a nickname. Willie's was "Buckduck" or, simply, "Buck," which the game's insiders would use for the next 30 years and more. None of them knew the origins of the name, but Aunt Ernestine did. "Buckduck" evolved from a family nickname, "Duck-butt." "He always had a high behind," Ernestine recalled fondly.[10]

He'd put what he learned into practice with kids his own age in pickup games wherever there was enough space to play. There was no organized baseball for young people in Westfield then—no Little League, Pony League, or other officially sanctioned, adult-run version of the game. Kids would just gather in an empty lot or a quiet street with a bat and a ball and their gloves (if they were lucky enough to have gloves) and play. In later life, Mays always maintained that this was a better way to learn the game, if only because unorganized sandlot players get a lot more playing time than Little Leaguers do. One plays on a child's schedule, which is to say practically any afternoon he wants to. The other only plays when the adults can manage it.

When Willie was 10, his father realized his dream. He bought a house in nearby Fairfield, Alabama, and moved the entire extended family into it. Aunt

Sarah continued to keep the house neat and clean, with help from Aunt Ernestine, who also worked as a waitress to add to the family income. She would often leave lunch money for Willie on his dresser late at night when her shift was done. When school let out for the midday meal, Willie, in turn, would buy the makings of a meal—"lunch meat, a couple of big loaves of bread, tomatoes, mayonnaise, and some cake"—and share it with a group of friends. "We shared all we had," he put it simply, in the knowledge that someone else would provide another day.[11]

In his new Fairfield neighborhood waited a new friend, Charley Willis. Willie and Charley shared a passion for comic books and a love of baseball that drew them out to the sandlot every day they could. With his strong arm and his knowledge of the game, Willie usually pitched, and Charlie was his catcher. As they walked to and from Robinson Elementary School together, they'd bounce a pink rubber ball back and forth between them.[12] Soon they were known as well for their skill at "playing peach." That was when a boy would sneak into one of Fairfield's many peach orchards and hurl ripe fruit over the fence to his waiting friends.[13] "I'd fill up a big bag in no time," Mays remembered.

It was Charley who first pegged Willie as a center fielder, the identity for which he would one day become famous. That first summer of their friendship, 1941, was a banner year for baseball: it was the year of The Streak, Joe DiMaggio's still-unequaled feat of hitting safely in 56 consecutive games.

Baseball fans across the country were enraptured by the Yankee Clipper's performance, and none more than a 10-year-old Alabama boy with baseball in his blood. As the streak continued, Willie would listen for news of DiMaggio's latest feats on Aunt Sarah's big console radio, a large box with a cloth front that covered the speaker and a hinged top that hid the controls. The memory of those days—of himself as a skinny kid by a big radio, straining his ears to root for a long-distance hero—remained with Mays for a long time to come.[14] Suddenly, he knew what he wanted to do and to be.

One day that summer, as he and Charley headed out to play ball, he said it out loud: "Call me DiMag."

"That means you got to play center field," his friend said dubiously.

"I don't care about center field. Just so long as I hit like him."[15]

So DiMag it was, at least among the kids who gathered to play ball in Fairfield's empty lots. Although children of different races were strictly segregated in the local schools, they made no such formal restrictions in the sandlots. "It didn't matter to me whether I played with white kids or black," Mays said later. "We thought nothing of it, neither the blacks nor the whites. It was the grownups who got upset. If they saw black kids playing on the same team with white kids, they'd call the cops, and the cops would make us stop."[16]

His son's passion did not escape the notice of Cat Mays, whose philosophy had always been to encourage a child's interests but never to force them. One day that summer, Mays spotted his boy, alone in an empty lot, running the bases in an imaginary game. It was obvious that the kid knew and loved the basics of the game—hitting, running, throwing, catching. The time had come for some real baseball instruction.

"Now, lots of things come natural in baseball," Cat Mays explained in their first training session. "Some things, you got to practice on more than others. 'Picking it up,' you can never practice that enough."[17] So began the first of many hours of father-and-son pepper games. Standing about 15 feet apart, the boy would pitch and the man would hit the ball back, over and over again. Cat would vary his hits—a pop-up, a chop, a liner, a bunt—and Willie would have to adjust, instantly, to field whatever came his way as his father shouted advice and encouragement. "Pick it up! You're dug in like a potato plant! How can you go to the side? Bend those knees!"[18]

Baseball was his passion in spring and summer, but it wasn't the boy's only interest. With football in fall and winter and basketball all year round, Willie was always in the thick of Fairfield athletics. Uncle Otis was one reason why. With a wink, he would often perform the household chores that Aunt Sarah assigned to Willie, freeing him to hone his skills on the field. "Willie, you're going to be a ballplayer," Otis told him seriously, the first person to show such faith in his abilities.[19] It was a harsh blow when Uncle Otis died in his sleep (by some accounts, while sharing a bed with Willie, who woke in the morning to find the older man cold and stiff beside him).[20]

Willie loved to watch sports as much as he loved to play, and he was a big fan of football. He didn't have the money to buy tickets, but he'd find other ways to see the local college games. When he was 12, he climbed a tree so he could watch the hometown hero, Cap Brown, playing for Miles College. Indestructible as he was on the field, the boy was all too human up off the ground; he fell out of the tree and broke his arm.[21] One of the few sports injuries he would ever suffer was incurred as a fan.

But once he recovered from the fracture, Willie leaped right back into all the sports he loved. If anything, his arm had gotten stronger, so much so that his father began to bring the 13-year-old along as an "extra man" whenever he played a local ballgame. Usually Willie would serve as the bat boy. But "if the score was lopsided or we didn't have enough players or something, I'd get to play." After the traditional passing of the hat, when the players would divide up the take, "even though I was just a kid and an extra hand, they always made sure I got a full share just like everybody else."[22] It felt good to contribute to the family income, even if it was only $10 at a time.

5

The notion of getting paid to play baseball, the teenager thought, was "just about the nicest idea that anyone ever thought up—like getting paid for eating ice cream."[23] Certainly, other kinds of work held no appeal for him. He did try—once. Willie accepted a job as a dishwasher in a local restaurant that lasted exactly one night. When he realized he would have to work the whole night through to clean the huge pile of dirty dishes, and that he'd have to repeat the process night after night, he bid the boss good-bye. "And don't worry about the one day's pay, either," he said, generously, over his shoulder.[24]

It was becoming clear to the teen, and most especially to his father, that sports would be his ticket to the future. And suddenly, there was hope for a career beyond the Negro Leagues, which had long been the limit for a black player. Within the black community, one of the biggest events of 1946 was the signing of a Negro League player to a minor-league contract in "the white man's game." Willie and his father avidly followed Jackie Robinson's success with the Montreal Royals that summer, and celebrated with all of black America when Robinson broke the color line with the Brooklyn Dodgers in 1947.[25] If Robinson could succeed, maybe Willie, too, could dream of a baseball career in the major leagues.

In the meantime, Cat Mays continued to guide his son's baseball development as he played more and more games with teams of men years older. Mays was determined to clear a path for his son that didn't involve work in Birmingham's steel mills. "Once you get in, you never get out," he would say.[26] But he didn't mind at all for his son to take a regular position on the mill's baseball team. In 1946 and 1947, the teenaged Mays and his 34-year-old father were playing side by side in the outfield for the Industrial League's TC&I team. In the summer, when school was out, the teen would play occasional games with the semipro Fairfield Gray Sox, along with his former football idol, Cap Brown.

That was only in the summer, though, because Cat Mays was adamant that his son should earn his high school diploma. Education was a source of both hope and pride within the segregated black community, and it was not something that the elder Mays would allow his son to ignore. Willie was attending Fairfield Industrial High School, overseen by the strict and imperious E. J. Oliver. The school didn't field a baseball team, but in his freshman and sophomore years Willie starred as a halfback on the school's varsity football team. Playing basketball in his sophomore year, he was the county's top scorer.

Much as he loved those sports, there was no professional future in them for a black athlete, and no way a black teenager in the 1940s could earn money playing them. Playing semipro baseball put his amateur status, and thus his eligibility to play for his high school teams, at risk, but it was a risk that Willie took.[27]

He was in Chattanooga with the Gray Sox in the summer of 1947 when he ran into Piper Davis, the star player and soon-to-be manager of the Birmingham Black Barons. Davis had a passing acquaintance with Cat Mays, since local players at all levels would often put a game together if the prospect of a crowd, and thus some cash, was involved. So he was surprised to meet Mays's 16-year-old son in the lobby of a segregated hotel so far from home.

"Don't you know if they catch you out here playing ball for money, they won't let you play high school ball no more?" Davis scolded him.

"I don't care," said the boy.[28] Even playing part-time, he was making at least $100 a month, more than twice as much as any of his friends could earn with their afterschool jobs. And he was earning it doing something he loved. It wouldn't be long before Piper Davis would be taking the teenager on the road with his own team, high school sports or no high school sports.

But first, there would be one last game with the factory team. In the second inning, an opposing batter "looped a long, sinking liner to left-center, the wrong field for him, and I heard my father say 'All right, all right, let me take it!' But then I was aware that the ball was sinking and he was too far back, and I knew if I cut in front of him I could handle it, so I did, and caught it off the grasstops."[29] It was the right play as far as baseball was concerned, but emotionally it was another matter: Willie had shown up his father on the field, and both of them knew it.

Cat Mays hung up his spikes from that day. He never played another game of baseball. He could see that it was his son's turn now: "One in a family is enough," he would say.[30] Cat made a phone call to Piper Davis.

NOTES

1. Willie Mays, as told to Charles Einstein, *Willie Mays: My Life In and Out of Baseball* (New York: E.P. Dutton and Co., 1966), 19. Many sources list his given name as William Howard Mays Jr. However, Mays' own autobiographies never use this name, only "Willie Mays."

2. Willie Mays, with Lou Sahadi, *Say Hey: The Autobiography of Willie Mays* (New York: Simon and Schuster, 1988), 7.

3. Donald Honig, *Mays, Mantle, Snider: A Celebration* (New York: Macmillan, 1987), 99.

4. Mays, with Sahadi, *Say Hey*, 7.

5. Ibid., 13.

6. Mays is circumspect about these details of his early life in his memoirs and in interviews, and this chronology is never directly stated by him. He does not mention his mother in reference to his childhood or teen years in any of his recollections. In Mays'

memoirs, his mother re-emerges later in his life without any note of a break in their contact.

7. "Last Rites for Mrs. May Slated Here This Week," *Birmingham World*, July 20, 1954; Mays, with Sahadi, *Say Hey*, 9. In this memoir, Mays suggests that Sarah and Ernestine were not his blood relatives. News accounts of Sarah's death in 1954 state otherwise.

8. Charles Einstein, *Willie's Time: Baseball's Golden Age* (Carbondale: Southern Illinois University Press, 2004), 151. (Original edition published 1979.)

9. Charles Einstein, *Willie Mays: Coast to Coast Giant* (New York: Putnam, 1963), 42.

10. Einstein, *Willie's Time*, 171.

11. Mays, with Sahadi, *Say Hey*, 11.

12. Ibid., 12–13.

13. Ibid., 17.

14. Mays, as told to Einstein, *Willie Mays*, 18.

15. Ibid., 59.

16. Mays, with Sahadi, *Say Hey*, 11.

17. Einstein, *Willie Mays*, 46.

18. Ibid., 46–47.

19. Mays, with Sahadi, *Say Hey*, 9.

20. Einstein, *Willie's Time*, 150.

21. Mays, with Sahadi, *Say Hey*, 12.

22. Mays, as told to Einstein, *Willie Mays*, 62.

23. Honig, *Mays, Mantle, Snider*, 99.

24. Mays, as told to Einstein, *Willie Mays*, 62.

25. Mays, with Sahadi, *Say Hey*, 21.

26. Mays, as told to Einstein, *Willie Mays*, 70.

27. Years later, some would claim that Mays played under a pseudonym in his teen years for just this reason, but Mays himself never admitted to this.

28. Mays, with Sahadi, *Say Hey*, 15.

29. Mays, as told to Einstein, *Willie Mays*, 70.

30. Ibid., 71.

LEARNING THE GAME

"He can play," Cat Mays said simply.

Piper Davis knew full well that Cat's son could play. He had seen him on the field with the Gray Sox. But he was cagey nonetheless. "He thinks he's DiMaggio," he pointed out. "More he copies himself after another man, more he's got to unlearn."

"Then unlearn him," said Cat. "But if Willie wants to play, let him play."[1] And so Willie Mays acquired a new baseball mentor, as well as the beginnings of a career.

Cat Mays had taught his son as much baseball as he could. He had steeped the boy in the game from infancy, sat with him on the bench during his Industrial League contests, played pepper for countless hours in empty lots. But he was wise enough to know when his limitations had been reached. He could see that the teenager's talents had the potential to take him far beyond industrial-league ball. To do that, though, Willie would need more than Cat could give him—more connections, and more opportunities.

When Cat got off the phone with Davis, he was just as direct with his son. "Piper Davis wants to see you at 11:30 Sunday morning." He didn't have to say where. Everyone in Birmingham knew that the Black Barons played a doubleheader each Sunday afternoon at Rickwood Field. That's where Davis would be found.

Since he was a child, Willie Mays had dreamed of playing for the Birmingham Black Barons of the Negro American League. The team wasn't the league's most famous, but it had a proud history, going back to 1917, and an avid fan

Seventeen years old and the starting center fielder for the Birmingham Black Barons, Mays is all smiles as he poses for an official portrait. *Memphis Public Library and Information Center, T. H. Hayes Collection, Memphis, Tennessee.*

base. Now, at the age of 16, Mays had a chance to make the dream come true. The 1947 baseball season was almost over. This was his tryout.

Davis had Mays step up to the plate for some batting practice. He dug in and took up his stance, very close to the plate, with his shoulder angled away from the mound. The pitch came in, an inside curve. It was a strike, but Mays hit the dirt.

Davis strolled out to him. "Know what pitch that was?"

"Curve," said Mays, scrambling up and dusting himself off.

"Then why'd you go down?"

"I don't know."

"You were overcrowding, that's why. You don't stand on home plate and peer at the pitcher. You lay back and *aim* on him."[2]

And that, more or less, was that. "He can't hit the curveball none," Cat Mays agreed.

"Well, he's got to learn by next season if he's gonna play with us," Davis said. "But I promise you, I'll give him a chance then."[3] We can only imagine the hours of father-son batting practice that fall.

There was plenty of time for such workouts: Principal Oliver had found out about the games with the Gray Sox and, sure enough, barred Mays from the high school football and basketball teams. His professional play "created an uproar at Fairfield Industrial," Mays said years later. "The kids at the school felt I had sold them out," imagining all the county and state championships that might have been theirs had he remained an amateur high-school athlete. "I guess maybe I had. But look at the chance I had been given—to play baseball, and to get paid for doing it."[4]

When the 1948 baseball season got underway, though, there was no word from the Black Barons. Once school let out in May, the 17-year-old Mays joined up with the Chattanooga Choo-Choos, part of the unofficial network of Negro "minor league" teams. He played infield positions, mainly first base and shortstop. But Mays was unhappy to be so far from home. Worse, the athletes only got paid for the games they actually played. When an entire series in Dayton, Ohio was rained out, the team spent three days in the town without any money for a decent meal. "We'd eat loaves of stale bread and sardines and crackers and RC Cola, and . . . I said to myself, if this ever gets over with, I'm quitting."[5] Mays borrowed bus fare from the team's owner on their return to Chattanooga and went right home to Fairfield.

While he was away, the Black Barons starting left fielder broke his leg. The Mays household received a phone call: once again, Piper Davis wanted to see Willie Mays at 11:30 on a Sunday morning.

This time, the teenager was handed a uniform when he came in the clubhouse door. It was faded—it had been worn by who knew how many before him—and far from a perfect fit. But it said "Barons" across the front and had a triple-B logo on the cap, and for the young replacement left fielder, that was plenty.

Davis sent the teen to the outfield to shag some flies before the double-header began, but that was all. Mays spent his first game with the Barons on the bench. "Watch what's going on," Davis instructed him. Mays sat alone and he watched. He'd felt confident and proud coming into the park, but now he felt like an outsider, and a kid at that. These were talented ballplayers at the height of their skills. They were all much older than he, most by at least ten years. They won the game.

For the second game, Davis wrote Mays into the line-up, batting seventh and playing left. There were grumbles from the squad when the players got down to "Mays-LF" posted on the line-up card, but Davis put a quick stop to that. He called out, "How's the lineup to you, fellas? Anybody doesn't like that lineup, well, there's the clubhouse."

To Mays he whispered, "Give it your best shot."[6]

No one was willing to challenge Davis openly. The Barons took the field. And Mays quickly proved the manager right. He got two hits off one of the league's top pitchers and played the outfield with his usual verve. The team was convinced, and so was Piper Davis. He hired Mays on the spot, at $250 a month with a $50 incentive for any month he hit over .300; he only cleared it with the team's owner, Tom Hayes, afterward. It was a handshake agreement—Mays was too young to sign a formal contract, at any rate—but Davis was as good as his word.

The only problem, as the manager saw immediately, was the position. "My center fielder could out-run Willie, but he couldn't out-throw him," said Davis.[7] "Nobody, and I mean *nobody*, ever saw anybody throw a ball from the outfield like him, or get rid of it so fast."[8] Mays played left field for a few weeks, but as soon as Davis had a chance (when center fielder Norman Robinson broke his leg) he installed Mays in center field. From then on, Willie Mays was the Birmingham Black Barons starting center fielder—when he was with the team, that is.

Because, even though he was now a professional ballplayer, Mays was still a full-time high school student, too. Cat Mays and Piper Davis worked out a deal. Willie could play with the team for home games only, and only for night games or weekends, when school was in session. In the summer when school was out, he would travel with the team.

Principal Oliver was not convinced. The semipro games of the previous summer had been bad enough. Surely the lure of a regular spot on the roster of a professional baseball team would keep the teenager away from the classroom. Oliver fumed, he lectured, he even threatened suspension. But eventually, Davis and Cat Mays convinced the principal that they, too, wanted Willie to get an education. He stayed in school.[9]

But he lived for the weekends and for the summer months, when, to his mind, his real education—his baseball education—continued. Both on and off the field, there was a lot to learn about being a pro. Some of his first lessons were tutored by the legendary Kansas City Monarchs in a series early in the 1948 season.

Mays began to learn ballfield bravado. In one of his first games, he was welcomed to the league in the time-honored way: he was decked by a pitch from Hilton Smith, a future Hall-of-Famer with the Monarchs. Usually, Mays' quickness and his acute peripheral vision gave him the ability to duck out of the way of such a throw, but this one nailed him in the arm and he went down. His emotions always ran close to the surface, and now they overflowed. Hurt and perhaps a bit embarrassed, the teenager began to cry.

Davis came out to the plate and stood over him. He didn't help Mays up. "Don't lie there crying," he said. "And don't let this guy show you up. I want you to get up and I want you to *run* to first base. And the first chance you get, I want you to steal second."[10]

Mays wiped away the tears and did as he was told. He ran to first, and a few moments later he stole second. As he stood there, he got it. Smith's pitch had been a message: *Don't think you can hit me, kid.* Mays' baserunning spoke right back: *Take me down, you'll pay for it.*[11]

Inspired, he stole third, too. Smith called over to him, "Now you're in the majors!"[12]

Mays learned that a player could make a difference in a game from the field, too. In one game, he threw out a baserunner with a spectacular throw from left center to third. Then he nailed another runner at home on a heave from right center. After that, the Monarchs would take no more chances on Mays' arm. In the late innings Buck O'Neil, their manager, held up a runner at third on a sharp hit to center with a shout: "Whoa, whoa, that man's got a shotgun."[13] Mays saved a run just by his presence in center field.

Most of all, though, Mays still had to learn to hit the curveball. His offseason work was put to the test by the great Satchel Paige, the legend-in-his-own-time pitcher with the Monarchs. The first time Mays came up against Paige, he smacked a fastball for a double. Mays was dusting himself off at second when Paige came off the mound and approached him. "That's it, kid," he muttered.

Mays was mystified, though he knew that Paige was famous for his inscrutable sayings. But in the teenager's next at-bat, Paige made his meaning clear. He threw nothing but off-speed pitches, "those crazy curves and his other soft stuff," and Mays struck out on three fruitless swings of the bat.[14]

Negro League teams were located all over the eastern United States, from New York City in the north to Kansas City in the west to New Orleans in the south. With their limited budgets, getting the team from game to game was always a challenge. Some of Mays' favorite tales from his Negro League days revolved around transportation.

There was the time the team bus—a cranky, creaking old school bus driven by Charlie Wood, the club's "batman," clubhouse manager, and all-around assistant—broke down on a road trip from Birmingham to Montgomery, Alabama. Next thing the players knew, Piper Davis had commandeered an ice truck. "Got to play a game, fellas!" he shouted as he ushered his players inside. "Can't go disappointing the people." They had to ride 40 miles standing in the back of the truck, "with the door open so we wouldn't freeze."[15]

Another time, the Black Barons were headed to New York City to play the Cuban Giants. As the bus groaned its way under the Hudson River through the Holland Tunnel, it shuddered to a stop. Smoke poured out from under the hood. Someone spotted flames as the team scrambled off the vehicle. Then Mays remembered that his suitcase, packed with four brand-new suits, had been left behind. Now that he had some money, Mays was becoming a bit of a clotheshorse, and "I wasn't going to leave them there. I ran back to my seat and came back with my bag, and everyone was laughing. Five minutes later, the bus blew up."[16]

The team showed up for their game without uniforms or equipment, but with Mays' new suits. The Giants lent the visitors everything from bats to gloves to their own road uniforms, and in Willie Mays' first game at the Polo Grounds he had the first of the many home runs he would one day hit there. Twenty thousand fans witnessed a double-header in which, it seemed, the visiting Cuban Giants beat the hosting Cuban Giants in one game, and then the home team triumphed over its visiting self.[17]

Mostly on those long road trips, though, the men talked baseball, and the teenager drank it all in. The year before, the talk of the bus had been Jackie Robinson's performance with the Brooklyn Dodgers. Most of the players knew Robinson somewhat as a member of the Kansas City Monarchs in 1945. He had not been especially well-liked among the Negro Leaguers, who found him aloof.[18] But they all knew what Robinson's career in white baseball might mean for them. If Robinson could cross baseball's color line, maybe other black players could do it, too. The Black Barons told the wide-eyed rookie about the abuse Robinson had endured, and was still enduring, from bigoted fans. They knew that some prejudiced opponents, and even teammates, had threatened to boycott any game in which Robinson appeared. But they had also seen how others in baseball had supported Robinson, and had encouraged the whole notion of integration. Once the baseball commissioner announced that any club refusing to play a game against a team with a black player would forfeit that game, the other teams fell in line. And no one could miss the fact that thousands of black fans were turning out to see Robinson play wherever the Dodgers went. Integrated baseball was making money, and money was green in anyone's hands.[19]

Midway through the 1947 season, the American League had introduced its own black major leaguer, Larry Doby of the Cleveland Indians. Now, in 1948, the players regularly spotted major-league scouts in the stands. Rumors flew over which Negro Leaguer might be signed next. For individual players, especially for young ones like Mays, the future looked brighter than ever. "We're too old," his teammates would tell him realistically. "You can make it."[20] But as black fans flocked to major league ballgames to cheer for their own, Negro League attendance began to decline.

It was a trend that worried the more experienced ballplayers, and it terrified the Negro League owners. But it didn't trouble Mays much. As he traveled with the team that summer, his joy in the game quickly made him a favorite. "I was enthusiastic, and young, and I guess I kind of bubbled," he remembered years later. "The older guys treated me like a happy kid—which is what I was—and I didn't do much brooding or sulking."[21] Most of the players felt protective of their ebullient young teammate, and one or another of the more trustworthy ones would be his Davis-designated chaperone on the road.

Once he felt comfortable as a member of the team, Mays began to truly sparkle on the field. On one ball hit deep into left field, both he and Norman Robinson—playing left field now that he'd recovered from his leg injury—went back for it. They came within inches of a serious collision. Robinson missed the ball. Mays lunged, leaped, grabbed it bare-handed, and in one fluid motion flipped it to the shortstop, who tagged the runner out at second base. Across the field in the dugout, no one knew what had happened to the ball until they saw it in the shortstop's glove.[22]

Mays became known for his aggressive baserunning, too. Davis loved to tell about the game in Memphis when Mays was running for home and "the catcher was blocking the plate. So Willie went into him with his spikes. Ripped the catcher's pants from under his crotch down to his knees. After that, nobody tried to block the plate on Willie Mays."[23]

In Mays' memory of the incident, he felt guilty about spiking his opponent, though at the same time pleased that he'd scored a run on the play. He returned to the dugout, sought out his manager, and tried to apologize for what he saw as unnecessary roughness. Davis used the moment to teach Mays another lesson of the game: "Willie, that's the man to hit. He's got all that equipment on and he beats up on everyone, so he's the one to tear up."[24]

The Black Barons had a great season in 1948 with Mays in the outfield, and as the summer wound down they found themselves in first place in their division, earning them the right to play in that year's Negro World Series against perhaps the most storied team in the league, the Homestead Grays. Not even Principal Oliver could keep Mays away from that contest. He played in the best-of-seven series despite the fact that high school was back in session.

Now that black athletes had played in the formerly white leagues for two seasons, black fans were abandoning the segregated game in droves. The 1948 Negro World Series would be the last one ever, as one by one the black clubs sold off their players and closed up shop. The Homestead Grays, a club that had won 12 pennants and three championships in its history, was especially hard-hit by declining attendance. There was by now so little interest in the team in Pittsburgh, where it was based, that none of the Grays World Series home games was actually played at home. Instead, in an effort to bring in as many paying customers as possible, the last Negro World Series hit the road, with games in Kansas City, New Orleans, and Birmingham.

The Black Barons won just one game in the series, a 4–3 victory at Rickwood Field. Mays was proud of his contribution: he hit a run-scoring single in the bottom of the ninth to help his team secure a comeback win. But when the Grays won Game 5, and the series, in New Orleans on October 5, Mays headed right home. After all, he had classes to attend at Fairfield Industrial High.[25]

During the winter, several of the Negro League teams dropped out of the league, hanging on only as barnstorming shells of their former selves. The Black Barons stayed on to re-form the Negro American League with nine other teams.[26] Birmingham was still a strictly segregated city, and would remain so for years to come. Because it had no major league baseball team of its own, local fans didn't have the choices that baseball lovers in Pittsburgh or New York enjoyed. Both these factors continued to make black baseball a viable business in Birmingham.

When the 1949 baseball season opened, Mays hardly cared who the opponents were. He was playing the game again, and that was what mattered. No longer a rookie but still, by far, the youngest member of the team, he happily boarded the creaking old bus for another summer of professional ball.

This year, more and more white scouts came calling to Rickwood Field to see the Black Barons play. The number of black men actually playing on major league teams was still very small. But the number signed to minor league contracts was growing fast. The Negro League owners made no secret that their best players' contracts were for sale. The major league clubs smelled a bargain, and out went the scouts. In June, a Boston Braves scout saw Mays play in Birmingham. The authority with which the 18-year-old played the outfield and ran the bases made him an interesting prospect, even though the consensus was he still couldn't hit the curve. But when the scout asked about the teen's availability, he was rebuffed. Mays had not yet graduated high school. Until he did, he was ineligible to sign a major league contract.[27] This was based on a general ruling from "Happy" Chandler, the sitting baseball commissioner, and many of the clubs were contesting it. If the Braves had pressed the issue, baseball fans might still be marveling at the champion Braves of the 1950s, with both Willie Mays and Hank Aaron in the outfield.

So "blackball" it would be for 1949. As the makeup of the Negro American League shifted to adjust for teams that folded or moved, the Black Barons had to travel as far west as Houston, Texas, to play. They spent more nights sleeping on the shuddering bus than ever before.

Piper Davis continued to school Mays in the finer points of the game, and Mays remained an eager student. Davis had a keen understanding of baseball's inner workings. In the long hours on the team bus and in countless sessions of fielding and batting practice, Davis had a rapt audience in Mays: "Bounce the ball when you're throwing from the outfield. When the ball skips off the ground, it picks up speed." "You've got those big hands, so use them. Barehand the ball and you'll get rid of it that much quicker."[28]

But the main skill Davis taught his young outfielder that summer was how to overcome the one remaining flaw in his game: hitting the curveball. Without the benefit of film or video playback, Davis could see exactly what Mays was doing wrong in the milliseconds when he swung and missed.

"You're knifin' in when the ball's coming in," he said, "and that causes you to fight two things—the ball, and the way you go after it."[29] Davis convinced Mays to straighten up at the plate and turn his body a bit toward the pitcher. After yet more batting practice, the new stance felt natural to him. It was a stance he would use for the rest of his career, and "the curveball didn't worry me after that."[30]

On May 15, 1950, Willie Mays graduated from Fairfield Industrial High School with a special certificate in clothes cleaning and pressing. Not that he had any intention of using these skills professionally. "I didn't have any heroes who folded underwear in a laundry,"[31] he said. Baseball was his future, he was sure of it. But apart from the inquiry of that one Boston Braves scout, no one in major league baseball seemed to know that Willie Mays existed.

All that changed in June when Eddie Montague, a scout for the New York Giants, rolled in to Birmingham. The club wanted Montague's opinion on the Black Barons first baseman, Alonzo Perry. It was the morning of yet another

Sunday doubleheader when Montague came to Rickwood Field to watch batting practice, as any good scout will do.

A few years later, when the discovery of Willie Mays had already become a part of baseball lore, Montague wrote out his memory of the day. "My eyes almost popped out of my head when I saw a young colored boy swing the bat with great speed and power, and with hands that had the quickness of a young Joe Louis [the era's most famous boxer] throwing punches. I also saw his great arm during fielding practice. . . . This was the greatest young ballplayer I had ever seen in my life or my scouting career."[32]

During the two games he watched that day, Montague tried to mask his disbelief. Why hadn't he heard of this kid Willie Mays before? Was there some weakness in his game? No, he answered himself as the innings went on, Mays had speed and fielding smarts too. Alonzo Perry was completely forgotten as Montague moved around the stands, watching Mays from every possible angle, including up on the ballpark's roof.

There Montague ran into the Barons owner, Tom Hayes. He arranged his best poker face and asked whether Mays's contract was for sale. Why, yes, was the reply from Hayes: it could be had for $15,000, but not until Mays had played out the 1950 season in Birmingham. Montague took a deep breath. That was some serious money for a teenaged ballplayer, and he knew full well that Hayes could try to use the added time to drive up the final price. But when he went to talk with Mays after the second game, Montague was "impressed by his likable attitude," and he resolved to get the Giants to sign him.

The next day's Black Barons game was in Tuscaloosa, Alabama, and Eddie Montague was not about to let the young ballplayer out of his sight. He got to the Tuscaloosa ballpark early—"if it weren't for the groundskeeper, I would have been lonesome"—and pounced on Mays the moment he got off the team bus.

"Would you like to play professional baseball with the New York Giants, Willie?" he asked, taking the center fielder off to the side so they could speak somewhat privately.

"Yes, sir!" Mays replied.

Montague felt he was off to a good start. "Well, then, I'll be speaking to Mr. Hayes about your contract, and . . ."

Mays cut him off. "What contract? Mr. Hayes don't own me."

If Montague's eyes had popped out the day before, he nearly jumped out of his skin with excitement now. This, in the days before free agency, was simply unheard of.

"Didn't you sign a contract with him?"

"No, sir. I didn't sign any contract with him. I just told him I'd play." This was true. Whether the result of sloppy business practices, a lingering reluctance to formalize a deal with a player so young, or a deliberate effort by Piper Davis to protect his protégé's future career, Mays had never gone beyond his original handshake agreement with the Black Barons ownership.

"Well, who should I talk to, then?" Montague demanded.

"My father and Aunt Sarah," said Mays, giving Montague his address and phone number in Fairfield.[33]

Montague sat through the Tuscaloosa game and marveled at his discovery. On the field, Mays sparkled. There was his future, sitting up there in the stands, and he put on a show, "hitting line drives to all fields and making a great catch and throw," Montague noted.

The scout noted something else, too: his counterpart from the Brooklyn Dodgers organization was also watching the Tuscaloosa game. No scout could possibly miss the star out there in center field. There was no time to waste.

The next morning, Montague telephoned the Mays home in Fairfield and spoke to Aunt Sarah. The family was asking for a $5,000 signing bonus, plus a monthly player's salary. It sounded more than reasonable to Eddie Montague, and to the Giants front office when he phoned them to approve the deal. That afternoon, when Cat Mays came home from his shift at the steel mill at 4:00 P.M., there was Montague waiting for him, contract in hand.

To Willie Mays, it was all a blur: the talk about the Giants organization, where he would go to play minor league ball "to gain confidence," and how long it might take him to make it to the majors. ("In two years, he'll be playing center in the Polo Grounds," Montague predicted. His guess would turn out to be a year too many.) Then there was a pen in his hand, and he was signing his first professional baseball contract. His father signed it, too, for good measure. Five thousand dollars up front, and $250 a month.[34] It was a good deal all around, even for Barons owner Hayes, who got a $10,000 check from the Giants to ensure he wouldn't put up a fight.[35]

For Mays, the money was secondary. He was 19 years old, and he was on his way to the major leagues.

NOTES

1. Mays, as told to Einstein, *Willie Mays*, 69.
2. Einstein, *Willie Mays*, 49.
3. Mays, with Sahadi, *Say Hey*, 16.
4. Ibid., 24.
5. Einstein, *Willie's Time*, 308.
6. Mays, with Sahadi, *Say Hey*, 21–24.

7. Dave Kindred, "From Miner to Majors," *The Sporting News*, June 30, 1997.

8. Einstein, *Willie's Time*, 309.

9. Mays, with Sahadi, *Say Hey*, 24–25.

10. Ibid., 34–35.

11. Ibid., 34–35.

12. Ron Rapoport, "Another Class in Hall that Definitely Has It All," *Chicago Sun-Times*, August 6, 2001. In the way of tales of the Negro Leagues, the pitcher in this story has varied in different retellings. Mays has said it happened with Chet Brewer, also of the Monarchs, on the mound. But he told it about Smith at the latter's Hall of Fame induction ceremony in 2001. Given the erratic record-keeping of the Negro Leagues, it's impossible to know for sure.

13. Mays, with Sahadi, *Say Hey*, 19.

14. Ibid., 19–20.

15. Ibid., 35.

16. Ibid., 35–36.

17. Ibid.

18. Mark Ribowsky, *A Complete History of the Negro Leagues: 1884 to 1955* (New York: Birch Lane Press, 1995), 275.

19. Peter Golenbock, "Men of Conscience," in *Jackie Robinson: Race, Sports, and the American Dream*, eds. Joseph Dorinson and Joram Warmund, 18–19 (Armonk, NY: M.E. Sharpe, 1998).

20. Dave Sheinin, "Repaying a National Debt; Negro Leaguers' Trail-Blazing Achievements Are Recognized," *Washington Post*, September 19, 2002.

21. Mays, as told to Einstein, *Willie Mays*, 78–79.

22. Mays, with Sahadi, *Say Hey*, 33.

23. Kindred, "From Miner to Majors."

24. Mays, with Sahadi, *Say Hey*, 34.

25. Rich Emert, "Lore of the Game: Pittsburgh was a Special Place in the History of Negro Leagues Baseball," *Pittsburgh Post-Gazette*, August 8, 2001.

26. Ribowsky, *A Complete History of the Negro Leagues*, 275.

27. Honig, *Mays, Mantle, Snider*, 99.

28. Mays, with Sahadi, *Say Hey*, 18.

29. Ibid., 20.

30. Ibid.

31. Ibid., 21.

32. Einstein, *Willie Mays*, 30.

33. Mays, with Sahadi, *Say Hey*, 39.

34. One source, Mays' *Say Hey*, asserts that the signing bonus was only $4,000. Most, however, including Montague's account, give the $5,000 figure.

35. Einstein, *Willie Mays*, 32–34.

COMING UP, 1950–1951

Willie Mays wasn't a Giant yet, though. First he would have to prove that Montague's observations weren't just a fluke. Like thousands of young ballplayers before him and thousands more to come, he would have to perform at the minor league level. For Mays there was an added complication, though: he would be the player to integrate one of those minor leagues.

Even though black and white men had been playing major league baseball as teammates for the past three years, the fight to integrate the national pastime was not over. In many parts of the country in June 1950, a mixed-race team was still seen as an affront.

Eddie Montague and the Giants weren't out to make history or change American society. They just wanted to put together a winning ballclub, and they thought Willie Mays had the talent to help them do that. Nurturing his talent was the next step, and minor league baseball was the place for that to happen.

But there were several levels of minor league ball to choose from, and several circuits of teams at each level. It took the Giants a few days to figure out where Mays should play his initial season of minor league baseball. Class A ball, a couple of steps removed from the major leagues, was their first choice. The class A Southern League, in which Birmingham's white Barons played, was out of the question; the Giants were not about to be the first team to dare to integrate the game in the Deep South. The Giants had a Western League class-A affiliate in Sioux City, Iowa that could have been Mays' first destination. It was that team's need for a first baseman that had sent Montague off to Birmingham to scout Alonzo Perry in the first place. But Sioux City was in the middle of its own kind of racial uproar at the moment: a Native American had just been buried in a "whites-only" cemetery. "The farm club refused to take me, fearing the consequences and 'bad' publicity," Mays later recalled.[1]

Class B was the next best option, the Giants decided. Their class B affiliate team was based in Trenton, New Jersey. Trenton wasn't far from New York City, so the front office could keep an eye on the new prospect's development. And the team was part of the Interstate League, which, while still whites-only in June of 1950, confined its member teams to the more tolerant Northeast, with clubs in Pennsylvania, New Jersey, Delaware, and a single team in Maryland. It wouldn't exactly be easy to be the first black player in the Interstate League, but the Giants didn't figure it to be an unbearable burden for their 19-year-old center fielder.

Mays, not entirely aware of these considerations at the time, felt a bit insulted by the assignment. "Class B ball? Why, the [Black] Barons played better baseball than that, probably as good as Triple A," he thought.[2] But he didn't lose any time joining the team, even though it meant skipping his senior prom. That Friday, June 23, just five days after Eddie Montague first laid eyes on him, Willie Mays boarded a train heading north. He was going to meet the Trenton Giants on the road for a weekend series in Hagerstown, Maryland.

The family had seen him off, and Aunt Sarah had pressed a bag of sandwiches into his hand, but on the train Mays was alone—and nervous. "I couldn't sit still on the train, and kept getting up from my seat, walking from car to car to help pass the time."[3] He knew he would miss his home and his teammates—despite the age difference, he had grown close to the other Black Barons players after two seasons together. But on the train, he was too excited to think much about it, or to eat a bite of sandwich.

When he finally disembarked in Hagerstown, it was late in the day and the game between the Trenton Giants and the Hagerstown Braves was already underway. One of Mays' new teammates, a tall righthanded pitcher named Ed Monahan, was on the platform waiting for him. Monahan was friendly, and as he guided Mays to the ballpark the two chatted about their hometowns. He showed Mays into the visitors' clubhouse, where a Trenton Giants uniform was waiting for the new prospect, with number 12 on the back. He suited up and joined the team in the dugout in the seventh inning.

Chick Genovese, his new manager, greeted Mays just as warmly as Monahan had. "You're starting in center field," he said, which was all Mays had been hoping to hear.[4]

After the game, though, Mays heard a piece of disquieting news: in Hagerstown, at least, the starting center fielder would not be allowed to sleep in the same building as the rest of his team. Hagerstown was located barely south of the Mason-Dixon Line, but it was no more integrated than the Birmingham that Mays had just left behind. The Giants had reserved a room for him at the Harmon Hotel on Jonathan Street, the heart of Hagerstown's one black neighborhood.[5]

Later, Mays would recall being "confused" at his room assignment. With the Black Barons and his other teams, he'd never been singled out on account of his race; he stayed where the team stayed and ate where the team ate, and while segregation was a fact of life, at least the separation was shared. In the big cities that Mays had visited with the Black Barons, like Baltimore, New York, and Washington DC, race hadn't seemed to him to be an issue at all. Having spent his whole life under Jim Crow, Mays was almost inured to its injustices and indignities.[6] So he hid his surprise, carried his bags to Jonathan Street, and settled in.

The rest of the team was more upset. "About midnight, about five of my new teammates knocked on my window"—having climbed a fire escape to do so—"to check whether I was okay," he remembered later.[7] Three of them stayed with him the rest of the night, sleeping on the floor, then headed out the window and down the fire escape at dawn to get back to their assigned hotel.[8] This gesture of kindness and camaraderie solidified Mays' feeling that his new team was happy to have him.

He would need every bit of those good feelings at the Braves ballpark that day. Mays hadn't played in the previous night's game, but he had been noticed. A local sports columnist told Hagerstown in that morning's local paper, "History was made last night as far as the color line is concerned when the Trenton Giants placed a colored player in uniform."[9]

It was all it would take to get the bigots in the crowd fired up, and they were ready and waiting for him. "When I walked onto the field for the first time, I heard someone shout, 'Who's that nigger walking on the field?'"[10] Mays didn't react to the taunts. "I didn't let it bother me . . . I had learned how to be thick-skinned," he said. In batting practice, he smashed the ball over the fence time and again. But as the game began, the shouts only continued. They made an impression on a young fan who was attending with his father. Years later, Bob Miller "remember[ed] distinctly hearing one fan yell 'crapshooter' and another yell 'watermelon man.' . . . I remember my dad saying later as we left, 'They sure were tough on that kid.'"[11]

Much as Mays wanted to prove himself to the crowd and to his new teammates, he was frustrated at the plate. He went 0 for 3 in this first game, and in the series overall he was "oh-for-Maryland," as he put it. "I wondered whether my showing confirmed some of those rednecks' feelings that I wouldn't do well in the big time. What a way to start."[12]

Not all the Hagerstown fans came away with a bad impression, though. One said, "I remember him running the bases faster than we had seen before and losing his cap as he rounded third and headed for home. He was powerful and graceful, and we knew he was a special talent."[13]

Mays' manager and coaches agreed. Chick Genovese was a former outfielder himself. He had played in the Red Sox farm system as a minor leaguer, but he'd never made the big leagues: his way had been blocked by Dom DiMaggio, the younger brother of the Yankee great. Genovese liked what he saw in Mays, and he made it his mission to get the young center fielder all the way to the majors. He identified Mays' problem in those first few games—he was pressing, over-eager to make a good impression. "Relax. Don't overswing. The hits will come," Genovese assured the teenager.[14] He counseled Mays to concentrate on making contact with the ball.

Genovese's advice was sound. Once the Giants left Hagerstown behind, Mays began to hit—but for base hits, not for power. His physical strength translated into fierce line drives, hit to all parts of the field, but not into home runs; he had not yet developed the ability to get under the ball and power it over the fence consistently. In the outfield Mays excelled, as he always had, and he began racking up assists as runners tested his arm and, more often than not, lost the challenge. (Mays ended up leading the league in assists with 17, even though he played just half the season.)

Mays took a room in a Trenton boarding house a few blocks from Dunn Field, the team's home ballpark. If he was homesick, he didn't talk about it. His life was the game—and, like his father, he had no use for drinking or smoking. Time not spent on the ballfield might be passed playing pool, going to the movies, or, like most teenagers, catching up on sleep. "I always seemed to need rest, even though I was strong and well built," he said. If he wasn't sacked out in his room near the ballpark, "I would pile the duffel bags in the back of the bus, lie down on them, and go to sleep."[15] This habit was so well-known that Genovese had to assign a teammate to wake Mays up in time to report to the field. It's a mark of the regard Genovese had for his young star that it was the human alarm clock, not Mays, who got chewed out the time Mays overslept anyway and missed the bus.[16]

Genovese wasn't the only one who protected, even coddled, Mays. The rest of the club, too, took special care of him. Because Mays was still the youngest player in the group, he picked up the affectionate nickname "Junior." With his high-pitched voice and his boundless enthusiasm, he seemed if anything younger than his years, singing on the team bus, tearing headlong after impossible fly balls. "What I wanted to do most in the world was play baseball. . . . Because it was fun for me, it was fun for the others, too," he said.[17] When he went on to *make* those impossible catches, his skills demanded the other ballplayers' respect, along with their affection. "Plenty of room, Junior! We'll let you know where the fence is," the left fielder, Mo Cunningham, would shout as Mays would start one of his patented flights, "crashing into fences, falling on the ground, just running my head off."[18]

He awed them, too, with the power of his throwing arm. "He could throw a ball two hundred feet and make your hand sting," said one of the Trenton infielders. "His pegs came at you like pitches: right on the money and humming."[19]

The other Trenton Giants were quick to come to Mays' defense when necessary. Brushback pitches are a normal part of the game, and every batter expects them. But Mays' close-in batting stance, his statistics, and his race combined to make him a particular target for pitchers that season, and he was continually dodging balls at the plate. Mays would make a point to glare back at the mound to show he wasn't intimidated—Piper Davis had schooled him well. When one opposing pitcher threw at Mays' head, however, the Giants were furious. "After I made out," Mays recalled, "[Eric] Rodin, a big right fielder, laid down a bunt toward first base, attempting to run into the pitcher and knock him down when he tried to field it. Luckily the ball rolled foul. . . . Here I was, the first black ballplayer in the league's history, and my team was ready to start a fight with someone over me . . . both benches emptied onto the field. It was a show of strength and support from my teammates, and it cleared the air."[20]

He rewarded them with incredible, game-saving plays, like one in a home game against Wilmington. The opponents' most dangerous slugger hit a sure home-run shot to dead center field. Mays raced back as far as he could go, leaped, barehanded the ball, bounded off the fence, and whipped it to home plate. It reached home on the fly.[21]

Meanwhile, Chick Genovese picked up where Davis had left off as Mays' baseball mentor. He shared the job with the team's general manager, Bill McKechnie Jr. On the long bus rides from city to city, when Mays wasn't singing or sleeping on the duffel bags, he was sitting with Genovese and McKechnie, talking baseball. Sometimes one or the other of the men would challenge Mays with a rapid-fire quiz on strategy: bottom of the ninth, score tied, it's your pitcher's turn at bat, do you pinch hit? Early in the game, one out, you're on second, there's a long fly to center, do you tag up? Where do you pitch a guy who's weak high and inside on a one-and-two count?

Eventually Mays grew impatient. "I burst out at McKechnie, 'Shoot, you got a *manager* to do that kind of worrying!' "

McKechnie answered, "Buck, someday you may be a manager."

Mays couldn't accept that. "Where? Negro league someplace? Gonna be no Negro leagues anyhow, time you get through raiding 'em."[22]

This was true, perhaps truer than Mays himself knew at the time. The decimation of the Negro Leagues was continuing. Shortly after Mays left Birmingham, Piper Davis's own contract had been bought by the Boston Red Sox. He was the first black man to play in the Red Sox organization and was with the Red Sox Single-A team in Scranton, Pennsylvania by the middle of the 1950 season. But like many Negro League stars, Davis found he could go so far and no farther in "the white man's game." The Red Sox released him the next year. "Too old, I guess," Davis believed. He was 32 at the time.[23] Nine years later, the Red Sox became the last major league team to field an integrated squad.

Mays' youth and undeniable talent meant that nothing—not age, and not bigotry—would hold him back. In 1950, though, he couldn't be sure of that. McKechnie was sure. He believed that Mays could go as far in baseball as his desire could take him. "You think I'm fooling with you," he said placidly. "I'm not. I say the day can come when you'll be a manager."

"And what if it don't?" asked Mays.

"Then you will have been a better player, because the more you understand about this game, the quicker you'll put your ability to maximum use."[24] It was a moment that Mays would always remember, because it made him realize that constant practice would help him hone his baseball mind, just as his father's pepper games had helped him develop his physical skills.

During the 1950 season, in 81 games with Trenton, Mays hit for a .353 batting average with 20 doubles. His average was the highest in the league, though he didn't have enough at-bats to formally win the batting title. His reputation was such that Horace Stoneham, the Giants owner, made several trips to Trenton just to see Mays play. Impressed, Stoneham made it known that Mays would not return to the team in 1951. He was moving up in the farm system, skipping the A and AA leagues and heading straight to Triple-A ball, one step below the majors.

Trenton's baseball fans knew it couldn't last. They savored every game. "We had big league ball in Trenton for a few months in 1950," as one local sportswriter put it.[25]

When the short Class B season ended, Mays headed home to Birmingham where—what else?—he played more baseball. Piper Davis called on him regularly to take the field against teams of barnstorming major leaguers. One of the teams that came through that year was led by Jackie Robinson and included such Brooklyn stars as Roy Campanella, Pee Wee Reese, and Ralph Branca. Another barnstorming team Mays played that fall included Monte Irvin and Henry Thompson of the New York Giants. Mays was glad to make these contacts, but even happier with the income the contests generated. "I made more money in these exhibition games than from playing all of the 1950 season for Trenton," he noted.[26]

When the barnstorming games petered out, Mays followed the lead of many ballplayers of the time and headed to Cuba to play winter ball. It was a chance to pick up some extra money, live in a warm climate for a few months, and play more baseball—perfect, he thought. The Giants had other ideas. As soon as the organization heard that Mays was in the Caribbean intending to play ball, the team sent word that he was forbidden to do so. They were not about to let their top prospect risk injury playing for some other team—in a foreign country, no less. Mays stuck around for a few weeks, hoping the Giants would relent, but the front office stood firm. No winter ball for him.[27]

While in Cuba, he struck up a friendship with Ray Dandridge, a longtime Negro League star who would be Mays' teammate on the Giants AAA team, the Minneapolis Millers. Dandridge, a disciplined hitter and an all-time great third baseman, had been the American Association's MVP in 1950.[28] His success in Minneapolis and in the AAA league had to come as a relief to Mays. Not having to be the first or the only black player on the team would free him to concentrate on the game.

Soon after he returned from Cuba, Mays headed to Sanford, Florida for his first formal spring training camp. The first day in camp, the Millers had a VIP spectator: Leo Durocher, manager of the New York Giants. Durocher strolled through the field as the players limbered up first thing in the morning. Known for his intensity, a carryover from his playing days with St. Louis's "Gashouse Gang," Durocher was sharp, forceful, and loud. After twelve years of playing and managing for the Brooklyn Dodgers and now for the Giants, he seemed the quintessential New York baseball man. He zeroed in on Mays. "Hey, kid, what are you going to show me today?" he barked.[29]

When the game began, Mays went all out to make a good impression on the man he hoped would one day be his manager. He hit a double his first time up, then clobbered a 450-foot home run. He threw out two baserunners from deep center field. He stole a base.

Durocher left the game in the seventh inning without a word, and Mays was crushed, convinced he had done something wrong.[30] The Millers played several practice games with members of the Giants that spring, but Mays didn't see Durocher again. Still, he "hit the hell out of the ball the rest of spring training,"[31] Mays said. He felt that he had to. The Triple-A players looked just as talented as the major leaguers, as far as he could tell.

Doubtful of his status within the organization, Mays was thrilled when Millers manager Tommy Heath told him he would be traveling north with the Millers once spring training ended. "I kind of have the feeling you're not going to be spending the whole summer with us," Heath said. "I think it's only a matter of time before the Giants call you up."[32]

On the train heading north from Florida to Minnesota, Mays felt like he belonged. As one of three black players on the Millers, he would not find himself alone in rooming houses or restaurants, and he wouldn't be breaking new ground. Dandridge and David Barnhill had both been stars in the Negro Leagues, and they had led the Millers to a league championship the previous year.[33] Mays thought that with them on the team, he would fit in easily. And the feeling of acceptance wasn't coming only from his teammates. The Minneapolis sportswriters who had been covering the Millers in Sanford had talked up Mays' skills to the fans back home, who were waiting to welcome him.

He was eager to start the season's first game, but was taken aback when he woke up on the morning of Opening Day and saw, for only the second time in his life, snow falling. Who plays baseball in a snowstorm? Mays went back to bed.

A few hours later, he was awakened by the telephone's ring. It was Heath. "We've got a game to play!"

"It was snowing, Tommy."

"But it stopped." A helicopter had been brought in to blow the snow off the playing field, and the fans were arriving.[34] Mays leaped out of bed, threw on some clothes, and made it to the ballpark in time for the game. The snow, the cold, and the lack of any warm-up routine didn't seem to bother him: he had a home run and a double. The Millers won the game.[35]

What's more, the fans seemed to adore their new center fielder. "The Minneapolis fans took me to their hearts," Mays said. Then again, "It's hard to be disliked when you're hitting .477," a league-leading pace that he sustained through his first month with the team.[36] In the first week alone, Mays racked up 12 hits. His slugging average was a jaw-dropping .799, as he hit 18 doubles, 3 triples, and 8 homers. He scored 38 runs and drove in 30. In Milwaukee, he smashed a line drive so hard that it actually punched a hole in the outfield fence. (Mays noted, with understandable pride, that "instead of repairing it they were going to put a circle around it and keep it as a memento."[37]) He started dating a local Minneapolis girl. Things couldn't be going any better.

Meanwhile, things couldn't be going worse for the Millers parent club. The New York Giants had been favored to win the National League pennant after a 1950 season they had closed by winning 50 out of 72, finishing third behind the Philadelphia Phillies and the Brooklyn Dodgers.[38] But in 1951, the team dropped their first 11 games. As the second month of the season wound down, the Giants were in fifth place with a 17–19 record. Their play seemed listless and uninspired. The irascible Leo Durocher thought his team needed a spark, a wake-up call. He had seen it in the person of a 20-year-old center fielder in a spring training game. He wanted Willie Mays.[39]

On May 25 the Millers were in Sioux City, Iowa for an exhibition game. Afterwards, Mays set off to find a movie theater. As he tells the story, either halfway through the movie or in between films in a double feature, "the house lights went on, and a guy came out on stage to make an announcement. 'If Willie Mays is in the audience, would he please report immediately to his manager at the hotel.' "[40]

Worried that an interruption like this could only mean bad news from home, Mays rushed to find Heath. When he did, the manager was beaming. "Let me be the first to congratulate you," he said. "The Giants want you in New York."

"Says who?" Mays asked.

"Leo. I just spoke to him myself," said Heath.

"Shoot. Man must be out of his mind."

Heath looked on quizzically as Mays "thought a moment, and then I got scared. 'Call him back. . . . Tell him I don't want to go to New York. I'm happy here, and we got a good chance to win the pennant.' "[41]

Heath was dumbfounded, but he wasn't about to bear this kind of bad news to Durocher. He got the Giants manager back on the phone and handed the receiver over to Mays, who said, "I'm not coming."

"What the hell do you mean you're not coming?" shouted Durocher, who continued sputtering on the other end of the line for two solid minutes.

"I can't hit the pitching up there," Mays said when Durocher paused for breath.

"What are you hitting for Minneapolis?" Durocher yelled.

".477," said Mays. There was silence on the other end of the line. Leo Durocher had been rendered speechless.

Finally he spoke, quietly now, either subdued at last or barely suppressing his rage: "Do you think you can hit two-fucking-fifty for me?"

".250? I think so," said Mays.

"Well . . ." began Durocher, who launched into another tirade that ended ". . . we're playing in Philadelphia and I want you there . . . so *get up here*!!" And he slammed down the phone.

Mays and Heath looked at each other. "I better get on a plane," Mays said.[42]

NOTES

1. Mays, with Sahadi, *Say Hey*, 40.
2. Ibid., 40.

3. Ibid., 41.

4. Mays, with Sahadi, *Say Hey*, 42.

5. Mark Kram, "Mays Enjoys Sunset Serenade; Hagerstown Welcomes Willie This Time," *Philadelphia Daily News*, August 10, 2004.

6. Einstein, *Willie's Time*, 298.

7. Mays, with Sahadi, *Say Hey*, 43.

8. Mark Kram, "Mays Enjoys Sunset Serenade; Hagerstown Welcomes Willie This Time," *Philadelphia Daily News*, August 10, 2004.

9. Ibid.

10. Mays, with Sahadi, *Say Hey*, 42–43.

11. Mark Kram, "Mays Enjoys Sunset Serenade; Hagerstown Welcomes Willie This Time," *Philadelphia Daily News*, August 10, 2004.

12. Mays, with Sahadi, *Say Hey*, 43.

13. "Sports Letters," *The News and Observer* (Raleigh, North Carolina), September 12, 2004 [letter from Andy Leo].

14. Mays, with Sahadi, *Say Hey*, 43.

15. Ibid., 46.

16. Ibid., 46.

17. Mays, as told to Einstein, *Willie Mays*, 78–79.

18. Mays, with Sahadi, *Say Hey*, 47.

19. Honig, *Mays, Mantle, Snider*, 103.

20. Mays, with Sahadi, *Say Hey*, 45–46.

21. Ibid., 119.

22. Mays, as told to Einstein, *Willie Mays*, 75–76.

23. Dave Kindred, "From Miner to Majors," *The Sporting News*, June 30, 1997.

24. Ibid., 76.

25. Honig, *Mays, Mantle, Snider*, 103.

26. Mays, with Sahadi, *Say Hey*, 63–64.

27. Honig, *Mays, Mantle, Snider*, 103.

28. T. Nicholas Dawidoff, "Big Call from the Hall," *Sports Illustrated*, July 6, 1987, 99.

29. Mays, with Sahadi, *Say Hey*, 48.

30. Ibid., 49.

31. Ibid., 50.

32. Ibid., 51.

33. James A. Riley, *The Negro Leagues* (New York: Chelsea House), 86.

34. Mays, with Sahadi, *Say Hey*, 51–52.

35. Ibid., 52.

36. Mays, as told to Einstein, *Willie Mays*, 84.

37. Ibid., 85.

38. Tim Kurkjian, "All-Star Break 1951: A Giant Flop," *Sports Illustrated*, July 19, 1993, 90.

39. Leo Durocher, with Ed Linn, *Nice Guys Finish Last* (New York: Simon and Schuster, 1975), 308.

40. Mays, with Sahadi, *Say Hey*, 56. According to Mays, he was alone; in later years, Ray Dandridge claimed to be with him in the theater.

41. Ibid.

42. Versions of this conversation, with slight variations, appear in both Mays' autobiographies *Say Hey* (56–57) and *Willie Mays* (85–86), as well as sources such as *Willie's Time* (25).

Monte Irvin (20) and Don Mueller (22) greet Mays as he crosses the plate after smashing one of his many Ebbets Field home runs. Dodgers catcher Roy Campanella (39) looks on. *National Baseball Hall of Fame Library, Cooperstown, N.Y.*

THE BIG LEAGUES, 1951

Mays raced to his room and threw a few items into a duffel bag: his spiked baseball shoes, his glove, underwear. He took along some favorite bats, too—34-ounce, 35-inch Adirondacks—stashed in a golf bag that had been a gift from the Millers booster club.[1] The team would send the rest of his things after him. There was just time to place a good-bye phone call to his local girlfriend ("I'll probably be back in a week," he assured her) before Mays was boarding a plane to New York.[2]

Next morning, he was ushered into the offices of Giants owner Horace Stoneham on Forty-second Street in midtown Manhattan. Stoneham was there to congratulate Mays, and to get his signature on a $5,000 contract for the season.[3] As was the custom in these pre–free agency days, there was no discussion of the contract's terms. Mays signed.

There wasn't much time for negotiation, in any case. Mays had to be on a train to Philadelphia for that day's game. Doc Bowman, the team trainer, was waiting in Stoneham's office to get the rookie to the ballpark on time. Stoneham introduced the two and shook Mays' hand in farewell.

"Thank you, Mr. Stoneham," Mays said. "I hope I can get in a few games, get a few chances to help. I hope you won't be sorry."

Stoneham was incredulous. *"Get in a few games—get a few chances to help?"* he repeated. "Don't you know you're starting tonight?"

"My tongue and the back of my mouth went dry," Mays remembered later.[4] Bowman hustled him out of the office and onto a train heading for Philadelphia. The train trip gave Mays two hours to get used to the notion that he was now a major league center fielder.

They headed to the hotel where the team was staying, and Bowman conducted Mays to the room he would be sharing with left fielder Monte Irvin. "Hiya, roomie," Irvin greeted him. They had met before, on the barnstorming circuit in Birmingham, but the way Durocher and Stoneham had been talking up the young center fielder, Mays found that all his teammates were well prepared for his arrival. It made him feel gratified, welcomed, and nervous all at once.[5]

One of Durocher's great skills as a manager was his ability to get inside his players' heads, to figure out what each man needed to motivate or move him. In his one meeting with Mays, and in the scouting reports he'd read on him before and since, Durocher had gleaned Mays' need to feel comfortable and reassured. To that end, he assigned Irvin to be something of a big brother to Mays—his roommate on the road, his lockermate in the clubhouse. Irvin, a fellow Alabaman who was 12 years Mays' senior, stepped into the role with enthusiasm. A genuine closeness grew between the two. The 20-year-old Mays looked to Irvin as someone to emulate, both professionally—Irvin was an excellent hitter who would lead the league in RBIs that year—and personally. "If [Irvin] wanted to eat somewhere that's where we ate," Mays said. "If I wanted to take out a girl on a date, she knew she'd have to meet him first, get his okay."[6]

When Irvin and Mays arrived at the visitors' clubhouse at Shibe Park, a fresh new uniform hung in the otherwise empty locker next to Irvin's. It had number 24 on the back. Mays suited up, and his jitters began to melt. "All of a sudden, I was in the major leagues and doing major league things," he recalled years later. "Someone passed a ball to me for my signature . . . I wrote my name on it: 'Willie Mays.' And then I added '#24.' It looked so . . . real."[7]

Mays stepped onto the field moments later as the Phillies were about to begin fielding practice. As Durocher put it, "I saw something then that I had never seen before in my life . . . every player there stopped dead in his tracks to watch him."[8] Word had gotten out to the Giants, and to their opponents as well, that this rookie's batting practice would be something worth seeing.

"[Mays] popped it up, hit a weak grounder, fouled one back. . . . Then all of a sudden he hit a rocket that landed in the middle of the upper deck in left field. Then he hit another rocket that went over the roof. Then he hit one that hit the . . . scoreboard [in right-center]," said then-teammate Bill Rigney. "He was amazing."[9] It was a display of power, and power to all fields, that was unlike anything these pros had seen before. It got the Giants in the rookie's corner from that moment: "You could see them relax. They knew this kid was the real thing," said Durocher. And it simply awed the Phillies; the man scheduled to pitch the next game, Robin Roberts, started "thinking, 'Wow, I've got to face this kid tomorrow night. How will I get him out?' "[10] Durocher penciled Mays into the line-up, batting third.

Batting practice was one thing; the game itself was another story. In his first big-league at-bat, Mays struck out looking. He was hitless in the game overall, going 0 for 5. Otherwise, observers were impressed with Mays' baserunning when he got to first base in an eyeblink on an error by shortstop Granny Hamner, and reporters noted a couple of fine catches in center field.[11] Mays fixated on the outfield play in which he bumped into Irvin as both went after a ball—"The thing should have been caught, but thanks to me it went for a double."[12] Still, the Giants won it 8–5, on a late-game rally.

The next day, with Roberts pitching for Philadelphia, Mays went 0 for 3. (Roberts fudged the question of how to pitch to the rookie: he walked Mays twice.) The Giants won 2–0. On Sunday, Giants ace Sal Maglie pitched a two-hitter. Mays, hitless again, went 0 for 4. But the Giants swept the series with another 2–0 win.[13] They had climbed over .500 and were showing signs of life at last. The New York press chalked it all up to the new kid in the outfield: one story began, "Inspired by the presence of their flashy rookie star, Willie Mays, the Giants rallied . . ."[14]

Meanwhile, back in Minneapolis, Millers fans were distraught over the loss of the phenom their team had had so briefly. That day, Horace Stoneham ran a full-page ad in the *Sunday Minneapolis Tribune* that said, in part: "We appreciate his worth to the Millers, but in all fairness, Mays himself must be a factor in these considerations . . . Mays is entitled to his promotion and the chance to prove he can play major league baseball."[15]

From Mays' perspective, he hadn't proven anything of the sort. He was oh-for-Pennsylvania, and visions of Hagerstown must have been dancing in his head. But when the team returned to New York the next night for Mays' first home game as a Giant, the fans at the Polo Grounds "gave me a big hand when my name was announced in the batting order. I turned to Irvin in the dugout and said, 'Is everybody crazy except me?' "

"[Irvin] said, 'They got it figured out. So long as you don't hit, we win. Only trouble will be if you ever get a hit.' He was laughing."[16]

The game was against the Boston Braves, and veteran lefty Warren Spahn was on the mound. On the first pitch of his first at-bat of the game, Mays guessed fastball, swung, and connected. He hit it clear over the roof that shaded the left-field stands for a home run, so fast and so far that it moved Durocher to comment: "I never saw a fucking ball leave the fucking park so fucking fast in my fucking life."[17]

It was Mays' only hit of the game, though, and it would turn out to be the

Giants only run as they lost 4–1. It looked as if the fans might be right—the team would win as long as Mays *didn't* hit.

The home run, while spectacular, didn't break the spell. The next day, in a double-header, Mays' hitless streak resumed, and it continued the next night for thirteen more at-bats in all. Mays was now 1 for 26. He had gone from a .477 batting average in Minneapolis to .039 in New York.

Finally, the tension became too much for him. The team wasn't even winning anymore when Mays' bat failed; they had lost that night's game 1–0. In the clubhouse after it ended, "I actually sat in front of my locker and began to cry."[18]

Herman Franks, one of the coaches, went to fetch Durocher. "You better do something about your boy," he said, embarrassed.[19]

Durocher ran out to Mays and, as kindly as he could, asked what was the matter. Mays' emotions seemed to spill over as Durocher patted his back. All his worries and fears tumbled out in a torrent of words that began in his ordinarily high-pitched tenor voice and only got higher as he went on: "Mister Leo, I can't help you, I can't even get a hit, the pitching is too fast for me, they're going to send me back to Minneapolis, I *told* you I couldn't hit this pitching. . . ."[20]

Durocher kept on patting Mays' back, both literally and figuratively, as he answered: "Willie, see what's printed across my jersey? It says Giants. As long as I'm the manager of the Giants, you're my centerfielder. You're here to stay. Stop worrying. With your talent you're going to get plenty of hits."[21]

Still, Durocher seized the moment as a teaching opportunity. As Mays' emotional flood subsided, he gave some practical advice: "Who do you think you are? [Carl] Hubbell? . . . The way you wear the legs of your pants, down around your ankles. Pull them up." When Mays asked why, Durocher explained, "You're making the umpires think your strike zone's down where the knees of your pants are. They're hurting you on the low pitch. Pull up your pants. If you do, you'll get two hits tomorrow."[22]

The next day, he did, and he did. With pants legs up, Mays had a single and a triple in a 14–3 Giants romp over the Pittsburgh Pirates. The day after that, Mays hit two doubles and scored the game's only run in another Giants victory. "From that day on, he just carried us on his back,"[23] according to Durocher.

This was not just another piece of Durocher hype. The stats bear him out. The first week that Mays started to hit, he went 9 for 24, a .375 batting average. On a road trip in late June, after he won a game for the Giants with a three-run homer in the tenth inning, Mays went on a ten-game hitting streak that included four home runs and 16 runs batted in. At one point in July, Mays had six hits over eight games—all of them home runs.[24] Slowly, the Giants gained ground in the standings, climbing step by step from fifth place in the league to second. All the while, the Brooklyn Dodgers, their crosstown rivals, remained on top.

Mays' contributions in the field are not so easy to quantify, but it's clear that he won games for the Giants that way, too. All those years of practicing the pickup with his father were paying off now. Mays seemed to get a preternatural jump on batted balls. Fans quickly noticed how he would start to run before the batter even swung, making him perfectly positioned to make the catch almost every time. That ability, plus Mays' speed, was absolutely essential in playing the Polo Grounds' cavernous center field, which was 483 feet from home at its deepest point and which featured left-center and right-center power alleys that were 455 and 449 feet deep, respectively. (Mays' secret: the second baseman, team captain Alvin Dark, would relay the catcher's signs to him, and Mays was a quick study when it came to sizing up a hitter's strengths and weaknesses. For example, if the catcher "signaled for a fastball against a right-handed hitter who had trouble with the pitch, he might swing late. That would send the ball to right," and Mays would take off in that direction.)[25]

For the fans, Mays' fielding and running made him, all around, a joy to watch. As one writer put it, his "pell-mell style made [outfield plays] look daring, turning him into the most crowd-pleasing and theatrical man ever to play center field. He ran the bases with equal flourish, often running out from under his cap as he whirled from first to third on a base hit."[26]

What's more, Mays stepped up his fielding when it mattered, when the Giants at last began to make a run for the pennant. Mays' best-known outfield play that season came to be called, simply, The Throw.

It came against the Dodgers on August 15. Just days before, the Giants had been 13½ games behind Brooklyn in the standings. But the Giants had begun to surge. They had a four-game winning streak going when the Dodgers came to the Polo Grounds for a three-game series. The Giants took the first game, and the second game was tied 1–1 in the top of the eighth with one out. Brooklyn's Billy Cox, a speedy infielder, was taking his lead off third base; pitcher Ralph Branca was on first. Carl Furillo lofted a fly ball to right-center at medium depth. It was deep enough to let Cox score the go-ahead run from third, even if it was caught.

Mays, expecting Furillo to pull the ball, was shading him toward left-center, so he had to pour on all his speed to reach it. He caught it in full sprint. Cox tagged up at third and ran for home. Because Mays' momentum was taking him toward his left, there seemed to be no possible way for him to throw Cox out—there was simply not enough time to stop, pivot, set, and throw to home.

So Mays cut out a couple of steps. He didn't stop, and he didn't set. He touched down his left foot, pirouetted, and threw, with his body now facing home and the momentum of the spin whipping the ball along. "That was the perfectest throw I ever made," he said after the game.[27]

"It wasn't a throw, it was a *pitch*," said teammate Whitey Lockman. "It was 85 miles an hour, minimum," agreed Giants catcher Wes Westrum.[28] By any name, it was precisely targeted. Westrum caught the ball and blocked the plate against a startled Cox. "Oh, shit, no," Cox said. He didn't even try to slide.[29] It was a double play like no other, and it got the Giants safely out of the inning. In the home half, who should be the first man up to bat but Willie Mays. He laced a single, Westrum followed with a home run, and the Giants won the game 3–1.

When reporters asked Brooklyn manager Charley Dressen what he thought of Mays' play, he said he couldn't comment, "because he'll have to do it again before I believe it."[30]

The Throw made the Giants feel as if they had momentum. They swept the series with the Dodgers and kept on winning over the next ten days as they put together a 16-game streak, the best the National League had seen since 1935.[31]

Winning always buoys a team's mood, but suddenly the Giants, a group that had previously been known as one of the most sullen and least communicative in baseball, had become relaxed, even cheerful—singing choruses of "It's Howdy Doody Time" in train cars, pulling practical jokes, laughing and talking. Always, one player's piping tenor and high-pitched laugh seemed to be part of the mix. Many observers swore that the real difference in the Giants had been brought about by the ebullient presence of Willie Mays. As a rival manager put it, "[Mays] can help a team just by riding on a bus with them."[32]

Durocher, certainly, believed that Mays had made the difference, and to keep his star's spirits high he pumped Mays' ego every chance he got. To the rest of the team, he explained it this way: "[Mays is] a young boy, he's a baby. But he's got more talent in five minutes than the rest of us will ever have in our lifetime. . . . I think it does something for Mays if I keep telling him, 'You're the greatest, no one can carry your glove . . . ' I think it makes him a better player, and as long as it does, buddy, he puts money in your pocket and mine."[33] As far as Durocher could see, the rest of the team understood. "Without exception, my players said, 'Just keep rubbing him, Skip. He's our boy, too.' "[34]

There's no denying, though, that Durocher had a special affection for Mays. As he put it, "If Willie could cook, I'd marry him."[35] Neighbors on Mays' Harlem block noticed how Durocher would walk the rookie home after games, then stay with him out on the stoop talking for hours at a time.[36]

Mays' living arrangements had been organized by the Giants front office, which went all out to protect the young star from the temptations of the big city and the pitfalls of fame. Frank Forbes, the club's official liaison with its black players, became Mays' combination adviser/bodyguard/nanny.[37] Forbes settled the rookie in with a retired couple, David and Anna Goosby, transplanted Alabamans who were now living in the Sugar Hill neighborhood a few blocks from the Polo Grounds.[38] After that, Forbes saw to it that Mays made it to the ballpark on time, he ran interference with the media, and he dissuaded overly ardent admirers (once, by "accidentally" overturning a double chocolate soda into a young lady's lap).[39] Other Giants officials kept an eye on Mays' finances and organized his advertising and TV appearances.[40]

It seemed that all of New York City was almost as enthralled with the rookie as Durocher and Stoneham were. The local press corps, which included reporters for several large-circulation daily newspapers, found everything about Mays newsworthy. His habit of greeting people with a jaunty "Say hey!"—a necessity when everyone around him, casual acquaintance or perfect stranger, would call him by name—led to an article in the *Journal-American* that dubbed him "The Say Hey Kid," a nickname that would stick for life (but would never be used to his face).[41]

The press was ecstatic when a photographer caught Mays in the street one afternoon playing stickball with the neighborhood kids. For the reporters, it was the embodiment of everything Mays represented to them: a boy in a man's body, playing ball for the pure joy of it. As Mays realized later, it cemented his persona in the popular imagination.[42]

Stickball, largely a New York City phenomenon, is a baseball-like game in which players use a broom handle to hit a small pink handball, or "spaldeen," for distance along the street, from manhole cover to manhole cover (or, as they'd say, "sewer to sewer"). To New Yorkers of the day, it was a pastime that was strictly for kids.

From Mays' point of view, playing street stickball was perfectly logical. He was, in fact, only 20 years old, surrounded by considerably older teammates with whom he had little in common. The Goosbys were kind and they made him feel at home, but Mays didn't have much in common with them, either. Ballplayers weren't big on weight rooms and formal workouts in the early 1950s, so what better way to kill the hours before or after game time than a few innings of stickball? "It isn't bad for your eyes, either, because it's a little ball and a thin stick you got to hit it with,"[43] Mays liked to point out. Ever the competitor, he took almost as much pride in his five-sewer stickball hits as in any of his big-league home runs.

But not quite, because Mays was part of a Giants team that was on a sustained tear of great baseball unique in the game's history. Improbably, from their low point 13½ games out of first place on August 11, the Giants were simply refusing to lose, denying Brooklyn the chance to clinch the pennant. The Dodgers were still playing well; their winning percentage was close to .600 in the second half of the season. But the Giants were playing brilliantly. In the season's last six weeks, their winning percentage was a phenomenal .841; the team won its last seven games in a row. When the dust cleared after the season's final games on Sunday, September 30, the two teams were tied for first, with 96 wins apiece. The pennant would have to be decided in a three-game playoff.[44]

Today, with multiple divisions, wild-card teams, and a multi-layered postseason, playoff series in baseball are routine. Not so in 1951, when the team in each league with the most wins took the pennant and went straight to the World Series. This was only the second time in National League history that, with two teams tied in the final standings, the pennant would be won by a playoff. It was all the more intense that the two teams involved were such bitter rivals in the same city, and that the winner would go on to meet New York's other team, the American League-champion Yankees, in the World Series.

Mays was not a major run producer in the Giants final dash for the pennant. After "carrying the team on his back" in June and July, his bat cooled considerably; he hit just two home runs in August and one in September. His bold baserunning had been a factor, though—in a game against the Boston Braves, he stole second base, then third, and scored on an infield grounder.[45] And, of course, his presence in the outfield made a difference, too. Runners around the league now knew better than to challenge Mays' arm.

The batting heroes of the pennant run were Monte Irvin and Bobby Thomson, and they continued to dominate in the playoff. The first game, held at Ebbets Field on October 1, was won by the Giants 3–1. Both Irvin and Thomson hit home runs off Brooklyn pitcher Ralph Branca, accounting for all of the Giants' scoring. Mays went 0 for 3, and Branca struck him out twice. "I didn't want to face [Branca] again," he recalled later.[46]

The series moved to the Polo Grounds for Game 2. It was a romp for the Dodgers as they shut out the Giants 10–0. Mays had one hit, his only hit of the series, as it would turn out. But he also committed an error.

With the series tied, it all came down to one game. It remains one of the most famous games in baseball history, partly because of its inherent drama, and partly because it was the first baseball game to be televised nationwide. The whole country was caught up in the excitement and the tension on October 3, 1951. And every baseball fan since has heard replays of Russ Hodges' play-by-play commentary so often it's become a cliché: "The Giants win the pennant! The Giants win the pennant!"

Yet it truly was a remarkable game. Brooklyn led 1–0 through the first six innings, and the Giants tied it up in the seventh. When the Dodgers scored three runs off Sal Maglie in the top of the eighth, the game seemed out of reach for the Giants.

In the bottom of the ninth, though, exhausted Dodgers ace Don Newcombe couldn't finish the Giants off. Alvin Dark and Don Mueller smacked hard grounders to right for successive singles. With a chance to tie the game, Irvin came to bat, but he popped up a foul ball that was caught for the first out. Next up was Whitey Lockman, who hit to left for a double. Dark came around to score, making it 4–2. But Mueller sprained his ankle on a bad slide into third. The game was delayed as he was borne off the field on a stretcher.

Dodgers manager Charley Dressen used the extra time to strategize. Two relief pitchers, sinkerballer Carl Erskine and Game 1 starter Ralph Branca, were warming up in the bullpen. The Giants had the tying runs in scoring position. First base was empty. Bobby Thomson, a slugger down the stretch who had touched Branca for a home run in Game 1, was up next. Willie Mays, the rookie who was 1 for 10 in the series, was on deck.

In perhaps the most second-guessed managerial move in baseball history, Dressen brought in Branca and, instead of having him walk Thomson intentionally, pitched to him. The first pitch was a called strike. The second one landed in the left field stands.

Willie Mays watched the whole thing from the on-deck circle, and his first emotion on seeing Thomson's home-run shot was relief. Terrified that the Giants' entire season would come down to his next at-bat, he had been so "scared I'd have to go up there with the game depending on me, that I was shaking, near sick to my stomach."[47] When Branca had foregone the intentional walk to Thomson, Mays had "nearly wept with gratitude."[48] Now as Thomson rounded second and the ballpark erupted, Mays' analytical side made him spring into action. He rushed to home and spread his arms wide, protecting the plate and keeping it clear so that Thomson could touch it before the rest of the Giants, already celebrating the victory, could sweep him away.[49] Thomson, who had been jumping rather than running around the bases, leapt down on the plate, and with the score 5–4, "The Giants win the pennant!"

They called it "The Shot Heard 'Round the World," and it certainly seemed that the cheers of the Polo Grounds faithful would carry that far. "The roaring sound of those Giant fans," Mays said later, "was something that will stay in my ears as long as I live."[50]

To fans and players alike, it seemed miraculous– from fifth place to first, from $13\frac{1}{2}$ games back to taking the pennant. The celebration was citywide. Even Mays had some champagne. (It was his first taste of it, he says, and "it was also my last. I didn't like it much.")[51] The euphoria was tempered somewhat by the fact that the Giants still had unfinished business to attend to. The World Series was set to start the next day at Yankee Stadium.

This series, too, would make baseball history, though not in ways that were apparent at the time. Yankee great Joe DiMaggio, 36 years old and past what he considered to be his prime, was planning to retire from baseball quietly once the season ended. This would be his final World Series appearance, and it would include the final home run and plate appearance of his storied playing days. The series also would mark the first World Series games for two rookies just beginning Hall-of-Fame careers, Willie Mays of the Giants and Mickey Mantle of the Yankees.

Before the first game, as players and press milled around the field, Mays only had eyes for DiMaggio. There was his childhood idol in the flesh, "but I was too shy to go up and introduce myself."[52] Finally an enterprising photographer made some mental connections—two centerfielders, rookie and veteran, black and white; not a bad shot—and came up to Mays, saying, "We want a picture of you with DiMag."

"What does he want to be in a picture with me for?" Mays asked.[53]

The photographer made the introduction, the two players posed together, and "I got the chance to talk with him for just a few minutes, a dream come true."[54] It was one memory that would stand out for the rookie, who felt that he played the series in a daze, unable to believe it was all really happening.[55]

Still riding high on the euphoria of the previous day, the Giants took the first game of the World Series in front of 70,000 fans, the biggest crowd Mays had yet seen. Irvin, as if to make up for his ninth-inning pop-out, was the star. He stole home, and he tied a World Series record with four hits in the game. The final score was 5–1 Giants.

The Yankees tied the series the next day 3–1, in a game that would have long-term consequences for one of its participants. Mays lofted a fly ball to right center in the top of the fifth inning, between DiMaggio in center field and Mantle in right. Mantle, who knew that DiMaggio was playing hurt, ran all out to reach the ball. DiMaggio called his teammate off and Mantle stopped short, then Mays saw him "suddenly fall as if he had been shot."[56] His spikes had caught in a drainage-ditch cover, and he had twisted his knee. DiMaggio made the catch; Mays returned, dejected, to the bench, still without a single World Series hit to his credit. Mickey Mantle was carried off the field. He was plagued with knee problems stemming from this injury for the rest of his brilliant career.

The teams headed across the Harlem River to the Polo Grounds for Game 3. The Giants took this one 6–2, due to an inning replete with uncharacteristic Yankee errors that allowed five Giant runs to score. The series stood at two games to one, advantage Giants.

The next day's scheduled Yankees pitcher, Johnny Sain, had been with the Boston Braves for most of the season. The Giants had batted against him before, and recently, giving them a decided edge. The game was rained out, though, and that gave Yankees manager Casey Stengel room to maneuver. With his pitchers granted an unexpected day of rest, Stengel was free to go back to his aces, Allie Reynolds, Ed Lopat, and Vic Raschi, to start Games 4, 5, and 6.

In Game 4, Sal Maglie was on the mound for the Giants when DiMaggio homered in the fifth—the last home run of his career, and the capper of a 4–1 Yankee victory. The exuberant Mays could not contain his joy on seeing his idol hit it out; out in center field, he stood and applauded.[57] But Mays hit into three double plays in the game. With the series tied at two games apiece, the Giants, exhausted after the long pennant race and the stressful playoff, began to fold. Game 5 was a humiliating 13–1 loss for them. Mays managed a walk, but he had a strikeout, too.

It came down to Game 6 at Yankee Stadium, do-or-die for the National Leaguers. The Yankees carried a 4–1 lead into the ninth, but in the top of the inning, the Giants awakened. They loaded the bases on two singles and a bunt, and Monte Irvin came up to bat. He hit a long fly ball that was caught in deep left field and scored the runner from third. Now—déjà vu all over again—the score was 4–2, there was one out and two on, first base was open, and Bobby Thomson was up. The Yankees tempted fate and pitched to Thomson. Again, he hit a monster fly ball to left center. But this one was caught as another run scored.

With two out and still trailing, the Giants were running out of options. Durocher sent a pinch hitter, Sal Yvars, to bat in place of catcher Wes Westrum, and he hit a liner that was caught for the final out of the series. On deck for the last out, once again, was Willie Mays.

"I played [the Series] like a twenty-year-old,"[58] Mays concluded, with a batting average of just .182 on four singles. He had played his first season like a pro, though, with 127 hits, a .472 slugging average, and 20 home runs. He headed home to Fairfield, soon to be named the National League's Rookie of the Year.

NOTES

1. *New York Times*, May 25, 1951.
2. Mays, as told to Einstein, *Willie Mays*, 87.
3. Mays, with Sahadi, *Say Hey*, 63.
4. Mays, as told to Einstein, *Willie Mays*, 88–89.

5. Mays, with Sahadi, *Say Hey*, 64.

6. Mays, as told to Einstein, *Willie Mays*, 146.

7. Mays, with Sahadi, *Say Hey*, 65.

8. Durocher, with Linn, *Nice Guys Finish Last*, 309.

9. Frank Fitzpatrick, "The Night This City Saw Greatness," *Philadelphia Inquirer*, May 25, 2001.

10. Ibid.

11. Ibid.

12. Mays, with Einstein, *Willie Mays*, 93.

13. Frank Fitzpatrick, "The Night This City Saw Greatness," *Philadelphia Inquirer*, May 25, 2001.

14. Einstein, *Willie Mays*, 62.

15. Mays, with Sahadi, *Say Hey*, 58.

16. Mays, as told to Einstein, *Willie Mays*, 93–94.

17. Honig, *Mays, Mantle, Snider*, 106.

18. Mays, as told to Einstein, *Willie Mays*, 94.

19. Durocher, with Linn, *Nice Guys Finish Last*, 309.

20. This conversation is related, with variations, in Mays's memoirs, Mays, with Sahadi, *Say Hey* (69), and Mays, as told to Einstein, *Willie Mays* (94), and in Durocher's autobiography with Linn, *Nice Guys Finish Last* (309–310). Mays's exact wording varies from source to source; this is a compilation.

21. Mays, with Sahadi, *Say Hey*, 69.

22. Mays, as told to Einstein, *Willie Mays*, 94–95.

23. Durocher, with Linn, *Nice Guys Finish Last*, 310.

24. Einstein, *Willie's Time*, 61.

25. Mays, with Sahadi, *Say Hey*, 75–76.

26. Honig, *Mays, Mantle, Snider*, 97.

27. Arthur Daley, "Reprieve for Willie," *New York Times*, May 19, 1952.

28. Einstein, *Willie's Time*, 62.

29. Ibid., 62.

30. Einstein, *Willie Mays*, 70.

31. Mays, with Sahadi, *Say Hey*, 81.

32. Einstein, *Willie's Time*, 41.

33. Durocher, with Linn, *Nice Guys Finish Last*, 310.

34. Ibid., 310.

35. Rick Reilly, "Say Hey, Again," *Sports Illustrated*, September 15, 2003.

36. William C. Rhoden, "Memories of Say, Hey in Sugar Hill," *New York Times*, May 7, 1996.

37. Gilbert Millstein, " 'Natural Boy' of the Giants," *New York Times Magazine*, July 11, 1954.

38. Mays, with Sahadi, *Say Hey*, 72.

39. Joe David Brown, " 'The Onliest Way I Know'," *Sports Illustrated*, April 13, 1959.

40. Gilbert Millstein, "'Natural Boy' of the Giants," *New York Times Magazine*, July 11, 1954.

41. "Obituaries," *The Sporting News*, February 5, 1990; Einstein, *Willie's Time*, 31–32.

42. Mays, with Sahadi, *Say Hey*, 72.

43. Mays, as told to Einstein, *Willie Mays*, 108.

44. Einstein, *Willie Mays*, 75.

45. Ibid., 77.

46. Mays, with Sahadi, *Say Hey*, 86.

47. Mays, as told to Einstein, *Willie Mays*, 16.

48. Ibid., 14.

49. Einstein, *Willie's Time*, 59.

50. Mays, as told to Einstein, *Willie Mays*, 15.

51. Mays, with Sahadi, *Say Hey*, 89.

52. Ibid., 90.

53. Mays, as told to Einstein, *Willie Mays*, 122.

54. Mays, with Sahadi, *Say Hey*, 90.

55. Mays, as told to Einstein, *Willie Mays*, 122.

56. Mays, with Sahadi, *Say Hey*, 91.

57. Carl Nolte, "An American Icon," *San Francisco Chronicle*, March 9, 1999.

58. Mays, with Sahadi, *Say Hey*, 96.

THE ARMY, 1952–1953

Mays returned to Aunt Sarah's house in Fairfield to find a letter waiting for him. It was news he had half expected, but after his incredible season in New York, it was the farthest thing from his mind. It came from the local committee of the Selective Service Board, and it could only mean one thing: Willie Mays was wanted by the U.S. Army. He had been drafted.[1]

Early in the 1951 season, Giants management had privately thought that Mays might be drafted that summer. Mays had not known it, but the fear of an untimely military call-up had been one of the reasons Horace Stoneham had sent Mays to Minneapolis that spring, rather than adding him to the New York roster as Leo Durocher wanted.[2] When the Giants got off to their awful start, though, Durocher had had his way, and the rest was history. Now, Stoneham's original fears were coming true—the difference being that now, Mays wasn't a little-known minor leaguer, but a nationwide star.

The drafting of able-bodied young men into military service had been done during times of emergency several times in the history of the United States, from the Civil War through World War II. Draftees had served with distinction—though not always with enthusiasm—in many conflicts. The "peacetime" draft of the early 1950s was another matter. A recent law, the Selective Service Act of 1948, had established a system of non-emergency military conscription to which young men over the age of 18 were subject. The memory of World War II was still fresh, American occupying forces were stationed around the globe, the Cold War was in full effect, and the United States was fighting in Korea. The need for troops was real, as was the sense of service and duty that most Americans felt when it came to the military's call. It was an invitation Mays could not deny.

Like many others, though, he did try to defer it. Mays was mainly worried about finances. His salary from the Giants was helping to support both Aunt Sarah's household and that of his mother, her frequently out-of-work husband, and their nine children.[3] Mays' baseball contract was good for one season only; it would be renewed if he played, but not if he didn't. A private's army salary would certainly not approach the amount the Giants would pay him for the 1952 season.

Mays believed that most young men claiming 11 dependents would be awarded a hardship deferment, no questions asked. But in his case, the draft board chose not to bend the rules, which required a man to live in the same house as his dependents. Never mind that Mays had never lived with his mother's family but had always taken some responsibility for them. Never mind that, as a ballplayer, his job forced him to live away from home for most of each year. Perhaps the draft board's members feared the appearance of favoritism toward the young major leaguer.[4]

So Mays went before the draft board in October 1951. He passed the physical as expected, but he failed the Army's written aptitude test.[5]

The AFQT, or Armed Forces Qualification Test, was in its second year of use at the time. Given to recruits through the 1970s, it was a relatively simple multiple-choice exam meant to gauge a military candidate's ability to perform certain tasks—mechanical, analytical, and so on. Its 100 questions also analyzed verbal and mathematical skills. The test results were used to match recruits with suitable military jobs or assignments.[6]

Did Mays botch the test on purpose? The draft board seemed to think so, though they did not declare it publicly. Mays was a high school graduate, after all, and he had finished in the top half of his class. He'd had as much education as many of the men who had served in the armed forces up to that time. Rather than declare him 4-F immediately and disqualify him from military service, which they could have done when they met with Mays on October 30, the board ordered him to take the AFQT a second time.[7] The retest was scheduled for January.

Meanwhile, Mays spent time with his family and friends in the Birmingham area, reveling in memories of the season just past and spending his $5,000 World Series bonus, the highest amount that the members of a losing team had ever earned. He bought furniture and household appliances for his mother's home and a portable record player for himself. Mays bought a car, too, even though he didn't know how to drive. Ostensibly the car was for his father. But as long as Mays was in Birmingham he had a friend from his teen years, Herman

Boykin, use it to chauffeur him around town. Finally, Mays decided to teach himself to drive. The car's manual transmission turned out to be a bit of a stumbling block, though: "I said the heck with it. I was going to drive the thing. So I hopped in and jerked down the streets of Fairfield to Big Tony's pool hall. They all laughed, but I told them I didn't need Herman anymore."[8]

In January, Mays took the AFQT again. This time, he passed.

Private Mays' two-year stint in the army would begin in the late spring. All he knew was that he would have to be ready when he got the call. Until then, he was going to wring everything he could out of being a New York Giant. He worked out at the Giants spring training camp in Arizona and prepared to start the season with the team.

With the loss of Mays looming, the Giants took another blow when Monte Irvin was badly hurt in a preseason exhibition game. It happened in Denver, where the Giants were playing the Cleveland Indians. With Irvin on first, Mays hit a sharp single. Irvin rounded second, slid into third, jammed his ankle on the base, and shattered it. There was no play at the bag; the outfielder hadn't even thrown to third. It was only an exhibition game, after all.

"I guess a couple of guys got to him before I did, but I was there—as fast as I ever ran in my life—and when I saw what had happened to him, I broke out crying," Mays recalled later.[9] From Mays' first day with the Giants, Irvin had been his friend and protector, especially when the team was on the road. On the field, Irvin was the engine that had powered the 1951 Giants. And there he was down in the dirt, doubled up and clutching himself in pain. "It was a horrible thing to see," Mays said. "He was on the ground and suffering and I couldn't do anything for him."[10]

It was immediately clear that without the big slugger and the sparkplug center fielder, the Giants would have an uphill battle in the 1952 season. Irvin would be out for a lengthy period; he was 33 years old, and the compound fracture that this proved to be had the potential to end his career. Durocher feverishly worked out various roster moves so that he could field a competent team in the absence of Mays and Irvin. It wasn't easy. "Without Monte's booming bat the Little Shepherd of Coogan's Bluff is in deep distress," were the words of a sportswriter of the day.[11] "Nor is his plight made any less acute by the fact that Willie Mays, his Infant Prodigy, is perilously close to being yanked into the Army."

But against all odds, the season began well for the Giants, as their pitching carried the team to the best start in baseball. Sal Maglie won his first nine starts, and the other hurlers were almost as good. With pitching like that, it didn't much matter that the Infant Prodigy hit just .236 with four homers in the 34 games he played with the Giants that season. Mays did have a memorable outfield play, though, in the Dodgers home opener at Ebbets Field on April 18.[12]

Bobby Morgan hit a long line drive out to left center that looked sure to hit the outfield wall for extra bases. But Mays got there first. With a flying leap, he nabbed the ball, crashed into the grass, and lay there, stunned by the impact. When he came to, Mays saw Durocher and several concerned teammates hovering over him, and Jackie Robinson strolling away.

"Jackie was coming out here to see if I was all right?" Mays asked, impressed.

"Are you nuts?" Durocher exclaimed at the idea of Brooklyn's fiercest competitor doing such a thing. "He only came out here to see if you still had the ball in your glove!"[13]

Mays' last game before his May 29 army call-up was played against the Brooklyn Dodgers at Ebbets Field. In a remarkable show of respect, the Brooklyn fans gave him a standing ovation after his final at-bat, a touching gesture Mays never forgot, and one that showed just how far he had gone in winning over New Yorkers' affections.[14]

The Giants sent Mays off with a portable radio from the team and a tie clip from Durocher, and he reported for duty at Camp Eustis, Virginia. He would be gone for the next two years.

"I was raised to say 'Yes, sir,' and I always respected authority," Mays said later, "so the Army and I got along very well."[15] Even though American troops were stationed all over the world in 1952, from Japan to Korea to Germany, Mays was not set to be sent overseas. After basic training—which he passed without trouble, unsurprisingly—he was assigned to the instructional division of the physical training department at Camp Eustis, leading other recruits in workouts. But his major task at camp was exactly as it had been in civilian life: he was there to play baseball. Here, he would be playing in the intercamp games that the army higher-ups enjoyed for the bragging rights that victory conferred on them. Mays had essentially traded a Giants baseball jersey for an army jersey.

Other ballplayers had similar military experiences in the early 1950s. Pittsburgh's Vern Law and Boston's Karl Olson played with Mays on the Camp Eustis team. As they visited and hosted other camp teams, they faced off against Johnny Antonelli of the Braves, and future Yankee Lou Skizas.[16] "If you didn't feel like soldiering they didn't mind," Mays said caustically of the army brass, once his military days were over. "But if you didn't feel like playing they got mad as hell."[17]

So he played, and played well. Mays hit .420 and .389 in his two 90-game "army-league" seasons.[18] Given the level of the competition, these stats aren't comparable to those of the rest of his career. The games weren't meaningful in the sense of contributing to a pennant drive or leading to a bigger contract. Still, Mays being Mays, he played all out. He stole a base in a game that his team was leading 14–0; he gave himself a slight ankle fracture on a slide play; he suffered a sprain while playing basketball with the camp team he led during the months he wasn't playing baseball.

Every time, just as if he was still in New York, he'd take a tongue-lashing from his anxious former manager. Somehow, Leo Durocher always knew when Mays had taken a needless chance on the playing field. Within hours Durocher would be on the phone, chewing out his long-distance prodigy. "When he got excited he would scream and talk so fast he sounded like Donald Duck," Mays remembered fondly in later years.[19] Sputtering and swearing, he would "ask me was I out of my —— —— mind."[20] Then he'd send a little cash in the mail to his favorite soldier, "I think," said Mays, "just to let me know he still cared."[21]

Through the rest of the 1952 season and even more so in 1953, it was as if Mays' power as the Giants' good-luck charm intensified with time. Now, though, it held when he was in no position to come off the bench and break the spell. If the Giants couldn't win without Mays, Durocher figured, he was going to do whatever he could—by phone, by mail, whatever means necessary— to keep Mays from getting hurt in the meantime.

For without Mays, the Giants faltered. Ten days after his departure, the team fell out of first place, never to regain it. They had a late-September surge upon Irvin's return from his ankle injury, but it seemed that their hearts weren't really in it.[22] They finished the season in second place, $4\frac{1}{2}$ games behind Brooklyn.

Speed and defense had been the hallmarks of the 1951 club's success, and without Mays the Giants were diminished in both departments. What was worse, everyone on the team knew it. Throughout 1952 and 1953, whenever a Giant outfielder missed a catch, he'd be met in the dugout with a mournful refrain: "Willie woulda had it."[23] It started with Durocher, who was never shy about burnishing the image of his favorite player. But then it caught on with the pitchers, and eventually with the entire team. No matter how impossible the play, the Giants were sure that any ball hit to any spot beyond the infield dirt would have been routine for the missing Mays. Be it screaming liner or pop fly, "Willie woulda had it."

It was a good mindset to have if you wanted a losing team. By the end of the 1953 season, the club was so listless that Durocher had players taking turns managing games, just to make things a little more interesting.[24] In the end, the 1953 Giants came in fifth, just as they had in their last pre-Mays season, 35 games out of first place.

Down in Virginia, Willie Mays kept on playing baseball, even though, increasingly concerned about his family's financial well-being, he had again appealed to the army for a hardship discharge.[25] Again he was denied.

51

He may have felt disappointed in the army's disregard for his family situation, but Mays still played all-out, continuing to amaze opponents with his abilities. For one opposing batsman, the memory was still fresh when he told the story almost 50 years later. His team was down by a run when he came to bat, bases loaded, two out, bottom of the ninth. He was a weak-hitting scrapper of a ballplayer, but he turned on a fastball down the pipe and "hit it square on with everything I had."

"I saw the center fielder turn his back on the ball. . . . He was running even faster than I was. And he ran and ran. When he finally caught up with the ball he made a spectacular catch going away in full stride." The hitter could hardly believe what he had just seen. He was frozen at second base as Mays jogged by, ball still lodged in glove. "That was some poke, Shorty," he said, smiling graciously.[26]

When Mays thought back on his army baseball days, the games against the Marines stood out in his mind. "They would knock you down all the time" with high-and-tight pitches, he remembered years later. "As soon as I step in the batter's box, bam, upside my head. I would hit it over the fence, come back up again, bam, back up in there." Once the game was over, though, there were no hard feelings. "They would carry me off the field and get me a couple of big steaks. They were fine when the game was over. But they were mean, boy. They were mean."[27]

Meanwhile, Mays' instructional work was taking an interesting turn. One of his charges had an odd way of catching a fly ball. Instead of holding the glove up and out at eye level, he held his glove at the belt, turned in. "You gotta be crazy," Mays declared.

"Try it my way," urged the kid, who threw a routine fly out to his instructor. Mays tried it, and caught the ball with the glove down low. "Doesn't make any difference, does it?" the kid called out.[28]

Oh, but it did make a difference, and Mays spotted the distinction immediately. Piper Davis had taught Mays to throw sidearm-fashion from the outfield. This new, non-traditional catching stance put his hands in the perfect position to make an immediate sidearm throw, without having to shift or set his body.[29] It would give Mays precious milliseconds on a runner headed for the extra base, a critical edge that he could not ignore.

And so the basket catch was born. It would become, like his cap-flying pell-mell flight around the bases, Willie Mays' signature play in the outfield.

"I have no pride in my Army career," Mays reflected later. "But I have no apologies for it either. I did what the man said, and when they needed my car they could have that too."[30] Once the camp baseball season ended in September, it was just a waiting game. Mays peeled potatoes and counted the days: *six more months till discharge . . . five more months till discharge. . . .*

Then came terrible news. In November 1953 Mays' mother, Ann McMorris, died in childbirth. She was only 41 years old. The baby, Diana, was her eleventh child.[31] Mays was deeply saddened—and, as the "big brother," he felt deeply responsible for the well-being of his remaining family. Now Mays had ten half-siblings to support, none over the age of 18, as well as Aunt Sarah. "It didn't help my final months in the Army," he noted.[32] His feelings may have been bitter, but he kept them to himself and served out his remaining time. On March 1, 1954, he would be free.

NOTES

1. Mays, with Sahadi, *Say Hey*, 98.
2. Durocher, with Linn, *Nice Guys Finish Last*, 308–309.
3. Mays, as told to Einstein, *Willie Mays*, 126.
4. Mays, with Sahadi, *Say Hey*, 99.
5. Ibid., 99.
6. "ABCs of the ASVAB" Web site, http://usmilitary.about.com/cs/joiningup/a/asvababcs.htm.
7. *New York Times*, October 30, 1951.
8. Mays, with Sahadi, *Say Hey*, 98–99.
9. Mays, as told to Einstein, *Willie Mays*, 146.
10. Mays, with Sahadi, *Say Hey*, 99–100.
11. *New York Times*, April 4, 1952.
12. Mike Getz, *Brooklyn Dodgers and Their Rivals, 1950–1952* (Brooklyn, NY: Montauk Press, 1999), 102.
13. Mays, with Sahadi, *Say Hey*, 82. This source claims a September 1951 date for the incident, but Morgan did not play for Brooklyn in 1951; other sources give the April 1952 date, which is consistent with Morgan's career.
14. Mays, with Sahadi, *Say Hey*, 100.
15. Ibid., 101.
16. Ibid.
17. Mays, as told to Einstein, *Willie Mays*, 148.
18. Mays, with Sahadi, *Say Hey*, 103.
19. Ibid., 102.
20. Mays, as told to Einstein, *Willie Mays*, 148.
21. Mays, with Sahadi, *Say Hey*, 102.
22. Mays, as told to Einstein, *Willie Mays*, 147.
23. Einstein, *Willie's Time*, 90.
24. Mays, as told to Einstein, *Willie Mays*, 148.
25. *New York Times*, January 27, 1953.
26. William T. Harper, "The Greatest Catch," *American Heritage*, November 1999.

27. "Still the Say Hey Kid," *New York Post*, May 3, 2001.

28. Mays, as told to Einstein, *Willie Mays*, 149.

29. Einstein, *Willie's Time*, 113.

30. Mays, as told to Einstein, *Willie Mays*, 148.

31. Mays, with Sahadi, *Say Hey*, 9; Einstein, *Willie Mays*, 42.

32. Mays, with Sahadi, *Say Hey*, 102.

THE CHAMPIONSHIP
SEASON, 1954

"In six—more days—we're gonna have Willie Mays. . . ." It was spring training in Phoenix, Arizona, and Giants vice president Chub Feeney was singing at the top of his lungs. The whole organization was happier than a fifth-place club had any right to be, all because of the impending return of a certain center fielder. Feeney made it his practice to count down the days to Mays' expected arrival by wandering through the hotel lobby, singing loudly to the tune of the traditional folk song "Old Black Joe" and changing his lyrics with each new morning.[1]

The din was beginning to get on the sportswriters' nerves, especially those who hadn't covered the team in Mays' rookie year. The *New York Herald Tribune*'s Roger Kahn was one of those who figured that the Mays legend had to be more hype than reality.[2] Kahn had covered the Dodgers in 1951, but was on the Giants beat now. He knew baseball as well as anybody, and of one thing he was sure: there was no way that one guy—a kid at that, not quite 23—would inspire a total turnaround in a team as lousy as the Giants had been in 1953.

While Feeney was singing in Arizona, Mays was still back in Virginia, packing his bags and counting down the days as well. He was so anxious to rejoin his team, he didn't even plan to visit the family in Birmingham once he was discharged on March 1, 1954. It was all arranged: the Giants' semiofficial Mays protector Frank Forbes would meet his charge at the gates of Camp Eustis, drive him to Washington, DC, and accompany him on the plane trip to Phoenix.

Finally the long-awaited day arrived. After 21 months in military service, Willie Mays was honorably discharged. Forbes was there to greet him, and right on schedule, they raced off to Washington.

Perhaps the most famous outfield play in baseball history: The Catch of September 29, 1954. *Frank Hurley/New York Daily News.*

When they got there, Mays' trip to the team training camp was nearly derailed. Just a few hours before, a group of Puerto Rican nationalists had opened fire from the gallery of the House of Representatives, wounding five legislators. The city was in a state of near-hysteria, and apparently the sight of two dark-skinned men attempting to board a plane was enough to arouse the suspicions of the police officers stationed at the airport. Mays and Forbes were detained for a while as their backgrounds were checked.[3] Finally they were allowed onto a flight. They arrived in Phoenix late that night.[4]

Next morning, slightly more than 24 hours after his discharge, Mays arrived at the Giants clubhouse, expecting to be welcomed with as much excitement as he felt about his return. Instead, the clubhouse staff, coaches, and some of his teammates made a show of treating Mays with indifference, like a no-name minor-leaguer up for a tryout. As man after man shrugged off his impassioned reminders—"Hey! It's me!" he was eventually shouting—Mays grew frustrated, then angry. As he tells it: "I busted my way in [to the batting cage]. I dug in, lined up on the first pitch. I hit it. I hit it downtown."[5]

Finally Mays heard someone call out, "Look, Leo, here comes your pennant!"[6] Suddenly there was Leo Durocher, enveloping Mays in a bear hug fit to break his ribs, and the rest of the team materialized to welcome him for real with back-slaps, handshakes, and—an element that had been missing from the Giants clubhouse in the previous two years—peals of laughter.

When the players took the field for an intrasquad game later that day, the Giants seasons of frustration and "what-ifs" evaporated. Mays got going with a catch of a low, humming liner that required him to charge the ball, dive, and somersault to get it into his glove. Next, at the plate, he smashed a 400-foot home run to left. Two innings later, he made an impossible one-handed catch in right-center, whirled, and threw the ball to first to snag the runner who'd been there in a double play. He followed that up with an over-the-shoulder catch of a ball that should have gone for a double. He wasn't the phenom kid who'd electrified the league three years before. He was better. The jaded New York sportswriters could barely contain their amazement: "a revelation," "an eye-opener," "incredible."[7]

His performance even won over the doubting Kahn, who began his coverage with the warning, "This is not going to be a plausible story, but then no one ever accused Willie Mays of being a plausible ball player. This story is only the implausible truth."[8]

Durocher was elated. "It's only 240 days to World Series time. In order to avoid the rush, let's start printing the tickets now," he chortled.[9]

Indeed, this was a Giants club that Durocher had built to his own specifications, and for that reason alone he was convinced that it would go all the way.

Ever since his arrival at the Polo Grounds in 1948, Durocher had been working to put together a team like this one, replete with high-average hitters, strong fielders, dominating pitchers, and baseball smarts all down the line. He'd come close to his ideal team in 1951. Now, as the 1954 season was about to get underway, he thought he had it.

In left field was slugger Monte Irvin, recovered from his ankle injury, though not quite as speedy as he had once been. In right was Don Mueller, who could hit for average and would lead the league in hits that year. The canny shortstop Alvin Dark was team captain in the dugout and on the field, positioning the defense. Hank Thompson at third could drive the ball. Whitey Lockman at first base and Davey Williams at second were both excellent position players. Wes Westrum had been a solid presence behind the plate for all of Durocher's Giants tenure, and this season he was the anchor for a pitching staff led by Sal Maglie and Johnny Antonelli, who had played against Mays in the service and who was poised for a breakout year. The bullpen included knuckleballer Hoyt Wilhelm. The bench was strong, too, with pinch-hitting specialist Dusty Rhodes at the ready.

But first and foremost, in Durocher's mind, was Mays in center field. His faith in Mays was such that he ordered the other outfielders, particularly Mueller, to give way to the center fielder any and every time Mays called for a fly ball.[10] This was against all baseball tradition, and for some on the team it rankled. But the manager made no secret of the fact that Mays had a special place in his estimations that went beyond mere appreciation of his baseball skills. "From the first moment I saw Willie, he was my boy," Durocher said later. "After all the fathers I'd had watching over me in my own career I had finally got me a son."[11]

Durocher wasn't even fazed by his "son's" new, unconventional, and risky-looking basket catch, which Mays showed off in camp. (The method certainly did appear to be daring, as many sportswriters commented, and for most fielders perhaps it would be an unsafe move. Not, it would turn out, for Mays, who used the basket catch for the rest of his career and who would admit to losing only two balls with the play.[12]) It's quite possible that Durocher didn't care if Mays was lunging at balls blindfolded and with his back turned, just so long as he was the man in center field. "Is [the basket catch] a flair?" a reporter asked the manager—that is, a bit of showboating designed to heighten the drama of a routine fly ball and garner the fielder some extra attention.

"Call it what you want," Durocher answered.

"Are you going to tell him to change back to normal style?" the questioner persisted.

"Why should I? He catches them, doesn't he?"[13]

The Giants spent most of spring training walloping the Cleveland Indians, the only other major-league team that worked out in the southwest.[14] As Opening Day approached, Mays was hitting .381 in preseason contests and "felt ready for anything."[15]

No one on the club was ready for an ugly incident that marred an exhibition-game trip to Las Vegas. After the game, in which the Giants beat the Indians again, the team was invited to visit one of the casinos for food and entertainment on the house. Mays took in a show with Roger Kahn, then wandered over to the dice tables, where he stood quietly watching the game. Suddenly a thuggish security man accosted Kahn, saying, "Get your friend away from the dice tables. We don't want him mixing with the white guests."

Kahn was indignant. The casino had asked Mays and the team to come in, after all. "Do you know who he is?" Kahn demanded.

"Yeah. I know who he is," said the security man. "He's a nigger. Get that nigger away from the white guests." The two were shouting now.

Kahn pulled out his press card. "I want to thank you," he said loudly, "for giving me a great story for the Sunday *New York Herald Tribune*." That was enough to bring out the hotel executives, desperate to get Kahn to drop the issue and not give the place bad publicity. The ballplayers quietly left. Seething, Kahn joined them on the team bus.

Monte Irvin approached him on the trip back to Arizona. Still protective of Mays, he too asked Kahn to keep the incident quiet. "Willie isn't Jackie Robinson," Irvin said. "He's a 23-year-old kid without much formal education. If you write what just happened, there could be an explosion and, you know, Willie isn't up to handling that."

Kahn understood. He did not publish a story about the casino episode until decades had passed. Mays himself never discussed it for publication. It was just one of many incidents of discrimination he preferred not to acknowledge.[16]

Mays had, without ceremony or negotiation, signed a contract with the Giants for $13,000—by custom, the same amount he had received in 1952, the year he had entered military service.[17] Some saw this as a mark of Mays's innocence or his blind faith in the club, but Mays understood that the practice was something of an insurance policy for all players subject to the military draft. At a time when there was no formal players' union to protect athletes' interests, customs like this one helped guarantee them some security. Mays accepted it without hesitation.

Mays and the rest of the club could hardly wait to get back to New York, where Opening Day would pit the Giants against the Dodgers at the Polo Grounds. Excitement was high in the stands and on the field, as it was whenever the two rivals met, and the pregame ceremonies included a players' parade to the center field flagpole and a first pitch thrown by New York's mayor, Robert Wagner.[18] The game was knotted 3–3 in the sixth inning when Mays hit his first home run of the season off Carl Erskine to pull the Giants ahead 4–3. It was a monstrous rising liner that kept sailing up and up until it was stopped short by the upper deck, high above the 414-foot marker in left field.[19] It turned out to be the game winner.

For Mays, it was a fitting reintroduction to baseball-mad New York, whose three major-league teams now boasted three future Hall of Famers in the premier center field position: Mickey Mantle of the Yankees, Duke Snider of the Dodgers, and again Mays of the Giants. That summer, practically every kid in the city and its swelling suburbs would spend hours arguing the merits of his or her favorite among the three. All three could hit for average and with power, though going into the 1954 season it was Snider who had the edge as a slugger. All of them played center with strength; Snider was known for his smoothness and Mantle for his speed. Now here came Mays, with his five tools and his penchant for the dramatic outfield play. The three of them would provide fuel for baseball debates for years to come.[20] Meanwhile, the man at the center of all the chatter had settled comfortably back into his life in New York. Mays again took a room with the Goosbys on Sugar Hill in Harlem, and again took up street stickball—because, as he said in seeming seriousness, "Somebody has got to get those kids to play right."[21]

Five days into the new season, the Giants and Dodgers met for another series, this time at Ebbets Field in Brooklyn. Once more Mays homered, this time for two runs, against Erskine. Again his hit was the game winner. But the Giants weren't getting off to the roaring start they had anticipated; they were in fifth place a month into the season. Despite hitting four game-winning home runs—one a clutch hit in the fourteenth inning—Mays' .250 average was part of the reason why. So Durocher got after him to alter his approach. Mays had to stop pulling the ball to left, stop trying to swing for the fences every time up. In the massive Polo Grounds outfield, that kind of predictability was a sure path to flyouts. A spray hitter, whose ability to hit to all fields would spread out defending fielders, was much more likely to get on base. A spray hitter with power might mix in a few homers, too.[22]

As much as his adaptability was a mark of Mays' talent, trust in his mentor, Durocher, was a mark of his personality. Mays altered his stance and suddenly both the hits and the batting average increased. The first day he tried to spray the ball, he drove a double to right field and hit a home run to boot. "I told ya," said Durocher.[23] To make the manager seem even more prescient, the Giants started to win. By the end of May, the Giants had pulled up to second place, and Mays was hitting at a .300 clip with 14 home runs.

As spring turned into summer, and as Mays continued to rack u'
the press began to do the math. Eleven home runs in May plu.
June; three full months of the season to go . . . could this be the year that
Ruth's 60-home run single-season record would be broken? Mays was actually
ahead of Ruth's pace, reporters liked to point out, because the Babe had to hit
a whopping 17 in the last month of the 1927 season to set the revered record.[24]
"The newspapermen . . . by now were jumping into the shower with me for extra
interviews," Mays noted dryly.[25]

To Mays, the important thing was that the team was performing as he had
thought it could. The pitching staff in particular was having a phenomenal year.
Antonelli, the new addition, was pacing the league in earned run average, and
the pitchers as a group were dominating the competition, well on their way to
racking up 19 shutouts and 22 one-run games.

All through June, the Giants and the Dodgers played at a level far beyond
the rest of the league as they battled for the first-place berth. It culminated in
a thirteen-inning game on June 29 at the Polo Grounds. The game included a
triple by Snider that would have been an inside-the-park home run but for Mays,
who grabbed the ball in deep right center and returned it to the infield in a
throw that reporters called "astonishing," holding Snider to three bases. Mays
was everywhere in that game, snagging line drives near the bleachers and rushing in for bloop flies behind second base. "Is there any way we can get that little
man out of there?" one Brooklyn fan complained.[26]

The Giants were leading 2–0 when, with two out and one on in the top of
the ninth, Brooklyn catcher Roy Campanella smashed a home run over the left-
field roof off Maglie to tie the game. The teams battled through three more innings as their managers tried to outmaneuver each other, their hitters worked
full counts, and their fielders turned inning-ending double plays. In the thirteenth, with two out, Brooklyn's weak-hitting third baseman Don Hoak hit a
solo home run to give the Dodgers the lead. But in the home half, with the Giants down to their last out and one man on, Mays and Irvin both walked on
3–2 counts. Durocher, whose moves had forced him to pull his first-string and
second-string catchers from the game, now replaced the Giants' third-string
catcher with pinch hitter Dusty Rhodes, a man who seemed to take a perverse
pride in his lack of fielding ability.[27]

"If we tie the score, who's going to be doing the catching?" Rhodes asked.

"You," said Durocher.

Rhodes grounded the third pitch into shallow center field. Irvin scored the
tying run, and right behind him came Mays from second, who had figured out
the consequences of a continued tie as Rhodes stood in the batter's box. "I never
ran so fast in my life," he said.[28] His heads-up baserunning won the contest,

and the dramatic game put the Giants in first place, a spot they held for the rest of the season.

When a week later they swept the Dodgers in a three-game series just before the All-Star break, it looked like the pennant was in the bag. Now the spotlight could shine directly on Mays, whose four home runs in the Brooklyn series sent the press and fans into paroxysms of delight. It was July 8; he was at 30 homers and counting.

Mays had been selected to play in his first All-Star Game on July 13. Snider had been elected as the starting center fielder, but that didn't bother Mays. He was proud to appear in the game, in which he was 1 for 2 with a single. He wouldn't miss another one for the rest of his career.[29]

The All-Star appearance was one marker of Mays' popularity. Another was the sudden spate of tribute songs that were produced in his honor during the 1954 season, including "Amazing Willie Mays" by the King Odom Quartet and "Say Hey Willie Mays" by the Wanderers.[30] The Treniers, an R&B act made up of four brothers from Mobile, Alabama, scored the coup of adding Mays's own voice to their song, "Say Hey (The Willie Mays Song)." When they recorded it on July 15 in a session supervised by a young Quincy Jones, Mays was there to interject an exuberant "Say, hey!" at key moments.[31]

Days later, Mays was hit with more bad news from Birmingham. His Aunt Sarah, his "second mother," died on July 17. Coming so soon after the sudden death of his birth mother, the emotional burden for Mays was staggering. He rushed home for the funeral, missing several road games with the team. The Giants sent Frank Forbes to accompany Mays, who was beside himself with grief. "Practically the whole time I was there for the funeral I stayed in my bedroom," he recalled years later. "About five hundred people paid their respects. The church overflowed . . . I was too upset, though, to go to the cemetery."[32] It was five days before he could pull himself together sufficiently to return to baseball. The Giants told the press that Mays had business to manage in Fairfield in the wake of his aunt's death.[33]

When he rejoined the Giants in Milwaukee, where the former Boston Braves were playing their second season since leaving their old home town, Mays seemed to pour all his energy and emotion into baseball. He smashed a home run off Warren Spahn to win the game, then hit two more homers when the team returned to the Polo Grounds later in the week. Meanwhile, he was *Time* magazine's cover story for its July 26 issue.[34]

The newspapers and national magazines were breathlessly covering Mays' home-run pace, but Durocher was looking at the bigger picture. The first-place Giants were still being pursued by the dogged Dodgers. To win the pennant, the manager knew they couldn't slack off for a moment. They had to keep scoring runs, as many as possible, game after game. To maximize runs, Durocher needed to create big innings and manufacture rallies. For that he had to put more men on base.

Durocher had noticed that opposing pitchers were on to Mays' home-run tear. They were beginning to keep the ball away from Mays now, painting the outer corners of the plate, reluctant to feed him any pitches he could drive deep.

With all this in mind, Durocher approached Mays for the second time that season to talk about his hitting. This time, the advice seemed counterintuitive at first: "Willie, I want you to stop going for home runs."[35]

Durocher explained that he wanted to move Mays up in the batting order, from sixth to third. This would give Mays more at-bats per game—more opportunities to get on base, to steal, and to move runners around. If he concentrated on hitting for average rather than swinging for the fences, Mays would help the team more. He might even contend for the batting title, Durocher said.[36]

"I really wasn't into the Babe Ruth thing," Mays said later; "I was naïve about records"[37] at the time. Durocher's logic made sense to him. Once again, Mays displayed his consummate adaptability: with a few minor alterations at the plate, immediately the home runs all but ceased. After hitting 36 of them over the season's first 99 games, he hit only five more in the final 55 contests of the regular season; one of those was an inside-the-park number. Meanwhile, just as Durocher had predicted, Mays' batting average spiked. He hit .379 during the final third of the season, pulling his overall average into the .340s.[38] With Mays now batting third, the Giants continued to win, staying just ahead of Brooklyn as the season wound down.

If the fans were disappointed in Mays' sudden drop in home run production, they didn't show it. When the Giants celebrated Willie Mays Day on August 8, 31,000 fans turned out to cheer him. Politicians made speeches, bands played, and the club presented Mays with gifts including an air conditioner, a TV set, a deed to a plot of land in New York's suburbs, and, from his teammates who knew of Mays' growing passion for jazz and swing music, a record cutter, which he could use to make his own acetate recordings. Mays hit only a single in the game, but the fans looked on the bright side: he extended an ongoing hitting streak to 13 games.[39]

By the end of September, the Giants held a comfortable five-game lead over the Dodgers. No playoffs necessary this time: there was no doubt that the Giants were headed to the World Series. It was an amazing turnaround from their dismal fifth-place finish the season before, a gain of 40 games in the standings, and many fans and writers couldn't help but feel that it was Mays who had made the difference, home runs or no home runs.

Now that the talk of catching Ruth's record had died, Mays was chasing another statistic—he was in the thick of a tight three-way race for the batting title. Duke Snider of Brooklyn, Giants teammate Don Mueller, and Mays were within percentage points of one another all through September, all hovering around the .345 mark.

It came down to the final game of the season, with the three men—Mueller at .3426, Snider at .3425, and Mays at .3422—in a virtual tie. The Giants were playing in Philadelphia and facing their ace and strikeout specialist, Robin Roberts. The Dodgers were at home in Ebbets Field, a park seemingly built for Snider's hitting proclivities, going against a Pittsburgh rookie pitcher with a 3–8 record. On paper, it looked like Snider had the title wrapped up.

But as the old saying goes, there's a reason why they play the games. Against all the odds, Snider went hitless in a Dodger defeat. The contest was between two Giants now, fellow outfielders Mueller and Mays, and the Giants' game went into extra innings, dragging out the suspense as each man got additional times at bat. Mueller singled, fouled out, and flied out twice. Mays singled in the early innings, grounded out, then hit a triple and a double. Both men stayed in the game for the tenth and the eleventh innings. Mueller doubled, then hit into a forceout. He was 2 for 6 in the game. When Mays was intentionally walked in the tenth, that decided it. He was 3 for 4 official times at bat, and with an average of .345, the National League batting champion. He led the league in triples and in slugging average for good measure and hit 41 home runs, the National League's third-highest total that year.

Mays rushed back to New York when the game was done and set off on a whirlwind tour of the national airwaves. Ushered by his constant companion Forbes, he was a guest on both CBS's *Ed Sullivan Show* and NBC's *Colgate Comedy Hour*, quite a feat since both shows were live broadcasts that aired simultaneously. (New York was the center of the television world at the time, so he only had to hustle across Manhattan to appear at the beginning of one show and the end of the other.) Next morning, Mays was a guest of the *Today* show. That night, he was interviewed on the *Tonight* show.[40] It was an all-out two-day media blitz.

It was not appreciated by Mueller, smarting at his second-place finish and put out by what he perceived as Durocher's favoritism toward Mays, all crowned by the season-long indignity of having to cede his right field turf to the center fielder.[41] In between TV appearances, when Mays reported to the Polo Grounds for a team photo shoot, Mueller sidled over to his teammate's locker, where Mays was tying his shoe. "Say, Willie, is it true you're the best center fielder in history?" he asked acidly.

"Best right fielder, too," Mays shot back, barely looking up from his laces.[42]

Before the World Series began, the Giants were cheered in a ticker-tape parade through lower Manhattan. This fall they were the only game in town: the Yankees, despite a 103-game-winning season, had fallen short of the pennant after five straight American League titles, and the Dodgers were the National League's runner-up. New York had only one ball club to celebrate, and celebrate the city did. One million fans filled the streets and shouted themselves hoarse. When it came time for speeches, and Durocher got up and told the throng that "Willie Mays is the greatest player I ever laid eyes on," Mays' eyes filled with tears.[43]

But there was business to attend to. The American League champions were on their way to play the first two games of the World Series at the Polo Grounds. This team had won an American League–record 111 games over the regular season. Their second baseman was the AL batting champion, and their pitching staff, which included two 23-game winners, had been dominant. The Giants had taken their league's title with a 97–57 record, and most observers expected another World Series win for the American League.

It would seem that none of those observers had been in Arizona in March, when the new American League champions, the Cleveland Indians, had regularly had the tar beaten out of them by the National League champion New York Giants.

The first game of the 1954 World Series was a beauty, a ten-inning battle that featured gutsy pitching and ended with a walk-off home run, but it is remembered today for The Catch, Mays' famous over-the-shoulder nab of Vic Wertz's long line drive in the eighth inning. As Mays has frequently, and with varying levels of patience, pointed out in the five decades since The Catch, he has never considered this the best fielding play of his career. If it hadn't been made in a World Series game, and televised nationwide, it would have gone unremembered. But the fact that it was done under such pressure, and with Mays' special brand of cap-flying theatricality, did make it a remarkable play, and not just in retrospect. Even those viewing it live knew they were witnessing a real feat. As play-by-play announcer Jack Brickhouse described it seconds afterward, it was "a catch which must have been an optical illusion to a lot of people."[44] Writers couldn't resist its symmetry as the perfect bookend to The Throw of 1951. However much Mays may downplay it, The Catch is a central part of his legend.

It came with the score tied 2–2 in the eighth inning. A tiring Sal Maglie had just left the game with runners on first and second and one out, and curveball-throwing reliever Don Liddle had come in to face Indians slugger Vic Wertz.

One of the reasons The Catch seemed so incredible was that Mays was playing Wertz close in, expecting him to hit the ball on the ground, as lefties often did with Liddle's curve. But Liddle's pitch came in shoulder-high, and Wertz drove it, forcing Mays to run all-out to catch up to it. He had judged its trajectory so accurately that the merest glance over his shoulder told him when to reach up with his glove and nab the ball.

Mays was far more worried about the two runners on base, the fast Larry Doby at second and Al Rosen at first. Doby, the Indians center fielder, seemed almost to expect Mays to reach the ball; he stuck close to second so that he could tag up and perhaps score. Rosen, too, was hovering around second, unable to pass Doby on the basepaths but, from the looks of it, convinced that Wertz's drive would go for a hit. Mays knew that to keep the runners from scoring, he had to get the ball back to the infield, and fast.

"If anything, I think the throw was the remarkable thing," Mays said later, "because the ball did get back there in a hurry, and I was a good 450 feet out when I caught it."[45] He did exactly what his sprint had given him time to plan: in one fluid motion he caught the ball, whirled about, and hurled. As one writer put it, "This was the throw of a giant, of a howitzer made human,"[46] and it was right on the money to second base. Rosen beat a quick retreat back to first; Doby, who had alertly tagged up and gone on to third, was forced to hold there as Davey Williams relayed the ball home. Mays' throw alone had saved at least one run, and perhaps two. Liddle was pulled from the game, and after some frenzied managerial moves and countermoves, the next Indians batter went down on a called third strike. End of inning, score still tied.

Jogging back to the dugout, Monte Irvin said, "Willie, that was a hell of a catch."

"I had it all the way," Mays grinned back.[47]

The game stayed tied through two more innings, with each team stubbornly hanging on to its two runs. Then in the top of the tenth, Mays made another incredible play, this one almost completely unremarked upon. Wertz walloped the ball low and hard, far out to left center. If it bounced into the far reaches of the Polo Grounds, it would be a triple for sure, maybe even an inside-the-park home run. But it never had a chance to go that distance, because there was Mays, deftly backhanding the ball on the bounce and firing a strike to Hank Thompson at third base. Wertz had to settle for a double. "That was a *real* play, one I'm proud of," Mays declared later.[48]

The Catch may have pricked a hole in the hot-air balloon of the Indians confidence, but this play of Mays' seemed to deflate them completely. They could not bring the runner home in that inning, a hallmark of a World Series performance in which the team would score only nine runs. In retrospect, as one observer noted, "When Mays again indicated he was not Mays, but Superman—[the Indians] must have known they were through."[49]

Indeed, in the bottom of the tenth the Giants secured the victory with a pinch-hit home run by Dusty Rhodes. It was a fly ball that would only be a home run in the Polo Grounds, which was just 257 feet down the right-field line. As Mays put it later, "Your daughter throws a ball farther than he hit that one."[50] But it counted, and the Giants won the game 5–2. The underdogs were up 1–0 in the Series.

In the clubhouse afterwards, the reporters were buzzing about Mays' catch. "Routine," Durocher said airily as their jaws dropped. "I've seen him make so many catches better than that I knew he had it all the way."[51]

The Indians, determined to come back in Game 2, started it off in style when Al Smith hit the first pitch of the game out of the park to put the American Leaguers up 1–0. The Giants' Antonelli would be shaky for much of the game, but with the backing of his fielders—including another spectacular throw by Mays that Indians manager Al Lopez thought was "the key play of the entire Series"—the pitcher escaped the first inning without allowing any further runs.[52] Meanwhile, Early Wynn of the Indians retired the first 12 Giants in order. Mays broke up the infant perfect game when he worked a walk to open the fifth inning. Hank Thompson followed up with a single; Mays, running on the pitch, took third. He tied the game when the next batter, Rhodes—pinch hitting again—singled to center. The Giants pulled ahead for good when Antonelli hit an infield grounder that plated Thompson, making the score 2–1. Rhodes iced the cake with a home run in the seventh.[53]

The teams traveled to Cleveland for the next three scheduled games of the Series, but the Giants would only need two to wrap things up. Mays had his first RBI—in fact, his first hit—of the Series in the first inning of Game 3 when he singled Don Mueller home. In the third the Giants rallied for three runs, two of them on a fierce single from improbable hero Dusty Rhodes. The Indians managed to score twice that game, once in the seventh inning and once in the eighth, but their inability to put together a big inning was taking its toll. With the Giants up 3–0 in the Series, the result looked inevitable.

In the fourth game, the Indians, perhaps jittery at the prospect of enduring a World Series sweep in front of the home crowd, made two costly fielding errors in the second inning that allowed the Giants to take a 2–0 lead. By the fifth inning, the Giants had piled on for five more runs. "We got a little careless after that," Mays said, and the Indians finally scored some runs, making the game 7–4.[54] It was too little and much too late, though. Wilhelm and Antonelli closed out the game for the Giants without any additional Indians coming around, and the New York Giants were baseball's world champions. It was only the eighth four-game sweep in World Series history.

What Mays remembered most about the World Series win was not his own performance. Apart from his outstanding play in the field, he'd had only five hits and three RBIs in 14 at-bats (though the stats don't quite tell the story of his impact on the team; of the 11 World Series innings in which the Giants scored, Mays was on base for eight of them).[55]

The detail that stood out in Mays' memory was Durocher's reaction. "Leo started to hug me when the game was over, and he didn't stop for the next ten hours, through a non-stop party," Mays would recall.[56] The victory was a vindication for Durocher, who had never won the championship in 16 years of managing. Mays knew how important it was to Durocher to be "in the record books with [John] McGraw and the rest of them," alongside all the great managers in baseball history.[57] Indeed, his work with the 1954 Giants would eventually be one of the credentials that earned Durocher his admission to the Baseball Hall of Fame. And as far as Durocher was concerned, there was only one reason for this crowning moment of his managerial career—his "son," Willie Mays.

NOTES

1. Einstein, *Willie's Time*, 99.
2. Roger Kahn, "For the Record," *Los Angeles Times*, October 25, 2002.
3. Einstein, *Willie Mays* (105) and Mays, with Sahadi, *Say Hey* (103). In the latter Mays describes the police confronting him outside a movie theater, but this is unlikely. All the shooters were apprehended at the scene and none were known to be evading police. However, accomplices might have been thought to be leaving the city by plane.
4. Mays, as told to Einstein, *Willie Mays*, 150–151. This and other sources describe Mays's trip by plane. Mays' other memoir, *Say Hey*, describes a train trip from Washington to Phoenix for 1954's spring training, but given the timing this seems improbable.
5. Mays, as told to Einstein, *Willie Mays*, 151–152.
6. Mays, with Sahadi, *Say Hey*, 105.
7. *New York Times*, March 3, 1954.
8. Einstein, *Willie's Time*, 100.
9. Durocher, with Linn, *Nice Guys Finish Last*, 314.
10. Einstein, *Willie's Time*, 101.
11. Durocher, with Linn, *Nice Guys Finish Last*, 306.
12. Mays, with Sahadi, *Say Hey*, 102.
13. Einstein, *Willie's Time*, 113.
14. Mays, as told to Einstein, *Willie Mays*, 155.
15. Mays, with Sahadi, *Say Hey*, 107.
16. Kahn, "For the Record"; Einstein, *Willie's Time*, 75–77.
17. Einstein, *Willie Mays*, 108; Honig, *Mays, Mantle, Snider*, 120.

18. Mays, with Sahadi, *Say Hey*, 110.

19. Arnold Hano, *A Day In the Bleachers* (Cambridge, MA: Da Capo, 1995 [originally published 1955]), 99–100.

20. Honig, *Mays, Mantle, Snider*, 120–121.

21. Gilbert Millstein, "'Natural Boy' of the Giants," *New York Times Magazine*, July 11, 1954.

22. Mays, with Sahadi, *Say Hey*, 111.

23. Ibid.

24. Ibid.

25. Mays, as told to Einstein, *Willie Mays*, 157.

26. Robert Creamer, "The Greatest Game I Ever Saw," *Sports Illustrated*, July 19, 1993.

27. Hano, *A Day In the Bleachers*, 161.

28. Einstein, *Willie's Time*, 97–98.

29. Mays, with Sahadi, *Say Hey*, 111.

30. "The Wanderers" Web site, http://home.att.net/~marvart/Wanderers/wanderers.html.

31. David Hinckley, "Hit Parade," *New York Daily News*, April 30, 2004; "RockDate July 15" www.rockdate.co.uk/jul15.htm.

32. Mays, with Sahadi, *Say Hey*, 111–112.

33. *New York Times*, July 23, 1954.

34. "Time Archive," Web site, www.time.com/time/covers/0,16641,1101540726,00.html.

35. Mays, with Sahadi, *Say Hey*, 113.

36. Einstein, *Willie's Time*, 100.

37. Mays, with Sahadi, *Say Hey*, 113.

38. Ibid.

39. *New York Times*, August 9, 1954.

40. Einstein, *Willie's Time*, 101.

41. Honig, *Mays, Mantle, Snider*, 121.

42. Einstein, *Willie's Time*, 102; Mays, with Sahadi, *Say Hey*, 116; Mays, as told to Einstein, *Willie Mays*, 159.

43. Mays, with Sahadi, *Say Hey*, 117.

44. "50th Anniversary: Mays' 'Catch' Might Not Rank Among His Greatest," *San Francisco Chronicle*, September 28, 2004; "Baseball Almanac" Web site, www.baseball-almanac.com/ws/yr1954ws.shtml.

45. Mays, as told to Einstein, *Willie Mays*, 161.

46. Hano, *A Day In the Bleachers*, 124.

47. "50th Anniversary: Mays' 'Catch' Might Not Rank Among His Greatest," *San Francisco Chronicle*, September 28, 2004.

48. Mays, as told to Einstein, *Willie Mays: My Life In and Out of Baseball*, 162.

49. Hano, *A Day In the Bleachers*, 144.

50. Mays, as told to Einstein, *Willie Mays*, 163.

51. Durocher, with Linn, *Nice Guys Finish Last*, 314.

52. Einstein, *Willie Mays*, 125.

53. *Staten Island Advance*, October 1, 1954.

54. Mays, as told to Einstein, *Willie Mays*, 164.

55. Einstein, *Willie's Time*, 104.

56. Mays, with Sahadi, *Say Hey*, 124.

57. Ibid., 125.

NEW YORK LIFE, 1955–1957

Once more, Mays returned to Fairfield as the celebrated hero. With extra money in his pocket—the winners' World Series share that season came to a record $11,147.90 per player—he intended to check on Anna Pearl, his oldest half-sister who was now in charge of the children his mother had left behind, and spread some of his good fortune around.[1] A crowd of family and friends met him at the airport on October 7.[2] Meanwhile, local officials had planned to use Mays' return as the centerpiece of a fundraising effort: Fairfield's official "welcome home" parade and barbecue would collect money earmarked for "a park for Negroes," according to news accounts.[3]

Mays was too exhausted to care much for official business. Since Aunt Sarah's death, he had funneled all his energy into baseball, and now he was spent. "I felt like collapsing," he would recall later.[4] But he stayed barely a week in the Birmingham area. With both his mother and Aunt Sarah gone, Mays' ties to his hometown were beginning to fray. Over the coming years he would continue to fulfill the responsibilities he felt to his family members, sending them up to a third of his Giants salary, but he would spend less and less time with them there.[5] Already, his father was spending the baseball season in New York to be closer to the younger Mays.[6]

He did have reason to be quickly on his way. Mays had agreed to participate in winter league baseball in Puerto Rico with Santurce, the circuit's best-known team. He'd accepted the offer, in part, for the money—or, as he put it, "baseball was my living, and where the chance was to make an additional living, there I went."[7] He was also going as a favor to Giants owner Horace Stoneham, who had a financial interest in the team, and to Giants third-base coach Herman Franks, who would be its manager. As the star attraction, Mays negotiated a deal: if the Santurce team was seven games up in the standings, he would be allowed to leave Puerto Rico and take a break. "I'd be able to stay in New York for a week or so at a time before jumping down to Puerto Rico for another week," he said later. "I commuted the whole winter."[8]

Mays wasn't the only top-quality talent on the team, which included Giants pitcher Ruben Gomez, Brooklyn's Don Zimmer, the Cubs Sam Jones, Milwaukee's George Crowe, and an up-and-coming local kid named Roberto Clemente, who was a few months away from his debut with the Pittsburgh Pirates. Still, Mays was the National League's batting champion and, most agreed, its probable Most Valuable Player, and his arrival in San Juan was a major event. "When my plane touched down . . . at six forty-five in the morning, a thousand fans were waiting for me," he noted with some pride.[9]

The team had great success on the field; "when you've got people like Gomez and Roberto Clemente on your side in the Puerto Rican League, you've got a chance to win, and we did win," Mays observed.[10] While in San Juan, Mays got word that he had, as expected, been named the National League MVP, the crowning achievement of an extraordinary year.[11]

Outside of the games, though, there were tensions on the Santurce team. They boiled over in January as the short season neared its end. The team was taking batting practice, and Mays and Gomez began to dispute who was next up. Gomez sat down on home plate and refused to leave. Mays stood off to one side in the batting cage and called for the pitcher, a local player, to throw to him. The pitcher did throw—at Mays' head. When Mays, shouting, started toward the mound, Gomez tried to get in between to calm the brewing fight. But Mays misread his intentions. "I thought Ruben was trying to defend his fellow Puerto Rican and I wrestled with him. I then knocked him down with a one-handed punch."[12]

Back home, the press covered the story "like the greatest donnybrook of all time," though Mays tried to downplay it, insisting that he and Gomez had made up in the locker room immediately afterward.[13] The next time Mays commuted back to New York, he was met at the airport by a phalanx of reporters and photographers, and he could not disguise his annoyance. "All those stories about a fight—phooey," he said as he hurried away from them. To the writers, this glowering man stood in stark contrast to the ebullient, joyous kid whose catch they had lauded a few months before.[14]

For Mays, the whole episode confirmed his doubts about participating in winter ball in the first place. He resolved never to do so again.[15] Certainly, there were less stressful ways to make extra money. He and Monte Irvin opened their own store, Willmont Liquors, in Brooklyn. Business offers, speaking engagements, and even a proposal for him to headline in a Las Vegas nightclub act came to Mays in a steady stream.[16] During the offseason, he also "wrote" his first memoir (it was entirely ghostwritten, actually, to such an extent that Mays did not even recognize his coauthor's name or recall the book's existence a few months later).[17] When Stoneham offered him a $25,000 contract for the 1955 season—and then raised the amount to $30,000 at the merest sign of protest from the star—Mays began to realize his financial value to the club.[18]

New worries were looming for Mays, though, about the leadership of his ball club. Now that Stoneham and Durocher had achieved their goal of a World Series championship, the cracks in their relationship were beginning to show. Mays began to hear "stories about how [Leo] didn't get along with Horace anymore, and that . . . Leo would quit baseball and get into private business."[19] Mays derived a great deal of security from Durocher's presence, and he feared his performance would decline without his manager's guidance. He extracted a promise from Durocher that he would not leave the Giants before his contract expired at the end of the 1955 season.[20]

In truth, the hiring of Durocher had been an anomaly to begin with. The New York Giants was one of the last family-owned clubs in major league baseball, and Horace Stoneham was known as much for his sentimentality about the "Giants family" as for his dedication to it. Stoneham's habit of hanging on to players once they passed their prime, or even reacquiring former Giants whom other clubs had given up on, drove the competitive Durocher to distraction. "Stoneham is loyal beyond the point of good business," Durocher would say after he had left the organization.[21]

Because Stoneham invariably chose his managers and coaches from within the "family," his 1948 recruitment of Durocher from the Brooklyn Dodgers, of all clubs, was a huge departure, especially so because the man he displaced as Giants manager, Mel Ott, had been the club's star slugger through the 1930s and its player-manager since 1942. Ott was a Hall-of-Fame hitter and a genuinely good man, but a poor manager—and the inspiration for Durocher's enduring aphorism, "Nice guys finish last."[22]

Durocher had served the Giants well, but there was no escaping that to Stoneham he was never quite "one of the family." Perhaps, then, it was inevitable that Stoneham and Durocher would break eventually. The hard-nosed Durocher could take it in stride. But the situation was distressing for Mays, who felt such great personal affection for Durocher and just as much professional loyalty to Stoneham. At the Giants spring training camp, the strain between owner and manager was obvious. As far as Mays was concerned, it meant that the 1955 season opened under a cloud that never quite lifted.[23]

The rest of the club seemed to be affected by the mood, too, and they got off to a slow start, hovering around a .500 winning percentage. Repeating his pattern of the year before, Mays had only three home runs in April, though the first two came in especially thrilling fashion, in a game against a resurgent Brooklyn.[24] The Dodgers had begun the season with a 22–2 record and were well on their way to their own World Series championship.

Compared to the success across town, the Giants looked even more listless, and Durocher began to worry that he wouldn't be allowed to play out his contract and keep his promise to Mays. In mid-May, Durocher asked his protégé for a favor: "Willie, I want you to start going for more home runs."[25]

Mays "was really shocked. All of the last season he had been worried about me swinging for the fences. Now that's just what he wanted me to do."[26] Ever adaptable, Mays rose to what he saw as a challenge. He hit 13 homers over the next month and his RBIs total climbed to 42.

As he pulled the ball more, though, he began to strike out more, and Mays' batting average fell below .300 and continued to drop. Opposing pitchers caught on to his new pattern and kept the ball on the outside corner. Mays soon found himself in a full-fledged slump, going 3 for 26, and an impatient Durocher told him he had to go with the pitch.[27] But Mays kept pressing at the plate, and unlike his previous slumps, this one seemed to hurt the other aspects of his game. He missed a shoestring catch and didn't run for the ball when it went past him (spurring some in the press box to peg him as a prima donna). He tried to tag up at first and take second base on a flyout to shallow left.[28]

To Durocher, Mays' sudden and uncharacteristic boneheadedness called for desperate measures. On June 19, he benched his star player for a game in Milwaukee. "He hasn't been helping the club, he has been making bad throws and running bases the same way," Durocher told reporters. "He may need a rest."[29]

Mays smiled for photographers as he "rode the pine" and declared that his manager knew best, but inside he was embarrassed and distraught. "There never was a longer game for me, sitting and watching," he remembered later.[30] It was the first time in his career he had ever been benched for poor play, and he resolved to make it the last. He was ready to listen when Durocher approached him with further instructions.

"Look, I've asked you but you haven't tried," the manager began. "If you go to right field you'll become one of the greatest hitters of all time. Maybe not percentagewise, but home-run-wise, powerwise. You can hit the ball out of any park. It'll be like an airport for you."[31]

Over the next few days, Mays concentrated on getting the bat on the ball. He stopped trying to get under it and loft it towards left; instead, he worked to drive it to the opposite field. Once again, Durocher's advice proved to be right. Mays hit two home runs in a game on June 29 (these, too, came at Ebbets Field), and the batting slump was decidedly over. He hit 31 home runs in the last half of the season and pulled his average back over .300, where it remained.

Mays quickly returned to form in the outfield, too. Perhaps more significantly, he sharply improved another aspect of his game: baserunning. Mays had never been much of a base stealer before the 1955 season, not because he lacked the speed, but because he lacked the confidence and knowledge to choose his spots well. The statistics tell the story: from eight stolen bases (and nearly as many times caught stealing) in 1954, Mays exploded to steal 24 bases (and just four times caught) in 1955. It was the second-highest total in the league that year.

Apart from the steals, Mays increased his baserunning aggression, too. On a play at the plate in a game against the Dodgers, he pulled what he called "the greatest single piece of base-running . . . of my whole baseball lifetime."[32] Brooklyn catcher Roy Campanella, ball in hand, was blocking the plate. Mays was barreling in from third. But instead of getting down in the dirt to slide, Mays leaped up in the air to reach home and yet avoid the tag. "I was kind of using his head as a fulcrum or something, and actually kind of ran up one side of him and down the other, and his hand with the ball kept aiming for me but never did touch me," Mays described it later.[33]

The umpire called him out. When Durocher put up one of his infamous, explosive protests, the implacable ump responded with pure logic: "You're telling me he did the impossible. . . . Well, I ain't fixin' to believe it."[34]

Partly, Mays ran more this season because he could; partly, he did it because he felt he needed to. The world champion Giants were hardly playing up to their title in 1955. Injuries took a toll; both shortstop Alvin Dark and second baseman Davey Williams lost significant stretches of playing time. The pitching staff was depleted when Sal Maglie was traded to the Indians midseason, and Johnny Antonelli threw hurt all year.[35] Once Mays emerged from his slump, he could see how much the team was depending on him to be the spark.

Mays used this same ability in that year's All-Star Game, held in Milwaukee. Once again, Duke Snider was the fans' choice as starting center fielder, but Mays was selected by the National League manager for the second year in a row. (Because Durocher was the NL manager in 1955, this was hardly a surprise.) The American League was leading 5–0 in the seventh when Mays came in to play center. He made his mark almost immediately when he leaped straight up at the outfield fence and speared a sure home run off the bat of the legendary Ted Williams. In the bottom of the seventh and again in the eighth Mays hit two singles off Yankee Whitey Ford to launch two separate rallies, coming around to score both times and helping the National Leaguers tie the game. Durocher's men finally won it in the twelfth on a Stan Musial home run.[36]

As Mays continued to drive the ball, he was racking up the homers. He achieved an important milestone on August 7 when he hit the 100th home run of his major league career. Coming in only Mays' second full season in the majors, it was one of the quickest rises to the 100-home-run level in major league history.

Still he continued to hit. Although Mays had gotten off to too slow a start for Ruth's single-season record to be in reach, he had a shot at the team's single-season home run record. Johnny Mize had set the mark in 1947 with 51. When Mays hit homers in six straight games in September, tying a major-league record and bringing his season total to 48 with a week to go in the season, it seemed possible.

The Giants were nearly 20 games behind the first-place Dodgers by this time, so Mays' exploits were one of the few things bringing the fans out to the Polo Grounds for the final contests of the season. He smacked two home runs on September 20, one in each half of a double-header, bringing his season total to 50. Then, going up on a rocketing fly ball hit by Dale Long of the Pirates, Mays collided painfully with the outfield wall.[37] The bruises he sustained to his thigh and back affected his swing, and with only five days to go on the season, Mize's record looked like it might be safe after all. Fifty homers was nothing to be ashamed of, Mays rationalized; he was only the seventh player in major-league history to accomplish it.

But Durocher wouldn't let him shrug off a chance at more. As always, the manager stepped in as Mays' cheerleader, pumping up his confidence and "telling me that the record was something I'd always be proud of."[38] But on the last day of the season, with the Phillies in town for a Polo Grounds double-header, Mays' total still stood at 50.

Robin Roberts, the Phillies top starter, was on the mound. He had won 23 games that season, the league's best. Mays was very familiar with Roberts: a strikeout specialist with great control, he was one to challenge hitters with his fastball. Mays knew exactly what to look for. In the first inning of the first game, "I got one of his strikes and tore into it. Homer Number 51."[39] Mays and Mize would share the team record for the next decade—when Mays would claim it for his own with a 52-home-run year.

The Giants won the first game of the afternoon. Halfway through the second game, the last game of the season, Mays finally heard the news he had been dreading all year. Later, he would call it "my saddest moment in baseball."[40]

Durocher beckoned him into the only private space to be had, the tiny players' bathroom tucked into the tunnel behind the dugout. The room was so small,

Mays had to crouch atop the toilet seat so both men could fit inside it and close the door.

"Now, son," Durocher began, "I want to tell you something. . . . You know I love you, so I'm prejudiced. There are other great ballplayers, there have been some fine ballplayers in our time. But to me you're just the best, the best ever. Having you on my team has made everything worthwhile."[41]

Mays must have looked at him quizzically, because Durocher went on: "I'm telling you this now because I won't be back next season."[42] By mutual agreement, Stoneham had not renewed Durocher's contract.[43]

Mays' eyes filled with tears as he pleaded with Durocher to stay. He felt like he was only just back from the army, that the Giants had only begun to get started; how could Durocher leave? "It's going to be different with you gone," Mays said. "You won't be here to help me."

Durocher responded with words that Mays would never forget: "Willie Mays doesn't need help from anyone."[44]

Then, as Durocher remembered it, "Willie leaned over and gave me a big kiss on the cheek. I tell you, I had to get out of there before I started to bawl myself."[45]

Despite the sad ending to the season, it had been a good one for Mays. His 51 home runs led the league, as did his 13 triples and his .659 slugging percentage.

All the while, he had been quietly dating a woman named Marghuerite Wendell, and their romance had deepened as the season progressed. Marghuerite was two years older than Mays. Originally from St. Louis, she was savvy and sophisticated, familiar with musicians and their nightclub world. Jazz legend Miles Davis, a longtime friend, praised her as "one of the hippest women I ever met."[46] Marghuerite had been married twice before, to a doctor and to the lead singer in the well-known group the Ink Spots, and she was the mother of a nine-year-old daughter, Billie. She was strikingly beautiful, having been a model for a time.[47]

In the off-season, Mays bought a home in upper Manhattan, finally moving out from under Mrs. Goosby's watchful eye. Then, on February 14, 1956, one week before he was to report for spring training, he and Marghuerite were married in a ceremony that had all the hallmarks of an impulse decision. They said their vows in Elkton, Maryland, where there was no waiting period for a marriage license. They were even stopped for speeding on the New Jersey Turnpike on the way there and had to pay a $15 fine before they could resume their journey.[48]

Perhaps it was the fact that Marghuerite was older, perhaps that she was twice divorced, or maybe it was just that people had a hard time picturing the Giants "natural boy" as a married man—whatever the reason, Mays believed that fans and reporters disapproved of his choice of a wife.[49] His sensitivity to this kind of gossip may have added strains to their marriage from the very beginning.

At the same time he was trying to adjust to married life, Mays had to adjust to a new manager. Bill Rigney had been a teammate on the pennant-winning 1951 squad. He had successfully managed the Giants' AAA farm club in Minneapolis for the previous two seasons. True to form, Stoneham had stayed within the "Giants family" for this hire.

Rigney had been an acolyte of Durocher's and credited the former manager with influencing his style of on-field generalship. But he planned to depart from Durocher's patterns when it came to the clubhouse. A utility infielder who had never been a star in his playing days, Rigney had not appreciated the system of praise and encouragement Durocher followed for Mays. Durocher left Rigney with only one piece of advice when he handed over the reins: that "the one thing he must never do [is] holler at Willie."[50] But that was about to change.

The very day that spring training camp opened, Rigney was quoted in the papers saying, "Aside from center field, shortstop, and rightfield, every position is up for grabs. And, if anyone can show me enough to move out Willie, Alvin [Dark] or Don [Mueller], even those spots may not be safe."[51] The sensitive Mays would completely miss the opening qualifier of that sentence, but the ending would ring in his ears: "even those spots may not be safe."

It got worse: in the middle of the club's first workout that spring, Rigney stopped play and publicly chewed Mays out for throwing a ball too high for the pickoff man. Then, in the words of Durocher (now watching from the sidelines as a broadcaster for NBC), Rigney "spent the rest of spring training telling the newspapermen that Willie was only one of twenty-five as far as he was concerned, which comes right out of the Old Managers Book of Wise and Pithy Sayings and should have been left there."[52]

Mays played hard in spring training, hitting at a .476 clip, but he was genuinely hurt by Rigney's attitude toward him. He could not see how his teammates might have been offended by Durocher's effusive praise and pumping: "Some people were saying that because [Durocher] treated me differently, other players in the locker room objected. If they did, no one ever told me about it."[53]

When Mays returned to New York and the season got underway, his hurt feelings lingered. Finally, Marghuerite Mays became so concerned about her husband's depressed mood that she called Durocher, whom she had never met, to ask for help. "I called Willie," Durocher recalled, "and did my darnedest to convince him that although Rigney's methods might be different than mine, he appreciated him every bit as much. Actually, I thought that Rigney was being stupid. But I didn't tell Willie that."[54]

While Mays was enveloped in his unhappiness, a radically different Giants team was taking shape around him. The change that affected Mays most directly occurred to his right. Monte Irvin had been traded, and Rigney installed Hank Sauer in left field. Sauer was a dangerous slugger at the plate but a defensive liability, so Rigney asked Mays to "shade" him on balls hit that way. Mueller was still in right field but was nursing a leg injury, so Mays felt that it was up to him to cover pretty much the entire outfield.[55] More trades were in the offing, too: two months into the season, Dark and Lockman were traded to the Cardinals for second baseman Red Schoendienst. The world champion Giants had almost disintegrated.

On Mays' 25th birthday, May 6, he finally snapped out of his funk. He "realized we were in sixth place and not getting any better. . . . I decided I had to do something to get us going. I really felt it was on my shoulders."[56] That day, in a game against the Cardinals, Mays stole five bases, driving their pitcher to distraction, firing up the fans, and getting him in position to score the winning run as the Giants took the game 5–4.

It was the beginning of a remarkable season on the basepaths for Mays, one in which he stole 40 bases and led the league for the first of four straight years. At one point in 1956 he had 13 steals in 13 attempts, a feat that spurred Ty Cobb, past master of the skill, to declare that Mays had "singlehandedly restored the art of baserunning to the game."[57] (Cobb had a point: the next man on the National League steals list that year came up with only 21, and Mays' mark topped that of the American League leader, too.) It was, Mays said, "just about the finest compliment I can remember," though perhaps misplaced: the man who had introduced the majors to the speed that characterized Negro League-style baseball was, of course, Jackie Robinson.[58] "He actually rewrote the book on how baseball is played, because of that basic defensive shift that came in because of him," Mays pointed out.[59] Mays was just walking a few steps farther along Robinson's path.

Mays had some incredible plays in the field this season, too, though by now it wasn't just Durocher who regarded his miracle catches as more or less "routine." One of them came at Forbes Field in Pittsburgh. Roberto Clemente hit a monstrous, towering fly ball to left center. The fact that Mays, playing in shallow center, even got close to the ball was enough to stun sportscaster Russ Hodges, "but in this case," Hodges said, "I swear the ball got there first. Willie— well, he kind of *overtook* it from behind. It was more than a great catch. It was an *impossible* catch!"[60]

Meanwhile, the home runs kept coming too, though not as thick or as fast as they had in 1955. In what was becoming a pattern, Mays' bat took a few weeks to warm up, but warm it did. By the end of the season, he had racked up 36 home runs. The combination of speed and power was unprecedented. Mays became the first man in baseball history to hit more than 30 home runs and steal more than 30 bases in a single season, inaugurating what is now known as the "30–30 Club."

Despite these personal achievements, Mays could not singlehandedly pull the Giants out of the hole they had dug for themselves in the standings. They were in sixth place in early May, and they remained mired in sixth place at season's end. The team's low point came on May 12 when they were no-hit by Carl Erskine at Ebbets Field. Not even the friendliest confines in baseball could help the listless Giants that afternoon, who were stymied by Erskine's slow curveball. The best Mays could do was work a walk in the first inning, which at least prevented Erskine from notching a perfect game. It was par for the Giants course that their frustration at the hands of the rival Dodgers was nationally televised as CBS's Game of the Week.[61]

For the third year in a row Mays was selected to the National League's All-Star team by its manager (Cincinnati's Gus Bell was the fans' choice). He hit a two-run homer in the fourth off Whitey Ford, then scored from first on a hit-and-run in the seventh, contributing mightily to the National Leaguers' 7–3 victory.[62]

Meanwhile, relations between Mays and Rigney had not much improved. Mays truly missed Durocher's encouragement and guidance. Later, he would admit that praise did make him a better player: "It's always seemed to me that when the fans cheered, I did better. I believe this is true of every ballplayer that ever lived."[63] Rigney, for his part, was in his first year as a big-league manager and having a hard time melding a disparate group of players into a cohesive team. He might be forgiven for lacking patience with a talented, high-achieving ballplayer who needed that much hand-holding.

The tensions between the two came to a head in the second half of the season, during a game in St. Louis. Mays popped up a high foul behind home plate. Rather than run it out, he stood in place and waited for the ball to come down. It did—in fair territory. The catcher grabbed it, and Mays was out. When he returned to the dugout, "I could tell right away that Rigney was upset. He looked at me and said, 'I'm fining you a hundred dollars for not running.' After the game I asked him why. 'You know why,' he said."[64] It seemed to Mays that Rigney was trying to make an example of him in order to assert authority over the team. If Rigney would fine a star and an on-field hustler like Mays, the other guys had better watch their step. "That fine upset me so much I called Leo," Mays recalled later. "He told me . . . that this was Rigney's style. But I never again had the same respect for Rigney."[65]

When the beat writers got wind of the incident, they besieged Rigney on Mays' behalf. Perhaps characteristically for that season, the manager's version of the story was very different. According to him, "Willie had returned to the dugout and said, 'I should be fined for that.' Whereupon Rigney had said, 'That's right. You are fined. Twenty-five bucks.'" Finally, Rigney announced that the fine was withdrawn, "because Mays is the hustlingest guy in the world."[66]

If the club was having any success on the field, it would have been easier to paper over such differences and personality clashes. As it was, the Giants played sub-.500 ball and were 26 games out by the end of the season. They were not a factor in the three-way pennant race that went all the way to the final weekend and that Brooklyn finally won. "I had never been with a second-division club before," Mays observed.[67] He did not enjoy the feeling.

Worse for Mays was his perception of the media's view of his season. Although he led all of baseball in stolen bases, his totals declined in other categories, and his batting average dropped below .300 (not that far below—it was .296). As far as the press was concerned, it was a subpar year, and when the reporters went fishing for causes, they came up with two: Bill Rigney and Marghuerite Mays. Either Mays wouldn't play for anyone but Durocher, or Mays couldn't play because of trouble at home. Both accusations would annoy Mays for years to come. "I don't concede it *was* a bad year to begin with," he protested when recalling the 1956 season.[68]

He would, however, concede that 1956 had been "one of my most difficult seasons . . . the first season where I put everything on my shoulders, and still I was worried that it wasn't enough."[69] With all his talent and all his accomplishments, Mays still felt the need for a mentor.

He was overjoyed, then, when in December banner headlines in all the New York papers screamed a piece of stunning news: Jackie Robinson had been traded to the Giants.

For ten full seasons, the fiercely competitive Robinson had been the Brooklyn Dodgers personified. He had endured the earliest, most difficult years of integration with spirit and dignity, and had helped the "Boys of Summer" win six pennants. News of his trade to the rival Giants transcended baseball. It was the end of an era, a major event.[70]

Dodgers fans were shocked and Giants fans (most of them) were thrilled, but for Willie Mays it was as if Christmas had come a week early. According to news accounts, he was "effusively optimistic about the aid and assistance he expected to get from Jackie as a teammate."[71] Some months later, Mays would say plaintively, "I need some one older to be over me . . . to watch me . . . the best thing would be to have Jackie Robinson for one year. I mean for Jackie to play with me just one year and tell me things. He'd tell me . . . he knew me when I come up and what I did."[72]

Robinson never did join the Giants. He had quietly planned to retire from baseball before the 1957 season began, and had already promised the exclusive story to a national magazine. The news of his retirement finally broke three weeks after the trade had been announced. "I'm very flattered that Willie Mays should even think I can help him," Robinson said graciously of his could-have-been teammate. "Willie is a very intelligent baseball player and I don't think he can be helped by talking to me."[73]

Compounding this disappointment were the unsettling rumors that Horace Stoneham was planning to move the Giants out of New York. Attendance at the Polo Grounds had plummeted in the two seasons since the Giants championship year, and revenues were falling along with them.[74] The Dodgers brash owner, Walter O'Malley, had been agitating for months to get municipal help to build his team a new stadium, but his demands were going nowhere. Stoneham, whose club was in even worse financial shape, found that the city government coveted the land below Coogan's Bluff more than it wanted to retain the team that played there.[75] Behind the scenes, as was his way, the Giants owner was looking to move.

When spring training began, though, the rumors were still only that—rumors—and the players had another season in New York to prepare for. One pleasant difference was that Rigney and Mays were settling into a more peaceful relationship, a result of increasing maturity on Mays' part and increasing confidence on Rigney's.[76] The manager was less concerned about appearances of favoritism now and more respectful of Mays' talents. This was apparent in 1957's preseason training sessions, when Rigney was overheard instructing the wannabe infielders vying for a slot on the roster: "When the ball is hit to the guy in center field, get to a base, because that ball is going to come in where it's supposed to. Trust him. Willie knows."

One of the bush-leaguers asked, "What does he know, skip?"

The question stumped Rigney for a moment. "I don't know what he knows, but Willie knows," he said at last. "So just get your ass to a base."[77]

For the Giants as a team, it looked to be another frustrating season. Three young players who were likely to make the '57 roster were instead called up for military service. That dashed Rigney's hopes of rebuilding. Instead, the 1957 club was a relatively old one, and it featured a number of "Giants family" members who had been traded away and then taken back, as Stoneham returned to his old hiring habits.

For Mays, it was another season replete with personal on-field achievements that were not matched by his club's success. As he continued to rack up the stolen bases, *Sports Illustrated* ran a four-page photo essay on his technique. "I never watch a pitcher's feet because they can fake you," Mays noted in the piece. "I watch the way he moves his head and I always watch the ball. Left-handers are the toughest . . . but then there's one advantage; with a left-hander, you can watch his eyes."[78] Once again, Mays would lead the league in steals, this time with 38—remarkable in that his .626 slugging average led the league as well.

Mays was an All-Star again, this time not without some controversy. He was leading in the fan balloting that selected the starting lineup until a sudden deluge of 550,000 ballots swept into the commissioner's office from Cincinnati. If those votes were counted, the National League's All-Star line-up would consist of Redlegs from top to bottom.[79] Coming on the heels of a similar though less dramatic tally in 1956, baseball commissioner Ford C. Frick felt he had to take action. He disallowed the late Cincinnati votes, making Mays a starting All-Star for the first time.[80] Eventually, Frick decided to remove fan involvement altogether. Not until 1970 would All-Star balloting be returned to the public.

The game itself was an exciting one, as the National Leaguers rallied twice in the late innings to pull ahead, only to see the American League stars put up a rally of their own to win it in the bottom of the ninth. Mays was a factor in both of his team's surges, hitting a single and scoring a run in the eighth, then walloping an RBI triple in the ninth.[81]

But the possibility of the team's upheaval nagged at the Giants, and the games they played seemed to take a back seat to the machinations of the league and their owners as discussions about a move continued. In May, the National League voted in favor of a resolution allowing the Giants and the Dodgers to leave New York City. After the All-Star break, Stoneham announced that he would recommend to his board of directors that the team be moved "elsewhere."

Minneapolis, where the club already had a Triple-A presence, was one candidate. Baseball's businessmen could not overlook the success that the Braves had had after setting up shop in Milwaukee, where the former money-losers from Boston had been setting attendance records. Perhaps the upper Midwest could support another team, too.

But California, and San Francisco in particular, was another strong contender. George Christopher, San Francisco's mayor, had made it his goal to bring big-league baseball to his town. The area had been a minor-league powerhouse for decades, so it certainly had a fan base. Now that air travel made cross-country road trips feasible, the businessmen and politicians of the West Coast cities, who dearly wanted to be seen as big-league in every way, could make a case for the expansion of major league baseball to their shores.

It was also no secret that the Brooklyn Dodgers were eyeing Los Angeles as their new home town. For California to acquire not just a team, and not just two teams, but a full-blown historic rivalry—now, there was a business proposition. All season long, Mayor Christopher pressed his case, as he and Stoneham discussed stadium plans, parking lots, and concession deals. Quietly, of course, because that was Stoneham's way.

On August 19, in an 8–1 vote, the Giants board made it official. The New York Giants were playing their final season. In 1958, the San Francisco Giants would take their place in the National League.

The reaction among the Giants New York fans ran from misery to outrage. The Giants were one of the founding clubs of the National League; they had played in New York since 1883. How could they leave all that history behind? Stoneham answered, "We're sorry to disappoint the kids of New York, but we didn't see many of their parents out there at the Polo Grounds in recent years."[82]

San Francisco's politicos had gotten what they'd wanted, but reaction among the city's baseball fans was decidedly mixed. A passionate baseball town, San Francisco had been the home of a successful minor-league club, the Seals, since 1903. As one reporter put it, "San Franciscans didn't get the team they sentimentally wanted (the Yankees), nor even the league they wanted (the American), but they did get a real live major league baseball club, and they did get the incomparable Willie Mays. So, like parents who hoped for a girl and got a boy, we'll make the best of it."[83]

The coming of the Giants meant the dissolution of the Seals, and some loyal Pacific Coast League fans were angry and resentful to have lost the club they had followed for decades. One local Seals fan complained at the prospect of giving up a first-place team for a sixth-place one. "I think that the Seals and the Giants should be made to play a seven-game series for the right to represent us in the major leagues," he said caustically.[84]

Back in New York, the rest of the season was a blur of last-ofs and farewells. The Giants would finish their final New York season in the same sixth place they'd held the year before, the same 26 games behind the pennant winners. Mays hit the last nine of his 35 home runs in the weeks after the move's official announcement. His 20 triples led the league, and his batting average was .333; with his combination of power and speed, he became the first player in major league history to hit at least 20 doubles, triples, and homers in a season.[85]

Still, Mays felt that he owed New York more. The Giants played their final game at the Polo Grounds against Pittsburgh on September 29. "I wanted to do something for the New York fans," Mays said afterward.[86] Pressing, he came to his last at-bat with nothing to show for the day, but the fans reacted with an ovation that made him blink back tears. "I didn't do anything—hit into a routine out—but I got that hand from the fans—that standing, prolonged hand-clapping and cheering as I returned to the bench," Mays recalled years later. "It's appreciation for a job well done, and for a happy time that you were given by someone else."[87]

It would be a long time before Mays would feel such warmth from the stands in San Francisco.

NOTES

1. Hano, *A Day In the Bleachers*, 166; Mays, as told to Einstein, *Willie Mays*, 171.
2. *New York Times*, October 8, 1954.
3. *New York Times*, September 4, 1954.
4. Mays, with Sahadi, *Say Hey*, 126.
5. Millstein, " 'Natural Boy' of the Giants."
6. Kahn, "For the Record."
7. Mays, as told to Einstein, *Willie Mays*, 171.
8. Mays, with Sahadi, *Say Hey*, 128.
9. Ibid., 127.
10. Mays, as told to Einstein, *Willie Mays*, 171.
11. *New York Times*, December 17, 1954.
12. Mays, with Sahadi, *Say Hey*, 129.
13. Mays, as told to Einstein, *Willie Mays*, 171.
14. *New York Times*, January 16, 1955.
15. Ibid.
16. Mays, with Sahadi, *Say Hey*, 126; *New York Daily News*, December 2, 1954.
17. Einstein, *Willie's Time*, 96.
18. Mays, with Sahadi, *Say Hey*, 130.
19. Ibid., 126.
20. Ibid., 127.
21. Robert Shaplen, "The Lonely, Loyal Mr. Stoneham," *Sports Illustrated*, May 5, 1958.
22. Mays, with Sahadi, *Say Hey*, 61–62.
23. Ibid., 130–131.
24. Mays, as told to Einstein, *Willie Mays*, 309.
25. Mays, with Sahadi, *Say Hey*, 131.
26. Ibid.
27. Ibid., 131–132.
28. Mays, as told to Einstein, *Willie Mays*, 172–173.
29. *New York Times*, June 20, 1955.
30. Mays, with Sahadi, *Say Hey*, 132.
31. Ibid.
32. Mays, as told to Einstein, *Willie Mays*, 102.
33. Ibid.
34. Ibid.

35. Mays, with Sahadi, *Say Hey*, 132–133.

36. *New York Times*, July 13, 1955.

37. Mays, with Sahadi, *Say Hey*, 134.

38. Ibid.

39. Ibid.

40. Ibid., 133.

41. Durocher, with Linn, *Nice Guys Finish Last*, 316.

42. Mays, with Sahadi, *Say Hey*, 133.

43. Robert Shaplen, "The Lonely, Loyal Mr. Stoneham," *Sports Illustrated*, May 5, 1958.

44. Mays, with Sahadi, *Say Hey*, 133.

45. Durocher, with Linn, *Nice Guys Finish Last*, 316. Mays' memoir *Say Hey* (133) recounts a nearly identical conversation, but in his version it is Durocher who bestows the kiss.

46. Miles Davis, with Quincy Trope. *Miles: The Autobiography* (New York: Simon and Schuster, 1989), 47.

47. In his memoirs, Mays is circumspect in describing his first wife and her past. Some information here was gleaned from newspaper articles and magazine profiles, including the *New York Times* (January 4, 1961 and September 20, 1974) and *Sports Illustrated* (April 13, 1959), and "The Original Ink Spots" Web site (inkspots.ca/ispress2.htm; nsafter52). It is not clear where Billie lived at this time, or during the Mays' marriage. On occasion, at least, she did make her home with the Mays family (*New York Times*, January 4, 1961).

48. Mays, with Sahadi, *Say Hey*, 137.

49. Mays, with Sahadi, *Say Hey*, 137; Mays, as told to Einstein, *Willie Mays*, 187–188.

50. Durocher, with Linn, *Nice Guys Finish Last*, 337.

51. *New York Times*, February 27, 1956.

52. Durocher, with Linn, *Nice Guys Finish Last*, 337.

53. Mays, with Sahadi, *Say Hey*, 136.

54. Durocher, with Linn, *Nice Guys Finish Last*, 338.

55. Mays, with Sahadi, *Say Hey*, 139.

56. Ibid., 138–139.

57. Einstein, *Willie Mays*, 138.

58. Mays, with Einstein, *Willie Mays*, 216.

59. Ibid.

60. Einstein, *Willie Mays*, 138.

61. *New York Times*, May 13, 1956; *Sports Illustrated*, May 21, 1956.

62. *New York Times*, July 11, 1956.

63. Mays, as told to Einstein, *Willie Mays*, 188–189.

64. Mays, with Sahadi, *Say Hey*, 140.

65. Ibid., 141.

66. Brown, " 'The Onliest Way I Know'."

67. Mays, with Sahadi, *Say Hey*, 138.

68. Mays, as told to Einstein, *Willie Mays*, 188; Jimmy Cannon, "If Only Mays Knew How Great He Really Is. . . . ," *New York Post*, June 27, 1958.

69. Mays, with Sahadi, *Say Hey*, 142.

70. Robert Creamer, "The Hot Stove Explodes," *Sports Illustrated*, December 24, 1956.

71. *Sports Illustrated*, January 14, 1957.

72. Cannon, "If Only Mays Knew How Great He Really Is. . . ."

73. *Sports Illustrated*, January 14, 1957.

74. *Sports Illustrated*, July 1, 1957.

75. Robert Moses, "Robert Moses on the Battle of Brooklyn," *Sports Illustrated*, July 22, 1957.

76. Mays, with Sahadi, *Say Hey*, 165.

77. Honig, *Mays, Mantle, Snider*, 111; Mays, as told to Einstein, *Willie Mays*, 169.

78. "Wondrous Willie," *Sports Illustrated*, August 5, 1957.

79. In a nod to the Cold War sensibilities of the day, the Cincinnati Reds had changed their name to the Redlegs starting with the 1953 season. They would revert to their original name in 1959.

80. *New York Times*, June 29, 1957.

81. *New York Times*, July 10, 1957.

82. *New York Times*, August 20, 1957.

83. *Sports Illustrated*, September 2, 1957.

84. Ibid.

85. Mays, with Sahadi, *Say Hey*, 148.

86. Einstein, *Willie Mays*, 140.

87. Mays, as told to Einstein, *Willie Mays*, 123.

Mays' teammates said that his throws from the outfield came in humming, like pitches off the mound. *National Baseball Hall of Fame Library, Cooperstown, N.Y.*

SAN FRANCISCO, 1958–1960

Mays decided to settle into his team's new hometown right away. House-hunting was the first order of business. He and Marghuerite traveled to San Francisco a few weeks after the 1957 season ended to begin their search.[1] They chose a newly built home on Miraloma Drive in the Sherwood Forest neighborhood, a short walk from Mount Davidson Park and close to the well-to-do planned community of St. Francis Wood. The modern three-bedroom brick and redwood house had a breathtaking view of the city and the Pacific Ocean beyond. It was three miles from Seals Stadium, Mays' new baseball home, and less than four miles from the site of the stadium that the city was constructing for the Giants on San Francisco Bay. The house's builder, Walter Gnesdiloff, agreed to sell the house to Mays for $37,500 cash.

But Sherwood Forest was an all-white neighborhood, and some of its residents wanted to keep it that way. When they heard that Willie Mays was moving in, they weren't impressed with his batting title, his World Series ring, or his Most Valuable Player award. All they could see was the color of his skin. "I stand to lose a lot if colored people move in," one Miraloma Drive homeowner told a reporter.[2] Several would-be neighbors pressured Gnesdiloff to break his deal with the Mayses, and the builder bowed to their demands. He told the couple that he would not sell the house to them after all.

Mays was stunned at Gnesdiloff's reversal.[3] This wasn't Birmingham, after all. That first minor-league game, marred by the jeers of segregated Hagerstown, seemed like a lifetime ago. Mays hadn't encountered this kind of clear-cut prejudice in Minneapolis, however brief his stay, or New York. Then again, he hadn't attempted to buy houses in "white" neighborhoods there.

If Mays was surprised, Marghuerite was enraged. "Down [South] where we come from, you know your place," which is bad enough, she said. "But up here it's all a lot of camouflage. They grin in your face, and then deceive you."[4]

The story was front-page news in the next day's papers and a tremendous embarrassment to the city's mayor. George Christopher had lobbied hard to bring a major-league team to San Francisco. He was chagrined that the team's star player should be treated so shabbily. Mayor Christopher immediately offered to let the Mayses stay in his own home as his guests, but Mays politely refused.

All the publicity made Gnesdiloff reconsider, and within another day he had changed his mind again. Willie and Marghuerite Mays purchased the home on Miraloma Drive after all.[5] When a brick was thrown through their front window after they settled in to the house in early January, it only confirmed Marghuerite's initial impression of the city. She never felt entirely comfortable in San Francisco. Mays chose to focus on the neighbors who called and offered their sympathy and support after this ugly incident. "I didn't feel concerned about racial tensions in my neighborhood once the season was about to start," he recalled later.[6]

Local fans had rabidly followed the careers of the Bay Area's ballplayers who had grown up or had made their names in the city by the bay, including Lefty O'Doul, Dom DiMaggio, and most especially the New York Yankees great center fielder Joe DiMaggio. Mays' childhood idol was raised in San Francisco, and he had played with the Seals in the Pacific Coast League. Now Willie Mays would be stepping into DiMaggio's own center field turf as the Giants temporarily took over Seals Stadium.

Seals Stadium was intimate, to say the least. It seated only 22,000 fans, and the roofless stands were right on top of the field—fans along the first-base line could practically reach out and touch the runners as they sped by. Just 400 feet to dead center field, the dimensions greatly limited Mays' opportunities for outfield theatrics.

Apart from the relatively close center field fence, the park's dimensions were similar to those of the rest of the league, but one unique factor made Seals Stadium a challenging place to play: the weather. Set on a peninsula surrounded by the Pacific Ocean and the San Francisco Bay, the city was famous for its dense fog and its chilly summers. For ballplayers, though, the winds would prove to be even more of a problem. Strong and capricious, the San Francisco winds could carry a pop fly over the fence, or push a towering home-run ball back into play—at random. Hitters, pitchers, and fielders alike would struggle with the conditions.

Eager to impress, Mays started the 1958 season on a tremendous hitting tear. In a ceremony-filled Opening Day game at Seals Stadium against their fellow migrants, the Los Angeles Dodgers, Mays was 2 for 5 and drove in two runs in an 8–0 Giants victory. During spring training, Rigney had predicted that Mays had a shot at breaking Babe Ruth's 60-homer record that season.[7] In early June, with a batting average over .400 and 14 home runs, he was on pace to make the prediction come true.

But some detected an undercurrent of mutual suspicion between the city and the transplanted ballclub. Quietly at first, the players grumbled about the stadium's amenities, the weather, and the local fans. "We were a big-league team with a minor-league audience," Mays would say later.[8] The fans picked up on this, and they resented it. The last thing they wanted was to be thought of as "bushy" by a bunch of New Yorkers.[9]

In fairness, the fans of Pacific Coast League baseball did have to get used to a different style when the Giants came to town. Power hitters were few and far between in the minor leagues, and infielders' skills weren't always top caliber. This meant that speed on the basepaths was critical in the minor-league game, and bunting for the base hit was so common that many fans expected to see the play regularly.[10] They even expected it of Willie Mays—who was speedy, to be sure, but as one of the premier power hitters in the game, he felt that his skills could be put to more productive use at the plate. Mays' lack of bunting was roundly criticized by the San Francisco press and fans in 1958.

It wasn't the only thing about him they criticized, either. For the first time in his career, Mays played for a home crowd that didn't adore him. After the ecstatic welcomes he'd received in Minneapolis and New York, Mays was hurt. He believed that the San Francisco fans resented everything about him: his "showboating" basket catch, his East Coast baseball pedigree, his effrontery in attempting to replace the great DiMaggio, and, in more than a few minds, his race.[11]

Instead of lionizing Mays, the local fans latched on to the rookie outfielder Orlando Cepeda. A promising 20-year-old whose father had been a baseball hero in their native Puerto Rico, Cepeda's lack of history in New York made him a blank slate for San Francisco's baseball dreams. His Opening Day home run, in his first major-league game, was all that was needed to make him San Francisco's new hometown hero. The fans celebrated the "Baby Bull's" .312 average and cheered his 96 RBIs during the first year of what would become a Hall-of-Fame career. (As well they should; Cepeda would be recognized as the NL Rookie of the Year in 1958.)

Mays felt that too few of the fans recognized how much Cepeda's place in the batting order contributed to his numbers: he hit fourth, behind Mays. When

Cepeda came up, more often than not there was Mays on base, ready to be batted home. With Mays on the basepaths, always a threat to steal, opposing pitchers were forced to throw Cepeda more fastballs, and he feasted on them. Fielders were pulled out of position to guard against a Mays stolen base, leaving holes in the defense; Cepeda took advantage, punching ground balls through for base hits.[12]

In mid-June, Mays entered one of his periodic slumps. His average began to drop, and his home run production ground to a halt. The fans let Mays have it: for the first time he could remember, he was booed at home. In the not-so-friendly confines of tiny Seals Stadium, he was sure he could make out every angry word.

Was it the fans' lack of support that depressed Mays that season, or stress over the move to a new city—or was it something else? As the slump continued, Mays began to feel tired for the first time in his career. He was only 27, and his non-smoking, non-drinking habits had helped him stay in great physical shape. But he had put some serious wear on his body. Already, he had played a decade of professional baseball with barely an injury to show for it—and hardly any rest in any of his seasons, either, appearing in more than 150 games, year in, year out. Perhaps he had good reason to feel tired. Instead, Mays worried that he might be really ill.

On a June road trip, Mays' worries finally got the best of him. He went to New York as the team played a series in Philadelphia and checked into a hospital for tests. They all came back negative: nothing was physically wrong with Mays. Relieved—and, after two days in the hospital, well rested—he rejoined the team.[13]

Emotionally, though, he was distraught at his performance, and at the way it was being discussed in the press. "They come and ask me if I'm having trouble with my wife," he said to a columnist he trusted from the club's New York days. "What about the rest of the ballplayers? Do they ask every guy in a slump if he's having trouble at home?"[14] And the slump continued, with Mays hitting at a .240 pace for July. It was a respectable average for the average player, but far below what Willie Mays expected of himself.

Then suddenly, for no reason he could pinpoint, the slump snapped. In August Mays' batting average—which, after his blazing start, had dropped to all of .320—began to climb again, and he hit nine home runs that month.

However worried he had felt during those dry weeks at the plate, Mays had remained his graceful and authoritative self in the field and on the basepaths. This season, he was also beginning to learn how to be a team leader. Apart from manager Rigney, only three other New York Giants had made the transition to the West Coast, all of them pitchers. The new San Francisco team was stocked with rookies and young players, and they looked up to the experienced Willie Mays.

He started by developing a relationship with Cepeda, who always credited Mays for assisting him on and off the field in that rookie year. "He helped me every way a man can help another man," Cepeda said later. "He put points on my batting average. He taught me plays. He even kept me out of trouble."[15] Such as the time in Pittsburgh when Cepeda tried to wallop the Pirates manager with a bat. Mays took the rookie down with a football tackle and sat on him until he could see reason.[16]

By season's end, the Mays-Cepeda line-up combination drove the team to an 80-win, second-place finish for the Giants. In spite of his two-month slump, Mays had a batting average of .347, the highest of his career. (He'd made a strong run at the batting title, but was beaten out by Richie Ashburn of the Phillies and his .350 mark.) Mays' 31 stolen bases led the league, as did his 121 runs scored, and he hit 29 home runs, more than any of his teammates. But he never could quite forget the fact that, when the San Francisco fans were asked to vote on the Giants most valuable player at season's end, they selected Orlando Cepeda.[17]

Mays' marriage to Marghuerite had been another source of stress during the season.[18] His wife was still uncomfortable in San Francisco, and neighbors overheard loud arguments between them. Because of his fame, even a run-of-the-mill spat between this husband and wife could fuel the rumor mill. Marghuerite was a strong woman, and she gave as good as she got. One unconfirmed story had Mays beating her; another had her beating *him*.[19]

Whatever the truth of these rumors, like many couples, the Mayses felt that a child would complete their family. Once they settled into their new San Francisco house, they began meeting with local adoption agencies. In January 1959, they brought five-day-old Michael home.[20]

Mays felt an instant connection with his son. "From the first moment I laid eyes on him, I knew this was it. And it's been that way ever since," he wrote when Michael was six years old.[21] He had always been close to his own father. Now that he was a father himself, Mays threw himself into the role with characteristic exuberance. He developed a special bedtime routine: loading Michael in his traveling crib into the back seat of the car and driving around the neighborhood until the baby fell asleep.[22] He changed diapers, too—not a common task for fathers of the day.

Mays had extra time to spend with his family soon after spring training began in February of 1959 when he suffered the first real injury of his major-league career. In an exhibition game, he slid into home and got tangled up in the catcher's shin guards. His leg required 35 stitches, and he sat out most of the rest of spring training at home in San Francisco.[23]

He had recovered by the time the season started and had another sterling year, this time without any protracted slumps. The Giants were still playing in Seals Stadium, which was as small and whose fans were, to Mays' mind, as cool to him as ever. But he was just a bit tougher now than he'd been before. Mays was developing an outer shell to protect him from fans' and writers' criticism. In later years, that attitude would be seen as crankiness or arrogance. In the 1959 season, it was toughen up or wilt under the constant pressure.

Remarkably, Mays was more warmly welcomed on the road. Opposing fans seemed to appreciate Mays in ways that the Giants hometown fans did not. Even as they cheered their own team, they would cheer his catches or steals or home runs. Mays was just so much fun to watch, they couldn't help but enjoy the show. In every city, fans would pack the stands when the Giants came to town. The team set road attendance records year after year, whether they were doing well or poorly in the standings.[24]

New Yorkers, who'd had an embarrassment of baseball riches for decades, were suddenly left with only the Yankees to cheer for—and no respectable National League fan would ever switch his or her allegiance to that hated American League juggernaut. ("Rooting for the Yankees is like rooting for U.S. Steel," as the saying went.) Instead, heartbroken New York Giants fans followed the San Francisco club any way they could: on radio broadcasts, in infrequent television appearances, and on the road.

When the team visited Philadelphia, the National League city closest to New York, Giants fans turned out in droves. The cities were less than two hours apart by train. The Philadelphia Phillies were an abysmal team that incited little fan loyalty. So when the Giants came to town, the cheers for the visiting team often drowned out those for their hosts.[25] To Mays, it almost made the Phillies Shibe Park feel like home.

In what was now an annual ritual, Mays was elected to the National League All-Star team for the sixth year in a row. This year, the leagues would play two games, one in Pittsburgh, the other in Los Angeles. The Pittsburgh game included his own favorite All-Star performance when he hit a game-winning triple to deepest center in Forbes Field. The irony of this was not lost on sportswriter Bob Stevens. In his wrap-up of the game, he described how an "unsmiling" Mays, frustrated at the plate three times through seven innings, attacked a high outside fastball from the Yankees Whitey Ford and sent it screaming out to right-center. Harvey Kuenn of the Detroit Tigers "gave it an honest pursuit," Stevens noted, "but the only center fielder in baseball who could have caught it just happened to hit it."[26] The triple scored Milwaukee's Hank Aaron, who had been on first, and won the game for the National League 5–4.

Later in July, in Pittsburgh again, Mays hit a home run with a back story. The pitcher, Harvey Haddix, was a fastballer with a long memory. In 1954, Mays had turned one of Haddix's occasional changeups into a 500-foot home run. Ever since, in meeting after meeting, Haddix had made it abundantly clear that Mays should not expect to see that pitch from him again. Now, five years later, in the eighth inning of a tight game, Haddix decided that the element of surprise was in his favor, and he unleashed the change. Somehow, Mays was ready for it: he smashed this one, too, over the left field fence.[27]

Two-thirds of the way into the season, in the thick of an extended pennant race, another explosive rookie joined the team. Willie McCovey was a first baseman, just like Orlando Cepeda. He hit for power as well as for average, and he was tearing up the minor leagues. Rigney wanted him—at any position. So up he came. McCovey was installed at first and Cepeda moved into left field, a position he'd never played professionally.

Offensively, Rigney's move paid off right away. McCovey was 4 for 4 in his first game with the Giants, he smashed 13 home runs in just 51 games, and his performance would earn him Rookie of the Year honors, as Cepeda's had a year before.

Defensively it was another story. Rigney knew that the fans would give Cepeda, still a local favorite, room to make mistakes as he learned his new position. Rigney also knew he had the league's best outfielder in center. Mays could be counted on to reach balls that Cepeda couldn't, and to back up the new left fielder on the ones he caught. Mays took to his responsibility as outfield general with gusto. His speed, and his preternatural sense of where a batted ball would land, gave him a confidence in the field that his teammates used to advantage. They would follow his lead as he positioned himself for each batter. It wasn't long before Mays was directing the outfielders' moves outright, pitch by pitch.[28]

In August, Mays broke his little finger sliding into first base in a game against the Reds. "I'll be able to play tomorrow," he told Rigney as he was removed from the game.[29] Instead of seeking treatment, or even sitting out for a few days, Mays let the broken bone heal on its own. He knew that opposing pitchers would continually jam him with inside pitches if they knew of his weakness.

Mays believed that the injury made him less able to swing away, so he tried to make up for the lack by pushing himself as a fielder and as a baserunner. He racked up 27 stolen bases and was caught stealing only four times on the season, leading the National League for the fourth year in a row.

In fact, though, the long balls kept on coming. Even hurt, Mays slugged 10 home runs down the stretch. His last one of the season was the 250th of his career.

The Giants had been in first place for much of the season, but the standings had been tight. In September, the top three teams—the Giants, the Braves, and the ever-competitive Dodgers—were separated by only two games. And in the final week, the Giants stumbled. They lost a three-game series to the Dodgers in Los Angeles, and another four of the final five games of the season. The Dodgers pulled ahead and grabbed the pennant right out from under their long-time rivals; the Giants ended up in third place.

It was tough to come so close to a pennant and lose it so late, though Mays knew that Rigney had done more with the team than anyone had a right to expect. And he was glad when, late in the season, the San Francisco fans gave him the kind of appreciative cheer he had once received routinely in New York and had missed so much. Mays had had four hits in the game, and Rigney decided to take him out for a pinch runner in the last of the ninth. The applause the fans gave him as he jogged off the field made Mays think that his new town was beginning to appreciate him at last.[30]

Between seasons, though, there were personal matters to deal with. For all the joy that Michael had added to his parents' lives, the Mayses' marriage had not improved. Marghuerite was still unhappy in San Francisco. In a last attempt to patch up their union, they sold the house on Miraloma Drive and moved back East. This time, Mays purchased a 15-room home in tony New Rochelle, a racially tolerant suburb just north of New York City. The house was Marghuerite's choice, and Mays was not fond of it. Even with his salary and the money he made from endorsements and speeches, buying the $125,000 property was a financial stretch.[31]

Officially, Mays planned to live in the New Rochelle house in the off-season and keep a San Francisco apartment for use during the rest of the year. But he was becoming attached to his team's new hometown and felt less drawn to New York than he once did.[32]

The whole Giants organization had high hopes for the 1960 season. They would be playing in a brand-new ballpark that had been built just for them; the team was stocked with exciting young players, including the league's last two Rookies of the Year; and they were led by a true star, Willie Mays. As spring training was about to begin, owner Horace Stoneham offered Mays $85,000 for the year, making him baseball's highest-paid player.

"You think I ought to have that much?" he joked with Stoneham.

"Yeah, I'm giving it to you because you're the best," Stoneham answered.[33]

It was another Opening Day filled with parades, pomp, and ceremony as the Giants inaugurated the brand-new Candlestick Park on April 12. Vice President Richard M. Nixon was there to throw out the first pitch (and to pitch his own presidential candidacy to his fellow Californians), and all-time great Ty Cobb attended as well.

The players were grateful to have a permanent baseball home at last. But their first workout on the new field gave them pause. The afternoon before Opening Day, the team returned from their spring training camp in the warm Arizona desert. The climate contrast was extreme. The damp chill of coastal Northern California seeped into the players' bones, and the wind was fierce. On Mays' first practice swing, he connected with a batting-practice fastball straight into the wind—and sawed his bat in two at the handle.[34]

Those winds would quickly become Candlestick's most notorious problem, one that would plague those who played there for its entire 40-year history. The capricious San Francisco wind had been an issue at Seals Stadium, too. But the new ballpark was located on Candlestick Point, a narrow spit of land right on the shore of San Francisco Bay. That made it all the more subject to strong and gusty winds. Even a light wind at Candlestick could swirl and eddy about, hurling a batted or thrown baseball in unexpected directions.

Mays felt personal reasons to gripe. Back in New York, the Polo Grounds had been perfectly suited to Mays' particular style of play, even though it had been built long before he was born. Now, as the Giants veteran star, he had hoped Candlestick would be designed with his talents in mind. Instead, it seemed to have been fiendishly calculated to thwart him. As a right-handed hitter, a short fence in left would have made an inviting home-run target for Mays. Candlestick Park was 330 feet down the left field line and 335 in right, making the ballfield almost symmetrical. With prevailing winds usually blowing in from left field, Mays' towering home-run shots often appeared to hit an invisible wall.[35] Some statisticians have calculated that Mays may have lost 165 home runs to the San Francisco winds during the rest of his career with the Giants, though like all baseball "what-ifs" this is open to dispute.[36] Mays also felt that an extra-deep center field, like the one at the Polo Grounds, would have given the Giants a defensive advantage, and would have allowed him to show off his unique fielding skills. Instead, the center field fence at Candlestick was set at a more conventional 410 feet.

The fans and the press soon came up with a litany of their own complaints. The cold was one: even at the height of summer, the stadium was always frigid, leading to jokes that parka sales went through the roof in the Bay Area that season. The radiant heating system that had been built into the floors of the press boxes and box seats never worked. There were too few restrooms or concession stands on the upper levels and too many at field level. Pipes leaked throughout the building.[37] The foul poles, complained the umpires, were set entirely in fair territory. And then the one that players and fans shared: the dugout bathrooms were built without doors—and were positioned so that fans in some box seats could see more of their heroes than they may have wanted to.[38] (This was one problem that ownership was able to correct, and did, quickly.)

Still, the first game of the season was a good one. Though Bill White of the St. Louis Cardinals christened the park with its first hit, Orlando Cepeda had a triple in the bottom of the first that scored two runs in a 3–1 Giants victory.

With the winds against him, Mays did not hit his first home run at Candlestick Park until three weeks into the season. Over the entire season, he would hit almost 60 percent of his homers on the road. During the first two months at the new ballpark, Mays went back to Durocher's old prescription: he tried not to pull the ball into the teeth of the left-field gale and go inside-out, toward right. He got results that way—by the end of April he was leading the league with a .425 average. But when the Giants went on the road, frustration set in. What worked at Candlestick wouldn't work elsewhere, and he found it hard to adjust from park to park. Eventually he stopped trying. "Now I hit the ball good on the road and I get my home runs," he said in September. "Back here [at Candlestick] I just swing and hope for the best."[39]

It took some doing to master the Candlestick outfield, but eventually Mays' baseball smarts prevailed. It wasn't the outfield's size or dimensions; there was not as much ground to cover here as there had been at the Polo Grounds, and fewer quirks. The trouble, of course, was the wind. Getting a good "read" on the ball had always been one of Mays' special talents. But if the Candlestick wind got hold of it, a ball's original trajectory became a moot point.

Here again Mays' speed would prove essential. Instead of getting a jump on the ball and moving to catch it at the earliest possible moment, Mays took a counterintuitive path: he waited. "When a ball was hit, I didn't move," he wrote in his memoirs, long after his playing days had ended. "From the moment it was up in the air, I started counting to five: one, two, three, four, five. At 'five' I began to run."[40] Only then would he gauge where the ball was going and whether the wind would take it in some unexpected direction, and he would rush to meet it. The technique made his on-field leadership-by-example even more critical to the team's success. Soon both infielders and outfielders were keying off Mays.

The Giants started strong, powered in part by Mays' hitting. Their winning percentage hovered around .600 through the first three months of the season. But the Pittsburgh Pirates, starring Roberto Clemente and Bill Mazeroski, started out even stronger. When the first-place Pirates came to town in late June and swept their three-game series with San Francisco, owner Horace Stoneham took out his frustration in time-honored fashion: he fired the manager.

After their first difficult season together, Mays and Rigney had settled into a peaceful coexistence. Mays had come to realize that he should not expect comfort, protection, or mentorship from his manager—or at least not from this one. Rigney remained respectful of Mays' talents. In later years he, like many other baseball professionals, would regularly say that Mays had been "the best ballplayer I ever saw." Observers believed that Mays actively disliked Rigney, but Mays denied it.[41]

Even though they had never been close, Mays said he was sorry to see Rigney go under such circumstances. "I thought the timing in firing him was very bad," he said later. "The season wasn't even half over . . . the only decision necessary was to keep things as they were."[42]

It was more dismaying to Mays that Rigney was not even properly replaced. Instead, Stoneham gained time by naming an interim manager. Tom Sheehan was a longtime employee in the Giants organization, having served primarily as Stoneham's personal scout. As a young man he had been a pitcher with the Philadelphia Athletics and with the New York Yankees in the glory days of Babe Ruth. It hadn't been a distinguished athletic career, but he'd gotten some great stories about the Babe out of the experience.[43]

More importantly, Sheehan was a drinking buddy of Stoneham's, whose problems with alcohol were well known. Rumor had it that he had been Stoneham's clubhouse spy during the tenures of both Durocher and Rigney. Some whispered that Sheehan had schemed to oust them.[44] True or not, the rumors made some of the players uneasy around Sheehan. Others were contemptuous of him. He had the respect of none, it seemed.[45]

Mays was elected to the National League's All-Star squad and started in both games, held this year in Kansas City and New York. The Nationals won twice, and Mays' eight at-bats included a home run, a triple, a double, and three singles; he stole a base, too. He was beginning to rack up some sizable All-Star numbers, not least because, as always, he played the games to win.

Another gifted rookie provided some excitement for the Giants and their fans. Pitcher Juan Marichal joined the club halfway through the season. His debut appearance on July 19 was a gem, the first of many Marichal would pitch for the team. In this game, the rookie right-hander beat the Philadelphia Phillies in a one-hit shutout that was a no-hitter into the eighth.[46] In less than half a season—just $81\frac{1}{3}$ innings—Marichal went 6–2 with six complete games. He struck out 58 batters, and had a 2.66 ERA. For the third year in a row, the Giants added yet another future Hall-of-Famer to the roster.

Marichal's performance aside, what had started out as a season full of promise in a brand-new ballpark quickly degenerated into something of a joke. It was obvious to the players that Sheehan could not be taken seriously as their leader.

"He didn't offer us any inspiration," Mays explained.[47] Sheehan would cycle unpredictably between laxness and harshness when it came to clubhouse discipline. One day he'd shrug off a raucous postcurfew card game; the next, he'd single out a player for criticism in a clubhouse meeting. Moreover, when he chose to be critical he didn't seem to know how to choose his battles. "Whatever you do is wrong," one player said. "He's the only manager I ever saw who criticized line drives."[48]

Sheehan's inconsistency was especially hard on Cepeda and McCovey. Both were first basemen by training and by inclination, but obviously both could not play the position at once. Rather than make a choice and take its consequences, and unwilling to lose either man's bat from the line-up, Sheehan kept moving them around from position to position. McCovey played at first base and as a utility infielder; Cepeda played at first and in left field. The constant shifting made it impossible for either one to develop his fielding skills. Worse, it hurt their hitting, too. McCovey was particularly affected—his batting average dropped by almost 120 points.

While Mays blamed Sheehan for the team's problems, there was plenty of finger-pointing to go around. Armchair psychoanalysis of the team became a popular San Francisco pastime. For many observers both inside and outside professional baseball, the trouble with the Giants came down to two things: clubhouse leadership and race. The issue of civil rights for black Americans was becoming ever more pressing, but in the racial climate of 1960 a national magazine could and did print the following: "The best ballplayers on the [Giants] are Negroes, yet the Negroes . . . could not lead because the whites would refuse to follow. Things being the way they are, this is something one can understand."[49] From this point of view, the Giants were less a ballclub than a collection of individuals, splintered into small cliques along racial and ethnic lines, and Mays, "a loner off the field" though respected for his skills, was the worst offender.[50]

Mays did achieve in 1960, though his team, whatever the underlying reasons, did not. He hit .319 with 29 home runs and 107 RBIs, and he led the league with 190 hits. The Giants' winning percentage sank under .500 for the months Sheehan managed, and they finished the season 16 games out of first place, fifth in the league. The underachieving Giants needed a fresh start.

NOTES

1. Mays, with Sahadi, *Say Hey*, 151.
2. Steve W. LaBounty, "Streetwise: Willie Mays on Miraloma Drive," Western Neighborhood Web site, http://www.outsidelands.org/sw5.html.

3. Mays, with Sahadi, *Say Hey*, 151.

4. Steve W. LaBounty, "Streetwise: Willie Mays on Miraloma Drive," Western Neighborhood Web site, www.outsidelands.org/sw5.html.

5. Ibid.

6. Mays, with Sahadi, *Say Hey*, 151.

7. Ibid., 150.

8. Mays, as told to Einstein, *Willie Mays*, 195.

9. Robert Boyle, "A Fine Romance With Some Hisses," *Sports Illustrated*, August 3, 1959.

10. Mays, as told to Einstein, *Willie Mays*, 191–193.

11. Mays, with Sahadi, *Say Hey*, 150.

12. Mays, as told to Einstein, *Willie Mays*, 196–197.

13. Mays, with Sahadi, *Say Hey*, 154–155.

14. Cannon, "If Only Mays Knew How Great He Really Is."

15. Einstein, *Willie Mays*, 145.

16. Mays, with Sahadi, *Say Hey*, 203–205.

17. Mays, as told to Einstein, *Willie Mays*, 197.

18. Ibid., 187.

19. Einstein, *Willie's Time*, 322.

20. Mays, with Sahadi, *Say Hey*, 157–158.

21. Mays, as told to Einstein, *Willie Mays*, 185.

22. Mays, with Sahadi, *Say Hey*, 157–158.

23. Ibid., 157.

24. Mays, as told to Einstein, *Willie Mays*, 79–80.

25. Einstein, *Willie's Time*, 111.

26. Mays, as told to Einstein, *Willie Mays*, 201; Bob Stevens, "The 1959 All-Star Game," *San Francisco Chronicle*, quoted in Charles Einstein, *The New Baseball Reader* (New York: Penguin, 1991), 409.

27. Einstein, *Willie's Time*, 64.

28. Mays, with Sahadi, *Say Hey*, 163.

29. Ibid., 159.

30. Mays, as told to Einstein, *Willie Mays*, 123.

31. *New York Times*, January 4, 1961.

32. Mays, as told to Einstein, *Willie Mays*, 202.

33. Mays, with Sahadi, *Say Hey*, 160–161.

34. Ibid.

35. Ibid.

36. Paul Campos, "Flickering Fans: 19th Hole the Readers Take Over," *Sports Illustrated*, September 25, 1986, 102.

37. Einstein, *Willie's Time*, 119–122.

38. "1960: Christening a New Stadium," San Francisco Giants Web site, http://san francisco.giants.mlb.com/NASApp/mlb/sf/history/sf_history_timeline_article.jsp?article=24.

39. Roy Terrell, "Old Pals in a Cold Wind," *Sports Illustrated*, September 24, 1960.
40. Mays, with Sahadi, *Say Hey*, 162–163.
41. Tex Maule, "The Giants Get Happy," *Sports Illustrated*, May 22, 1961.
42. Mays, with Sahadi, *Say Hey*, 165–166.
43. Einstein, *Willie's Time*, 123.
44. Robert H. Boyle, "The Sad, Bad Giants," *Sports Illustrated*, July 18, 1960.
45. Roy Terrell, "Old Pals in a Cold Wind," *Sports Illustrated*, September 24, 1960.
46. David Bush, "Marichal's Legacy Begins," *San Francisco Chronicle*, June 1, 1999.
47. Mays, with Sahadi, *Say Hey*, 166.
48. Roy Terrell, "Old Pals in a Cold Wind," *Sports Illustrated*, September 24, 1960.
49. Ibid.
50. Ibid.

CHEERS BY THE BAY,
1961–1962

After such a lackluster season for his team, Mays was relieved to learn that real leadership was coming to the Giants at last. When Stoneham chose a new manager, he again stayed within the "Giants family" to hire Alvin Dark.

In Dark, Mays knew, his own drive for victory would be more than matched. Dark had been the Giants shortstop and the team's captain when Mays came up from the minors. Over six seasons, the two had worked well together. On the field, Dark would use hand signals to let Mays know what pitch the Giants catcher had called for. Then Mays could set himself for the hit that might be coming.[1] In the clubhouse, Dark had been lighthearted with Mays, following Durocher's lead he would kid around with the center fielder to keep his spirits high.[2] At the same time Dark was known as an intense competitor, and his reactions to Giants losses ("losing turned in his stomach and would eat away at him," as Mays put it) were well known.[3] He deserved the nickname Mays continued to use for him even now: "Cap," for captain.

A few days after Dark's appointment, Mays received a short letter from his new manager: "Just a note to say that knowing you will be playing for me is the greatest privilege and thrill any manager could hope to have."[4] It was flattery and sweet talk, and Mays probably knew it, but it worked all the same. "I had never gotten a letter from a manager before," Mays would recall later. "It impressed me and made me really want to play for him."[5] Clearly, this was a manager in Durocher's mold.

At the same time, Mays' home life was disintegrating. He and Marghuerite were more at odds than ever. Mays was unhappy in their rambling house in sub-

Mays swings for the fences in Candlestick Park. *National Baseball Hall of Fame Library, Cooperstown, N.Y.*

urban New York. Marghuerite's daughter Billie, now 14, was living with them there, as was one of Mays' teenage half-brothers and the two-year-old Michael. But the children were not enough to hold the marriage together. "Basically, Marghuerite had trouble adjusting to my way of living, and I guess I didn't adjust to hers," was all Mays would say about the breakup.[6] On New Year's Eve, he moved out of their New Rochelle home.[7] Divorce proceedings would drag on for nearly two years, and Mays began to live in their Spruce Street apartment in San Francisco year-round.

Besides the emotional strain, Mays' finances were becoming precarious, too. He signed another $85,000 contract with the Giants, but the upkeep on two separate households was costly, and both he and Marghuerite had developed some expensive tastes over the years.[8] Mays' special weakness was for clothes: his suits had to be hand-tailored and impeccably pressed. Fairfield Industrial had schooled him well; reporters noticed how Mays "seems to feel a real pain when he sees wrinkled clothing."[9] Rather than cut back or economize, Mays would borrow funds from the ballclub as the need arose.[10] He paid little attention to the mounting debt.

As spring training neared, an airline strike made it difficult for the ballplayers to get to their Arizona camp on time. With Dark's letter fresh in his mind, Mays "made it a point to be there and I drove over from San Francisco . . . to show the rest of the team that I supported him."[11] He was pleased to find a number of the 1951 Giants waiting for him in camp. Dark had hired Whitey Lockman, Wes Westrum, and former pitcher Larry Jansen as coaches.

The New York memories made things comfortable for Mays and for Dark, but may have alienated some of the San Francisco sportswriters. As a result, Mays believed that the local media were overly critical of Dark, just as he felt they had been to him.[12]

Meanwhile, Dark continued to endear himself to Mays with praise. As Mays put it, Dark "became a one-man advertising agency for Willie Mays . . . the lengths Dark went to in his first season as manager to enhance the figure of Willie Mays were lengths that few people suspect."[13] In public interviews and private conversations, Dark repeated the sentiments of his letter over and over. Mays knew full well that Dark's goal was to buoy his confidence so that he would produce—the strategy was "a fairly obvious thing."[14] But he was glad to have a manager who understood his needs so well.

Dark had heard the stories about the lack of team unity the previous year. One of his first decisions as manager was to rearrange the players' dressing cubicles in the Giants clubhouse. Before, the white players' lockers were in one area, the blacks' in another, the Latinos' in yet another. Dark broke up the cliques. "We'll all get to know each other better this way," he said.[15] Some found it notable that a white Southern man like the Louisiana-born Dark would make such integration a priority, but it didn't surprise Mays. He knew that this was not so much a matter of philosophy for Dark as a matter of winning. A cohesive team would win more games than a divided team would. The Giants sense of team spirit increased quickly after that.

Another of the manager's early rules put a damper on the Giants moaning about their home field: no complaints about the weather. Dark realized that the team's vocal unhappiness about conditions at Candlestick Park alienated the fans and gave the athletes a smokescreen for poor performances. Over time, the power of positive thinking seemed to kick in, and the players began to learn how to deal with Candlestick Park's quirks.[16]

Dark's overall seriousness of purpose had an effect, too. For him, team workouts were for working out, not for chatting with reporters. He went to bed early and rose early. He didn't drink or smoke.[17] He didn't shout at his players; he didn't need to. His authority was clear. "He talks very low, so you got to listen hard when he says something, and everybody does," one player told a reporter.[18] Explosions, when they came, were rare, and he held himself to the same standards of conduct as he expected of his players.

What it came down to was that all the Giants, from their star center fielder to their rawest rookie, wanted to perform for the new manager. Over the first dozen games of the season, though, they didn't, mainly because the sluggers— Mays, Cepeda, and Sauer—weren't slugging. Rather than respond with a lecture or a tirade that might result in the players pressing even more, Dark instead asked his team to play "little ball"—to run, steal, draw walks, whatever it took to get on base and move runners along. That flexibility, his willingness to find any way to win, was an inspiration for the players.

Frustrated at bat, Mays continued to make his spectacular "routine" plays in the field. The Giants first trip to Los Angeles that season included a Mays throw from deepest center that caught Maury Wills, Mays' heir to the base-stealing crown, at home. The throw came in so accurately that it put Giants catcher Tom Haller in perfect position to block the plate, saving the run. As Dark said, Mays "couldn't have thrown it better if he'd walked to the plate, surveyed the situation, and *placed* the ball in Haller's glove."[19]

Still, the team was unhappy about their cold bats at the season's start, and never more so than on April 28, when they were no-hit by the 40-year-old Warren Spahn in Milwaukee. Spahn was hardly a lights-out pitcher. "He's not fast. He's not even sneaky fast," Mays said after the game. "But . . . he mixes them up real good. You never know what to expect. He's amazing."[20]

For his part, Spahn enjoyed beating Dark's team. The two had come up to the majors together 15 years before, and talked a lot of strategy in those days.

This was almost like a chess match between old friends. Spahn even felt it necessary to change his whole signal system for the contest, since Dark knew all his signs. "The night before the game," he said, "I tried to remember all the things we talked about so I could figure out Alvin's thinking during the game."[21] Spahn thought that the only bad pitch he threw was a screwball that stayed high and could have been belted out of the park. The hitter, though, was the slumping Mays, who merely tapped it back to the mound.

Dark was dejected after the loss. "I did all I could to break it up," he said. "Everything. [Spahn] earned it."[22]

The no-hitter turned out to be the team's low point, though. The next day, the Giants offense finally exploded. Still in Milwaukee, they racked up five home runs and 15 hits in a 7–3 win.[23] Every man in the batting order hit safely—except for Mays.

Another of Dark's team-building innovations was to room Mays with the young Willie McCovey on the road. (Rigney and Sheehan had allowed Mays the star's privilege of a solo hotel berth.) After the game, McCovey tried to cheer Mays up by taking him out for a walk and then picking up a late-night snack to share in their hotel room. He got them a double order of ribs.

A few hours after eating Mays woke, miserably ill. McCovey called in the team's trainer, but there was little anyone could do—Mays had food poisoning. He was up for much of the rest of the night vomiting. When he went to the ballpark the next morning for the day game that was scheduled, Mays was sure he would have to sit it out. "Cap, I'm weak as a cat," he told Dark.[24]

Still, he stepped into the batting cage, took a few cuts, and felt a bit better than he'd expected. When Dark asked, Mays said he'd be able to play after all.

He did, and then some: Mays burst out of his slump with four home runs in the game, tying a major-league record. All four were monstrous 400-foot-plus shots. Even the Braves fans were excited to see Mays become the ninth man in major league history to perform the feat; when the game ended with Mays on deck, they booed their own pitcher for retiring the last Giant and not giving Mays another at-bat.[25] Mays' eight RBIs contributed heavily to the Giants' 14–4 win. The eight homers that the Giants hit as a team that day tied one major-league record; the 13 they hit over the two games after the no-hitter set a new one.

"How 'bout some more ribs?" McCovey offered Mays on his return to the dugout.[26]

Once again, Mays was the toast of baseball. CBS flew him to New York to appear on the *Ed Sullivan Show* that night. Then he had to rush on to Pittsburgh to join the team for the next stop on the road trip.

Good as it felt to be hitting again, Mays was lonely, too. The separation from

Marghuerite was looking permanent now. While he was in New York, Mays spent time with the basketball player Wilt Chamberlain, a friend. "Know any girls in Pittsburgh?" Mays asked. Chamberlain did.[27]

When Mays reached the city, he called the number his friend had passed along. "You don't know me," he began when Mae Louise Allen came on the line, "but I'm Willie Mays."

"And I'm Martha Washington," she answered, and hung up. Then she happened to glance down at a copy of the local newspaper. The sports page was headlined "Mays & Co. In Town To Play Bucs."

"And I said to myself, oh, my good God, what have I done?" she would say later.[28]

Eventually Mays called her back, and they met for lunch the next day. Mae, in her mid-twenties, was a graduate student in social work. She had a wide range of interests, and the two found they could chat easily about everything from sports to adoption. They began dating during that season, and Mae would remain an important part of Mays' life in years to come.[29]

The four-homer game went a long way toward restoring Mays' confidence at the plate. He continued hitting the home runs, but this season they tended to come in spurts. Mays had two home runs in a game or in a double-header four times in 1961; in a single game at Philadelphia on June 29 he hit three homers. The pattern contributed to the notion that Mays was a "streaky" hitter, but however the long balls came, Mays was glad to have them. He would rack up 40 home runs during the year, and on July 4 he reached another career milestone with homer number 300. Now he was in some very select company: at the time, fewer than 25 ballplayers in history had ever hit so many.

What's more, he had managed to come to some kind of peace with his home field. In 1960, Mays had fought Candlestick Park. Rather than work with its quirks and challenges, he'd thrown up his hands and accepted it when 60 percent of his home runs came on the road. This season, he was more willing to adapt his hitting style as conditions demanded, pulling the ball when he could and hitting to the opposite field at other times. In 1961, he hit equally well at home and away: 21 home runs at Candlestick, 19 in other ballparks. The pattern would hold for most of his subsequent seasons in San Francisco.

The angst Mays was suffering at the plate in the early part of the season had no effect on his confidence in the field. Especially graceful had been a game-ending play at Candlestick on May 13. The Giants were leading the Braves 8–5 in the top of the ninth. With two out, the Braves last batter popped up to shallow center. Second baseman Chuck Hiller, eyes on the ball, went back for it: Mays, eyes on the ball, charged in for it. It was a recipe for a dangerous collision, but for Mays' acute peripheral vision. At the last possible moment, Mays put up his glove while circling Hiller counter-clockwise, then ran off the field. He knew he had caught the game's final out.

Hiller didn't. Neither did the umpire. The play happened so quickly, and was performed so deftly, it was as if the ball had disappeared into thin air. "I found myself grinning as I just kept going," Mays said later.[30] He was in the shower by the time the rest of the ballpark had it figured out.[31]

Once again, the major leaguers would play two All-Star Games during the season. One of them was set for Candlestick Park on July 11, the other for Boston's Fenway Park on July 31. Unlike the All-Star contests of a later era, these games were played to win. Players were much more loyal to their leagues at the time, and they felt that the All-Star Game put their league's reputation at stake. Mays would often meet with his fellow outfielders Henry Aaron and Roberto Clemente to talk strategy before the game. "We knew we had to keep playing until the game was decided one way or the other," Mays would say.[32]

That commitment to victory was put to the test in San Francisco, when the American Leaguers were rudely introduced to the realities of Candlestick Park in a ten-inning contest that included a record seven errors, most of which were committed after the winds kicked up in the eighth inning. One relief pitcher, the Giants' Stu Miller, was even blown off the rubber (it was called a balk), proving that familiarity with the conditions was not always much help.[33] By the time it was all over, the Yankees Roger Maris was telling any and all that he'd quit the game if he had to play 77 games a year at Candlestick, and other American Leaguers echoed the sentiment.[34] The experience enhanced Mays' reputation within the ballplaying fraternity. As the Cubs Don Zimmer put it, "For him to do what he does here, he's just got to be the best in the world."[35]

The game had begun, in warm temperatures and still winds, as a pitcher's duel between Warren Spahn and the Yankees Whitey Ford. By 1961 it was well established that Mays hit Ford as few others could, even though they faced one another no more than once or twice a year in All-Star play. Early in the game, Ford had an 0-2 count against Mays on two 450-foot foul balls that had screamed just outside the left-field line. On the next pitch, Mays was looking for the curveball. Instead, he got what he called "the craziest pitch I ever saw. . . . It started for my shoulders and I ducked away," expecting it to hit him. Mays fell to the ground as he twisted to avoid the ball. "All of a sudden, the ball dropped across for a strike," and Mays was out, ending the inning.[36]

Later, he learned the whole story. Ford and his teammate Mickey Mantle had run up a $1,200 tab at Horace Stoneham's golf course. To settle the bill, Stoneham offered Ford a bet: double or nothing that Ford couldn't get Mays out during the next day's All-Star Game. On that 0-2 count, Ford felt he had no choice but to throw Mays a spitball.[37]

So *that* was why Mantle could be seen "jumping up and down like a little boy" out in center field while Mays was still sprawled on the ground.[38] "What the hell is that SOB in center field clapping for?" Mays demanded as Ford jogged by.[39]

Despite this moment of American League triumph, the Nationals won the game 5–4 when Mays doubled in the tenth inning and Roberto Clemente singled him home. With that, Mays set a new record for career runs scored in All-Star contests, but the All-Star records he was continuing to break and set "didn't mean that much to me. Every time we won, that's what mattered."[40]

Mays had a chance to see Mantle and Ford again two weeks later, when the Giants traveled to New York for an exhibition game against the Yankees. Except for the 1960 All-Star Game in the previous season, Mays had not played ball in the city since the team left the Polo Grounds four years before. For most New York baseball fans, this was their first chance since 1957 to see Mays play. Fifty thousand packed Yankee Stadium in the pouring rain. When the weather let up and the teams were announced, the crowd went wild at the mention of Mays' name. "They rocked and tottered and shouted and stamped and sang," wrote the *San Francisco Examiner*'s reporter.[41]

Years later, when Mays looked back over a career filled with great moments, this outpouring of affection from the fans in New York stood out. "You couldn't hear a thing except their cheering. It lasted for about a minute and I was frozen. I had tears in my eyes. New York hadn't forgotten me."[42]

The season's second All-Star Game at Boston was a quiet affair compared to the battle in Candlestick Park. The teams were tied 1–1 when the game was called due to rain after nine innings of play. It was the first tie game in the contest's 31-year history. Mays singled and walked, adding to his formidable list of All-Star records.[43]

As the season wound down, and the baseball world buzzed about the home-run derby Maris and Mantle were mounting at Yankee Stadium, it was clear that the Giants weren't in the running for the pennant. The race was between the Cincinnati Reds—an excellent all-around team—and the Dodgers, who were hanging on to second place thanks to strong pitching, fleet baserunning, and the passion of a coach named Leo Durocher. The Giants finished a respectable third, eight games behind the Reds, after spoiling L.A.'s chances near the end of the season with a series at Candlestick Park.[44]

Mays led the league in runs scored, with 129. His 40 home runs were second only to Cepeda's 46. His 123 RBIs were the most he'd racked up since the move to San Francisco. He had played in every one of the Giants 154 games and both All-Star Games, and he had come to terms with his home field.

If only he could be so proud of the state of his personal finances. Mays' money problems were coming to the breaking point. Despite a $90,000 contract for the 1962 season, he was on the verge of bankruptcy. The maintenance of two homes, legal fees for his impending divorce from Marghuerite, and the prospect of alimony and child support payments meant that Mays' money was spent as quickly as it came in. On top of all this, the Giants presented Mays with a bill for the funds the club had advanced him over the years. The amount came to $50,000.[45] All during the next season, these problems gnawed at Mays.

While Mays' psyche was burdened by his personal worries, he tried to keep them off the field, and he largely succeeded. The Giants began the 1962 season on a tremendous tear, winning 40 of their first 55 games.[46] Mays excelled, too: in his first at-bat of the new season he hit a home run off Warren Spahn. He hit another homer in his first at-bat next day, then another one two days after that. In all, he hit seven home runs that April. In terms of the long ball, it was his best start ever.

"We were a fighting, kicking, battling team," Mays said of the 1962 Giants.[47] The club had shored up its pitching staff over the winter when they acquired Billy Pierce and Don Larsen in a trade. With an offense led by Mays and Cepeda, the Giants were in the pennant hunt from the very first.

It would be a long season, though. The National League had expanded to 10 teams, and with the addition of the New York Mets and the Houston Colt .45s the schedule had had to grow, too. This year, for the first time, the National League teams would play 162 games.[48] In response, Dark vowed to give his everyday players regular chances to rest. After his 154-game season the year before, Mays welcomed the notion. He was 31 now, after all.

But crossing his star center fielder off the line-up card proved more difficult than Dark had anticipated. The Giants played well from the beginning, but the Dodgers did too, and after San Francisco suffered a slump in June the teams found themselves in a season-long battle for first place. How can a manager in that situation bench the league's top slugger?

Also, the notion was growing in San Francisco that the Giants had never won a game that Mays hadn't started. Sportswriters and fans were convinced of this, and Mays believed it too.[49] (Of course, since Mays had played more than 150 games in each of the last eight seasons, there were precious few games he hadn't started.) How can a manager bench his team's good-luck charm?

So despite Dark's best intentions, once again Mays played game in, game out. The difference this season was that his stress level had increased exponentially. The divorce case was now in court, and periodically Mays had to appear for hearings and other procedures. His financial picture was also worrisome. Worst of all, he felt obliged to keep all these concerns to himself. Kids looked up to him; fans respected him. He couldn't bear the thought of their disapproval if they knew he couldn't pay his bills.[50]

At one point when the team was on the road, Mays felt so emotionally overloaded and anxious that "I couldn't sleep. I had the shakes. I found myself, for no reason that I knew, on the verge of tears."[51] The day before, he had missed most of a game because of a court appearance; the team had lost, and Mays blamed himself. (It made it all the worse that the opposing team had been the Dodgers, that a key play had been a line drive over the replacement center fielder's head, and that Dodger coach Durocher kept crowing after the game how "Willie woulda had it.") Alone in his hotel room, Mays called his manager.

Dark was soothing and calm. "Come on up," he said. The team trainer was there when Mays arrived and fed him a few sleeping pills. Dark insisted that Mays remain with him and kept talking until Mays finally slept.[52] Dark's compassion and understanding at moments like these touched Mays, to the point that he would remark with some surprise, "I never thought I'd say this about anyone—but I actually think more of Cap than I did of Leo!"[53]

Perhaps that was why Mays finally began to wear a batting helmet this season, after Dark "put it on the basis of a flat order," thus becoming the last major leaguer to take to the protective device.[54] Even though Mays was, by far, the Giant most thrown at by opposing pitchers, he had always disliked the weight and bulk of a helmet. Instead, he had worn a liner inside his cap and relied on his reflexes. Dark, worried that those reflexes were bound to slow sooner or later, could no longer allow Mays to take such a risk, and Mays saw the wisdom in that. "As I was getting older, all the fastball pitchers in the league seemed to be getting younger," he said ruefully.[55]

The Giants first encounters with the Mets were at Candlestick Park in late May. The expansion club, which was quickly establishing a reputation as the most hapless collection of losers in baseball history, didn't stand much chance against the Giants, who swept the series, though New York did force one game into extra innings. Two Mays home runs made the difference for San Francisco in that contest. "It wasn't the one in the tenth that wowed me," Mets manager Casey Stengel said of Mays' game-winning homer. "It was the one he hit in the eighth—he hit that one one-handed!"[56]

Two days later, Mays found himself fighting in one of the few on-field brawls of his career. It happened at Candlestick Park in another game against the Mets. Cepeda was at bat and Mays was on second, dancing off the bag and interfering with pitcher Roger Craig's timing. The Mets second baseman, Elio Chacon, nursed a grudge against Mays from the previous season, when Mays had spiked him in a hard slide. Craig made four throws over to second base; each time, Mays jumped back just in front of the tag. Finally, Mays was caught off guard and had to dive back to the base in a head-first slide. It was too much for Chacon. "All of a sudden instead of just trying to tag me, Chacon was beating on me with his fists," Mays recalled later.[57] Craig and Cepeda both rushed out to protect their respective teammates, but it all ended quickly. Mays, who had at least twenty pounds on the wiry second baseman, took no swings; he more or less picked Chacon up and dropped him in short center field.[58]

After their initial meeting in San Francisco, both teams traveled to New York for a series at the Mets temporary home field—the Polo Grounds. It was the first time Mays had been back to the old ballpark since 1957, and he was overwhelmed with emotion as the 43,000 fans cheered his every move, from his batting-practice hacks to the three home runs he would hit the four-game series, which the Giants swept again. These fans were mainly here to cheer their Mets, though. The team was hopeless—the losses to the Giants capped a 16-game losing streak—but it had already attracted a rabid local following of former Dodgers and Giants rooters.

Mays continued to parlay his knowledge of the game and his fellow athletes into great plays. One of the most amazing occurred at Candlestick Park in a game against the Braves. Hank Aaron was on first base, and the batter hit a long fly ball into deep right center. Aaron, running on the pitch, rounded second. When Mays overtook the ball and caught it, Aaron had to scramble all the way back to first. But Mays, who had grabbed the ball with his back to the infield, rifled it not to first base, but to second. Shortstop Jose Pagan, heeding Rigney's long-ago lesson, was there to receive it, but didn't know what to do with it until Mays, still deep in the outfield, pointed forcefully to the ground. Pagan stamped on second base, and the umpire called Aaron out. He had neglected to touch second on his way back to first.

Mays had had his back turned while Aaron was running. How on earth had he known that Aaron had missed the base, reporters wanted to know after the game? Simple, Mays replied. "I know the way he runs."[59] Mays himself thought this might have been "the greatest play I ever made."[60]

By midseason, Mays had slugged 26 home runs, on pace to exceed his 1955 total. Once again, he poured all his emotion—his anxieties over money, his sadness at separation from Michael, his frustration at the drawn-out divorce case—into his work on the field. His performances in the season's two All-Star Games, though, were below his usual standards; he was hitless in both contests. The first one, held in Washington, DC in the new District of Columbia Stadium, was a 2–1 National League win. It included a leaping catch by Mays that was featured in sports pages across the country. The second All-Star contest took place in Chicago's Wrigley Field. This one was taken by the AL team 9–4.[61]

The fight for first place had been stalled since June, with the Dodgers ahead by a healthy margin, when a new development gave the Giants hope. Sandy Koufax, the Los Angeles ace who was leading the league in strikeouts and in ERA, went on the disabled list with a circulation problem. He was not expected to return until the end of the season, if at all. "With Koufax out, there was no question in my mind but that we could make a run at the Dodgers," Mays said later.[62] Indeed, shortly thereafter the Giants swept a three-game series against L.A. at Candlestick Park, keeping the two teams close.

The Dodgers believed that these losses had more to do with Dark's creative groundskeeping than with their own skills. To slow both ground balls and L.A.'s league-leading base stealer, Maury Wills, Dark had the infield so heavily watered for the series that he was given a new nickname: the Swamp Fox.[63]

When the Giants headed to Cincinnati for the beginning of their season's final road trip on September 12, they had won seven in a row and were half a game behind Los Angeles in the standings, with the Cincinnati Reds close behind.[64] The pressure was high, and the hot, humid weather seemed to compound the tension.

Without warning, in the top of the second inning, Mays collapsed in the Giants dugout. He passed out briefly, then regained consciousness. "I just feel like I don't want to move," he said when he could speak again. "I *can* move, but I don't want to."[65]

An ambulance rushed Mays to a local hospital, where doctors ran batteries of tests that night and over the next two days. They found what Mays had expected them to find: nothing. There is no medical test for tiredness, and Mays was simply "exhausted. Mentally, physically, emotionally, every other way."[66] He had sat out one game so far that season.

Almost immediately, the rumor mill cranked up. The stories varied wildly: Mays was an alcoholic. He'd had a heart attack. He'd had an epileptic seizure. He'd been punched out by a teammate.[67] Writers and fans had a hard time believing that a healthy 31-year-old man, the league's top home run hitter and the star of a team in the thick of a pennant race, could simply be too tired to go on.

The doctors prescribed three days of bed rest for Mays. Dark told the insistent media that Mays would be back in the line-up when he felt ready to play. The Giants lost every game they played without him. Still, Dark never pressured Mays to leave the hospital.

Once again, Mays was deeply grateful for his manager's understanding. "After that, I wanted to play for Dark very badly," he said.[68]

He rejoined the team in Pittsburgh and hit a clutch home run that sent the game into extra innings, but the team's momentum had been thrown; the Giants lost three more games with Mays back in the line-up. "We just plain fell out of the pennant race," Mays said.[69] For him, the nadir came in the season's final week, when he killed a possible Giants rally by wandering off third base, thinking there were three outs when there were really two, and getting tagged.

But there was one thing that kept the standings tight: the Dodgers were in a free fall, too. So were the Reds. The press started calling it "The Pennant Nobody Wanted."[70] Once again the season came down to the last day of play. With the Giants half a game out of first place, the Dodgers fate was in their own hands. If they won, whatever the Giants did, Los Angeles would have the pennant. If they lost, a Giants victory would force a playoff.

The Giants were at home for their last game, playing Houston. Before the game, Joe Amalfitano, who was with the Colt .45s after several seasons with the Giants, asked Mays, "Can you score a run?"

"I think we can," Mays told him.

"Then you've got the pennant," Amalfitano said. "Those Dodgers are *never* going to score another run."[71] Houston had just finished a series in Los Angeles.

The Giants had to score two, actually. They and the Colts played to a 1–1 tie through seven innings. In the bottom of the eighth, with nobody on, Mays hit a tremendous home run into the left-field seats—one of the longest he'd ever hit, Mays thought—and that was the ballgame. The Giants won it 2–1.

"I was really excited when I hit that home run," Mays said years later, "but . . . I didn't want to show my emotions. I can't be jumping around."[72] They hadn't won anything but a game yet.

Now it was up to the Dodgers, who were playing in their brand-new ballpark in Chavez Ravine. But Amalfitano's prediction proved correct: St. Louis beat them 1–0.

The Giants, listening to the game on the clubhouse radio, reacted with stunned surprise. "Wahoo," Dark said, softly.

"Well, we owe the Giants something," Duke Snider mused back in Los Angeles.[73] Just like 1951, it would be the Giants and the Dodgers in a three-game playoff for the National League pennant.

The first game was played at Candlestick Park, and all of San Francisco was caught up in the excitement. As one local wit had put it five years before, San Franciscans "traditionally will pay anything to see a champion but won't walk two blocks to see a second-rater."[74] At long last, they were close to getting their champion, and now Mays was sure of the fans' affection.

Still, the echoes of New York in 1951 were inescapable. Once again, it was the Giants and the Dodgers in a playoff to decide a season that had come down to the very last game. Once again, Durocher was in the dugout—though this time on the Dodger side of the field. Once again, Alvin Dark was directing the

Giants on-field action, with Westrum and Lockman at his side. And once again, there was Willie Mays in center field.

For Game 1 the Giants sent the veteran Billy Pierce to the mound. Pierce had gone 15–6 over the season in what would prove to be his last productive year in baseball. He would be battling Sandy Koufax, who had returned to the team. Koufax wasn't the same pitcher, though. In the first inning Koufax gave up a double to Felipe Alou. Then Mays came up. He worked the count to 3–1 and waited on Koufax's fastball. When it came, Mays powered it over the fence in right center. After that, the Giants just piled on as Dodgers manager Walter Alston threw the bullpen at them. The final score was 8–0 Giants. Mays went 3 for 3 with two homers, a single, a walk, and a stolen base. The home runs brought his total to 49 and gave Mays the home-run crown (the playoff games' statistics were added to those of the regular season under the rules of the time).

The teams traveled to Los Angeles for the next two games of the series. The Dodgers had not scored in 30 straight innings and were feeling desperate. Coach Leo Durocher called on that old baseball standby: superstition. He pulled out of dusty boxes all the clothes he had been wearing during the 1951 Giants-Dodgers playoff and announced that he would once again wear the T-shirt, socks, and undershorts that had last been used on the day of Bobby Thomson's home run.[75] Meanwhile, the Los Angeles fans prepared for the game their own way. They brought duck calls and feathers to razz Alvin Dark, the Swamp Fox.[76]

The Giants built up a 5–0 lead early in the game, but the Dodgers roared back with a seven-run rally in the sixth inning. "Maybe Leo's underwear was working," Mays thought. He couldn't help but be amused at Durocher's tactics.[77] The Giants tied the game in the top of the ninth, but the Dodgers finally pulled out an 8–7 win.

Baseball voodoo being what it is, it seemed almost inevitable that once again these two teams would meet in a do-or-die situation. Adding to the mysticism, the date was October 3, eleven years to the day from Thomson's "Shot Heard 'Round the World."

Juan Marichal was on the mound for the Giants, while Johnny Podres started for Los Angeles. Neither team wanted to give an inch: runs came in ones and twos, and a total of 20 men were stranded on the bases. When the Giants came up in the top of the ninth, the score was 4–2 Dodgers. (Shades again of 1951, when the score was 4–1 Dodgers in the bottom of the ninth.)

Dark sent Matty Alou in to pinch-hit for Don Larsen, who had relieved Marichal in the eighth. Alou singled to right. Kuenn, up next, hit a ground ball that got Alou at second for the first out. Then Ed Roebuck, the Dodger pitcher who had come in for Podres in the sixth, walked the next two Giants to load the bases. Up next was Willie Mays. He had drawn two walks but was hitless in the game.

"I wanted to be up," Mays said later. "I wanted it to be on my shoulders. No scared rookie now, I knew what had to be done."[78]

He smashed a hard liner back at the mound that tore the glove off Roebuck's hand. The ball stayed in the infield, but there was no play. Everyone was safe, Kuenn had reached home, and the bases were still loaded with Giants. The score was 4–3.

Alston sent in a relief pitcher, but Cepeda, up next, hit a high sacrifice fly to right that scored the tying run. It was 4–4, two out, two men on. The jittery reliever next threw a wild pitch that allowed Mays to advance to second, putting two men in scoring position.

In hopes of setting up a double play, Alston had the next Giants batter intentionally walked to load the bases again. But Williams, not known for his control, unintentionally walked the next man up, sending home the go-ahead run and placing Mays on third. When Pagan hit a ground ball toward second base that the Dodgers fielder fumbled, it was all the margin Mays needed. He raced home, making the score 6–4.[79]

Billy Pierce shut the Dodgers down in the bottom of the ninth on a grounder and two fly balls to center. Mays pounded his glove, caught the last out chest-high, and tossed the ball into the stands in what was, for him, an unusual celebratory display.

In the raucous clubhouse afterward, as champagne flowed and players whooped in English and Spanish, someone asked Mays why he hadn't used his basket catch for the final out. He shrieked with laughter. "You crazy? That was $15,000 a man!"[80]

When the Giants flew home that night, their plane was unable to land at the terminal. The tarmac was mobbed by thousands of fans—estimates ranged from 50,000 to 75,000. The pilot brought the plane down near a maintenance building, and the fans ran to catch up. The players piled into the team bus and a couple of taxicabs just as the joyous San Franciscans reached them, shouting, "We want Willie! We want Willie!"[81]

"It had taken them only five years," Mays observed.[82] But coming after his emotionally bruising season, the affirmation mattered to him.

San Francisco went just a bit crazy over the Giants pennant win. It was the first time any of the city's major-league sports franchises had done so well. Downtown, church bells pealed, fireworks exploded, and happy crowds filled the streets. When the World Series itself started at Candlestick Park on October 4, it felt to many like an anticlimax.[83]

Mays put it this way: "The Giants couldn't have cared less . . . any team that a week earlier was trying to figure out how to win second-place money, and instead now would get a World Series share if it *lost*, wasn't going to be particularly tense at the prospect of facing the Yankees."[84]

The New York Yankees had won the American League pennant easily, by five games. Well rested, unlike the Giants, they were favored to win the Series. Many expected the Series to be marked by fireworks at the plate, given the teams' stats. Both teams had led their leagues in batting average. The Giants led the NL in home runs; the Yankees were second in the AL. Mays' 49 homers led his league; Mantle's .605 slugging average was the highest in his.

Instead, the pitchers came to the fore. The first World Series game ever at Candlestick Park pitted Whitey Ford against the Giants Billy O'Dell, the one Giants starter who had had only limited work in the previous four frantic days. O'Dell gave up a two-run double to Roger Maris in the first inning, then settled down. The Giants scratched back, a run at a time, in a game that developed into a Mays-Ford duel. Once again, Mays hit Ford well, going 3 for 4 with a home run to dead center, though Ford did rack up a single satisfying strikeout against his nemesis. But the Yankees put up four runs in the last three innings to win the game 6–2.

Game 2 had the Giants 24-game-winner, Jack Sanford, pitching against the Yankees 23-game-winner, Ralph Terry. The Giants cobbled together a run in the first inning, but that was all the scoring there would be for six more innings, until McCovey lofted a soaring home run to right. In the end, Sanford shut out the Yankees on three hits, and the Giants evened the Series on the 2–0 win. A contributing factor had been Dark's use of the "Ted Williams shift" against Roger Maris, who had had two hits and two RBIs in the first game of the series. Because Maris was such a strong pull hitter, Dark had shortstop Pagan play to the right of second and second baseman Chuck Hiller positioned closer to first base. The maneuver, and Sanford's pitching, effectively handcuffed Maris.[85]

The teams traveled to New York for the next three games of the Series. Game 3 was scoreless through six innings as Bill Stafford led the Yankees against Billy Pierce and the Giants. In the seventh, Pierce finally weakened, giving up two singles, then a two-RBI double to Maris, who eventually scored when Hiller bobbled the inning-ending double-play ball. The Giants answered with two runs in the top of the ninth on a double by Mays and a home run by catcher Ed Bailey, but that was the best they could do. The game ended as a 3–2 Yankee victory.

Game 4 finally provided some hitting excitement when Hiller hit a grand slam in the seventh inning. Before that, the game had been yet another pitching duel, this time between Marichal and Ford. Hiller's clout put the Giants ahead in the game for good, even though both teams added a run apiece in the ninth, making the final score 7–4. Don Larsen, who came into the game after Marichal smashed a finger in a bunt attempt, got the win for the Giants on the sixth anniversary of the perfect World Series game he'd pitched for the Yankees in 1956. The Series was knotted again 2–2.[86]

The next game was rained out, giving the players an extra day of rest but interfering with the pitchers' preparation plans. Sanford was especially bothered by the unexpected day off. When he took the mound for the Giants on October 10, he felt that his rhythm had been affected. Still, he pitched well through seven innings, allowing just two runs, as did the Yankees Terry. But in the eighth inning Tom Tresh hit a three-run home run for the Yankees, and the Giants only answered with a single run scored in the ninth, giving the Yankees a 5–3 edge.

By this time, Mays' outlandish outfield plays were so expected they were barely commented on, but he would always remain proud of a throw he made in this World Series. It was on a screaming liner that Moose Skowron hit out to the Yankee Stadium monuments, 460 feet from home plate. Mays dug the ball out, then rifled it to Pagan. If the shortstop hadn't hesitated, Mays was sure, he would have had Skowron at third. As it was, the Yankee first baseman was credited with a triple, and Mays was left with only the satisfied memory of how he "just threw the twine off the ball."[87]

The Series went back to San Francisco, which was being battered by a record-breaking storm system. Game 6 was rained out for three days as the teams waited impatiently. When the skies cleared on October 15, Candlestick Park really was a swamp—poetic justice, perhaps, for Dark's machinations earlier in the season. Helicopters were brought in to dry the outfield, but they weren't much help.[88] The drenched conditions would play a role in the next two games.

In Game 6, Ford got the start against Pierce. Once again, the contest began with three scoreless innings. Then the Giants broke through for three runs in the fourth inning and two more in the fifth. The Yankees only scored twice as Pierce held them to three hits. One factor in the game was Mays' fielding, to which Yankee third baseman Clete Boyer paid tribute after being robbed of a probable triple. "I hit the ball and . . . I was measuring how far it would roll when it hit and whether I'd get a double out of it or a triple. And then, running toward first base, I said to myself, 'Oh, hell, *he's* out there'. . . . And when I looked up, he was lobbing the ball back to the infield after the catch."[89] The Giants won 5–2 and the Series was even again.

It all came down to Game 7 in a World Series that had now lasted 13 days, equaling the longest on record. It was Sanford versus Terry for the third time in the tightest game of all. Sanford held the Yankees to a single run on seven hits. Terry held the Giants scoreless as he pitched a complete-game shutout. In the bottom of the ninth, San Francisco had its last, best chance as Mays lashed a double down the right-field line with two out and Matty Alou on first. It might have gone for a triple had the field been less waterlogged, but the muddy turf and Roger Maris' excellent play prevented that. Alou held up at third. With the tying and winning runs in scoring position, McCovey hit a fierce liner that was caught by Yankee second baseman Bobby Richardson, ending the game and the Series. The Yankees won it, four games to three.[90]

Still, Mays would always remember the 1962 Giants as "the best all-around type of team that I ever played on."[91]

NOTES

1. Mays, with Sahadi, *Say Hey*, 168.
2. Tex Maule, "The Giants Get Happy," *Sports Illustrated*, May 22, 1961.
3. Mays, with Sahadi, *Say Hey*, 168.
4. Mays, as told to Einstein, *Willie Mays*, 204.
5. Mays, with Sahadi, *Say Hey*, 169.
6. Mays, as told to Einstein, *Willie Mays*, 187.
7. *New York Times*, January 4, 1961.
8. Mays, as told to Einstein, *Willie Mays*, 251.
9. Brown, "The Onliest Way I Know."
10. Mays, as told to Einstein, *Willie Mays*, 252.
11. Mays, with Sahadi, *Say Hey*, 169.
12. Ibid.
13. Mays, as told to Einstein, *Willie Mays*, 210.
14. Ibid., 211.
15. Tex Maule, "The Giants Get Happy," *Sports Illustrated*, May 22, 1961.
16. Mays, with Sahadi, *Say Hey*, 172–173; Tex Maule, "The Giants Get Happy," *Sports Illustrated*, May 22, 1961.
17. Mays, with Sahadi, *Say Hey*, 170.
18. Tex Maule, "The Giants Get Happy," *Sports Illustrated*, May 22, 1961.
19. Einstein, *Willie Mays*, 163.
20. Tex Maule, "Everything Seemed Easy," *Sports Illustrated*, May 8, 1961.
21. Ibid.
22. Ibid.
23. Einstein, *Willie Mays*, 164.
24. Mays, as told to Einstein, *Willie Mays*, 225.
25. Mays, as told to Einstein, *Willie Mays*, 226; *New York Times*, May 1, 1961.
26. Mays, with Sahadi, *Say Hey*, 175.
27. Ibid., 261.
28. Einstein, *Willie's Time*, 323.

29. Mays, with Sahadi, *Say Hey*, 261.

30. Mays, as told to Einstein, *Willie Mays*, 230.

31. Einstein, *Willie's Time*, 156–157.

32. Jack Curry, "Mays Recalls All-Star Games That Had Passion," *New York Times*, July 13, 2003.

33. Bruce Jenkins, "Blown Away in '61," *San Francisco Chronicle*, August 24, 1999. When the story is retold, Miller is often said to have been "blown off the mound," but this is an exaggeration.

34. *Sports Illustrated*, July 24, 1961; *New York Times*, July 12, 1961.

35. Bruce Jenkins, "Blown Away in '61," *San Francisco Chronicle*, August 24, 1999.

36. Mays, with Sahadi, *Say Hey*, 282.

37. Steve Serby, "Serby's Sunday Q&A with . . . Whitey Ford," *New York Post*, October 24, 2004. The amount of the debt varies from telling to telling, but it was certainly significant.

38. Mays, with Sahadi, *Say Hey*, 282.

39. Steve Serby, "Serby's Sunday Q&A with . . . Whitey Ford," *New York Post*, October 24, 2004.

40. Jack Curry, "Mays Recalls All-Star Games That Had Passion," *New York Times*, July 13, 2003.

41. Einstein, *Willie's Time*, 135.

42. Mays, with Sahadi, *Say Hey*, 175; Mays, as told to Einstein, *Willie Mays*, 237.

43. *New York Times*, August 1, 1961.

44. Walter Bingham, "No Pennant for Platoons of Dodgers," *Sports Illustrated*, September 18, 1961.

45. Mays, as told to Einstein, *Willie Mays*, 253.

46. Einstein, *Willie Mays*, 172.

47. Mays, as told to Einstein, *Willie Mays*, 238.

48. *New York Times*, October 27, 1960. Expansion, and the expanded schedule, had come a year earlier for the American League.

49. Mays, as told to Einstein, *Willie Mays*, 128.

50. Ibid., 255.

51. Ibid., 254.

52. Mays, as told to Einstein, *Willie Mays*, 253–254; Mays, with Sahadi, *Say Hey*, 210–211.

53. Mays, as told to Einstein, *Willie Mays*, 222.

54. Ibid., 117.

55. Mays, as told to Einstein, *Willie Mays*, 117; Einstein, *Willie's Time*, 246–247.

56. Einstein, *Willie Mays*, 172.

57. Mays, as told to Einstein, *Willie Mays*, 284.

58. Mays, with Sahadi, *Say Hey*, 203; Einstein, *Willie Mays*, 173–174; date cited in Jack Lang and Peter Simon, *The New York Mets: Twenty-five Years of Baseball Magic* (New York: Henry Holt, 1986, 1987), 30.

59. Einstein, *Willie's Time*, 63. This source misidentifies the infielder as Tito Fuentes,

who did not join the Giants until 1965; the 1963-published *Willie Mays: Coast to Coast Giant* (136) also tells the story, with Pagan as the fielder.

60. Mays, as told to Einstein, *Willie Mays*, 68.

61. "All-Star Game," MLB.com Web site, http://mlb.mlb.com/NASApp/mlb/mlb/history/mlb_asgrecaps_story_headline.jsp?story_page=recap_1962a.

62. Mays, with Sahadi, *Say Hey*, 178.

63. Mays, with Sahadi, *Say Hey*, 185–186; Tom C. Brody, "A Miller-Hiller-Haller-Holler-Lujah Twist," *Sports Illustrated*, September 17, 1962.

64. Einstein, *Willie's Time*, 168.

65. Mays, with Sahadi, *Say Hey*, 179.

66. Mays, as told to Einstein, *Willie Mays*, 240.

67. Einstein, *Willie's Time*, 168–169.

68. Mays, with Sahadi, *Say Hey*, 180.

69. Mays, as told to Einstein, *Willie Mays*, 241.

70. Tom C. Brody, "A Giant Shot that Forced a Playoff," *Sports Illustrated*, October 1, 1962.

71. Mays, as told to Einstein, *Willie Mays*, 241–242.

72. David Bush, "Remembering the 1962 Giants," *San Francisco Chronicle*, May 31, 2002.

73. Tom C. Brody, "A Giant Shot that Forced a Playoff," *Sports Illustrated*, October 1, 1962.

74. "San Francisco 1 Los Angeles 0," *Sports Illustrated*, September 2, 1957.

75. Mays, with Sahadi, *Say Hey*, 188.

76. Tom C. Brody, "A Miller-Hiller-Haller-Holler-Lujah Twist," *Sports Illustrated*, September 17, 1962.

77. Mays, with Sahadi, *Say Hey*, 188.

78. Ibid., 189.

79. *New York Times*, October 4, 1962.

80. Einstein, *Willie's Time*, 172.

81. Einstein, *Willie Mays*, 182; Mays, with Sahadi, *Say Hey*, 190.

82. Mays, with Sahadi, *Say Hey*, 190.

83. Einstein, *Willie's Time*, 172–173.

84. Mays, as told to Einstein, *Willie Mays*, 246.

85. Mays, with Sahadi, *Say Hey*, 193.

86. Roy Terrell, "The Pitchers Stand and Fight," *Sports Illustrated*, October 15, 1962.

87. Mays, as told to Einstein, *Willie Mays*, 114.

88. *Sports Illustrated*, October 22, 1962; Mays, as told to Einstein, *Willie Mays*, 246.

89. Mays, as told to Einstein, *Willie Mays*, 169.

90. Mays, with Sahadi, *Say Hey*, 194–196.

91. David Bush, "Remembering the 1962 Giants," *San Francisco Chronicle*, May 31, 2002.

CAPTAIN MAYS, 1963–1964

The extra-long World Series capped an extra-long season, but Mays still had more baseball to play. He had committed to a postseason barnstorming trip through the Midwest, which he joined the day after the Series ended. Even then, he didn't take it easy; in his first game of the week-long trip, he singled and homered to win the game for the National League side.[1]

Once the barnstorming tour was over, Mays checked himself into San Francisco's Mount Zion Hospital. "I wanted to ease my mind—and, I suppose, everyone else's—that there was nothing wrong with me physically," he explained.[2] He believed that the Cincinnati doctors had been right, and that his September fainting spell had been the result of exhaustion, nothing more. Mays' all-out style of play was the same whether the game was a preseason intrasquad match or Game 7 of the World Series. It took a lot out of a 31-year-old body.

The medical tests proved Mays right. The doctors' reports declared that he was "in superior physical condition" and "perfectly healthy."[3]

The hospital stay gave Mays a period of forced relaxation that alone helped him feel better. It also gave him a chance to think. He knew that the stresses in his personal life, as much as the demands of his profession, had been a factor in his exhaustion problem. When he left the hospital, he began to face the issues that had haunted him all season long.

The most complicated and vexing problem was that of his finances. The Giants needed Mays to pay back the $50,000 he owed the club. Once the settlement of the debt was figured in, his 1962 salary of $90,000 was barely enough to pay his taxes, let alone his living expenses and legal fees and alimony, now that the divorce had been finalized.[4] Reluctantly, Mays decided that the only way out was to declare bankruptcy.

For all the money Mays had made, he had never had any professional financial advice or guidance. The Giants front office paid him and advanced money when he asked for it; Mays spent it. He bestowed cash on family and friends, bought the occasional piece of real estate, and sank some funds into friends' business ventures. That was the extent of his budgeting and investment policy.[5]

At last, he realized, he needed help. He found it in a local San Francisco bank president, Jacob Shemano. Mays felt that Shemano had imagination, as well as good sense, and late in 1962 he laid the whole monetary mess on his desk. The banker "helped me get organized again," as Mays put it—no small task, beginning with the problem of the taxes.[6]

Shemano convinced Mays to avoid bankruptcy, arguing that the process would hurt Mays' image and, in turn, damage his future earning potential. Over time, Mays reined in his spending, paid off his debts, and learned how to make long-term investments. He was grateful for Shemano's guidance, which greatly eased his mind over the next several seasons.[7]

Another troubling factor during the 1962 season had been loneliness. Living apart from his family, and especially from his son Michael, was painful. Mays had not fought Marguerite for custody, believing that "a young boy should be with his mother." Michael was only three years old now, Mays reasoned; when he was school age, they would spend more time together. For now, though, the child's short visits weren't enough. "I wanted to have someone with me all the time," Mays said.[8]

So, he decided, he would bring his father to San Francisco to live with him. Mays bought another house in his team's home city (undoubtedly with the tax benefits of such a purchase very much in mind) for Cat Mays and himself.[9] Over the years, he would welcome other family members into his home, just as Aunt Sarah and Aunt Ernestine had once done for him.[10]

There may have been another factor involved in his father's cross-country move, one that Mays would not discuss publicly: the state of race relations back home in Alabama. The issue of civil rights for black Americans was roiling the nation, and nowhere more so than in Birmingham, which Martin Luther King Jr. called "the most thoroughly segregated city in the United States" and where blacks' churches and homes were being firebombed on a regular basis.[11]

Willie Mays was, by all accounts, a politically indifferent man.[12] He did not speak out about racial injustice, unlike Jackie Robinson, who was now making regular speeches on behalf of the National Association for the Advancement of Colored People (NAACP). But Mays was not blind to political reality. Since 1954, he had not returned to Fairfield or to Birmingham to celebrate any of his records or even to mark the Giants pennant win. Friends believed that his avoidance of his hometown was a statement itself: he would not allow the city's white power structure to use him to bolster their own civic pride.[13] Moving his father from the city seemed to be a kind of statement, too.

Instead of making public pronouncements, Mays was more comfortable taking private action to help his community. He was a familiar figure in youth centers and children's hospitals, and would spend time with individual kids and teens in hopes of setting an example for them. One such teenager was a talented athlete whose involvement in his neighborhood's gang culture was threatening a potentially bright future. As O. J. Simpson told the story years later, Mays showed up unannounced at his home shortly after he'd been picked up by the police for gang activity. Mays had been called in by a youth counselor from the neighborhood. He didn't lecture the 15-year-old; he just took the kid along on an afternoon of errands and meetings. Simpson idolized Mays, who seemed to him a paragon of unattainable wealth and success, and their day together had a long-lasting effect on his life. "To have that hero pay attention to me, it made me feel I must be special too," he said. "After spending time with him, my dreams became realistic goals . . . he became a guy like me, with problems—his clothes weren't ready at the cleaners. [But] he made me realize that we all have it in ourselves to be heroes."[14] The very ordinary afternoon convinced Simpson that he, too, could succeed. He left the gang life behind and became a college and NFL football star, before murder accusations in the 1990s made him a controversial figure.

When the year turned, Mays felt he could look toward spring training and the 1963 season with a clear head and a rested body. The challenge would lie in getting through another 162-game schedule the same way.

He was pleased about his salary, which at $105,000 was again the highest in baseball, and thought to be a record amount.[15] It was rumored that this figure was as much the product of Horace Stoneham's competitiveness as it was a reward for Mays' own performance. Because Mickey Mantle had signed with the Yankees for $100,000, the story went, Stoneham wanted once again to have the game's highest-paid athlete.[16] Mays, however, believed the contract was offered strictly on his merits. After all, he pointed out, "It was after my $105,000 for '63 was announced that Mantle's $100,000 was announced."[17]

But he was disturbed at the way the club was treating Orlando Cepeda so soon after the Giants pennant-winning season. Cepeda was offered a contract at less than half of Mays' salary, and he was upset. He'd batted in 114 runs and scored 105 more. In terms of overall production, he ran a close second to Mays on the league's best team. He felt, with some justification, that it was unfair for him to earn so much less than his teammate. So Cepeda held out on signing his contract and did not appear for spring training.

Instead of trying to make peace or soothe Cepeda's hurt feelings, Alvin Dark seemed to take the holdout personally. Dark's ideas on team discipline and clubhouse behavior sometimes clashed with the players' sensibilities, particularly those of the ballclub's Latino members. His attempts to regulate the players' speaking Spanish or playing Latin music in the clubhouse had had little success, and Dark and Cepeda feuded frequently.[18]

Still, Mays was appalled by the manager's next move. Dark called a press conference and revealed some statistics he had been keeping on his players. His "key production system" was essentially a way to monitor clutch hits. According to Dark, Mays was the most productive clutch hitter on the team. Third baseman Jim Davenport was second. Cepeda was down toward the bottom of the list.[19] The charge upset Cepeda so deeply that he filed a libel suit (unsuccessfully, it would turn out) against the magazine that reported it.

A friend asked Mays whether he thought there was anything to Dark's stats. Mays answered, "Shit, a man hits .300 and bats in 100 runs, how you gonna say he can't hit?"[20]

Eventually, Cepeda signed the contract and returned to the team. He remained distrustful of Dark, however, and the incident gave Mays cause to wonder about Dark's judgment when it came to player relations.

Soon enough, Mays had other things on his mind as he got off to what seemed to him to be his worst start ever. He hit under .300 for the entire first half of the season and had only seven home runs in April and May. Of course, what was a slump for Mays would represent a career year for many other ballplayers. His "bad start" included a three-home-run game at St. Louis on June 2.

He was touched when the New York Mets honored him—a visiting player!—with "Willie Mays Night" on May 3. Several of his New York teammates, including Monte Irvin and Bobby Thomson, were on hand for the celebration.[21] Mays was still emotional whenever he played at the old Polo Grounds, and he was on the verge of tears the whole game. "I really wanted to do something special" for the 49,000 fans who turned out, Mays lamented, "but the most I could manage was a double as the Mets beat us."[22]

Mays had a close relationship with the Mets owners, who had been members of the New York Giants board of directors. Still, he was unprepared for the amount of affection they poured on him that night. In the speeches that preceded the game, Bill Shea, for whom the team's new stadium would be named, took the microphone. "We love you, Willie," he said to the fans' wild cheers. "When, Mr. Stoneham, are you going to give us our Willie back?"[23]

The Giants as a team had a good start, staying within a couple of games of first place, and sometimes in the top slot themselves, for the first half of the season. They were humbled, though, by a no-hitter at the hands of Sandy Koufax in Los Angeles on May 11. A month later, their defensive work helped secure a no-hitter for Marichal, but they could score only one run themselves in the 1–0 victory over Houston.[24]

Another 1–0 Giants win, this one in the beginning of July, exhausted them and their opponents. The game lasted 16 innings, and it was notable because both starters went the distance, each of them pitching a complete game, and each of them pitching a shutout until the very last at-bat. It happened in Candlestick Park. The pitchers were Juan Marichal for the Giants and the veteran Warren Spahn for the Milwaukee Braves. Neither starter trusted his bullpen enough to cede the ball. And, as Marichal told Dark in the ninth inning, "I'm 25. That old man is 42. If he's going back out there, I'm going back out there."[25] Finally, just after midnight, Mays came up with one out in the bottom of the sixteenth. Spahn had thrown 276 pitches, and Mays knew he had to be tired. When Spahn offered up a screwball, Mays powered it out of the park for a game-winning home run.

Still, Dark perceived an overall lack of effort on the part of his players. He responded with clubhouse lectures, benchings, and fines, but it seemed to Mays that the players were beginning to tune their manager out. Despite the success of the previous season, Dark inspired less confidence than he once did, and the more desperate he got, the less willing his players were to listen.[26]

"I wondered if Dark was losing his ability to communicate with his players," Mays would say later.[27] Dark, too, seemed to recognize the worsening problem. In an unusual move, he set up a players' committee, with Mays as chairman, that the teammates could use as a private forum. "[Dark] felt that there are times players would prefer to discuss some things without bringing him in," Mays explained.[28] If they wouldn't talk to the manager, at least he could give them the means to talk to each other.

The All-Star break, when it came, was a relief to Mays. By now his annual selection to the team seemed an inevitability; 1963 marked his tenth consecutive annual appearance as an All-Star.[29] It was one of the few years that Mays was selected and Whitey Ford was not. In recognition of Mays' .700 average against him, Ford sent Mays a telegram when the All-Star choices were announced. It read: "DEAR WILLIE—SORRY—WHITEY."[30]

Ford missed quite a performance by his friendly archrival. Mays was a marvel in the 5–3 National League victory. He scored two runs, batted in two more, stole two bases, and was named the game's MVP. When it was over, Mays' All-Star Game batting average stood at .417 for the 14 games in which he had played.[31] Better still, as far as Mays was concerned, was that the All-Star Game seemed to reawaken his bat. After the break, his batting average climbed above .300, where it would remain for the rest of the season.

Behind the scenes, though, Dark continued to have trouble keeping his feelings in check when confronted with frustration or, worse, defeat. In early August, the manager's explosion at Mays marked a low point. The team was playing in Chicago and had a six-run lead in the eighth inning. When a long fly ball headed past Mays in center, he didn't go after it in his usual pell-mell fashion. It was late in the game, and the Giants were so far ahead, he reasoned; why risk getting hurt? The hit went for a double that sparked a Cubs rally. They tied the game and won it in extra innings.[32]

Afterward, Dark was apoplectic. "You laid down on me," he snarled at Mays.

Mays was already angry at himself, and he didn't need this from his manager. "I didn't cost you no seven runs," he snapped.[33]

"In a way, we were both right," Mays would say, charitably, much later.[34] The two did not speak for several days after that. Then they went on as if nothing had happened. To Mays, the incident was another sign that Dark was losing control of his emotions and his team.

Mays' power numbers, which had returned to their accustomed levels in June, continued strong, so much so that at the end of August he approached another milestone: his 400th career home run. A TV crew happened to be filming a documentary about Mays during the last week in August. The filmmaker interviewed Mays in his car on the way to Candlestick Park the afternoon of August 27. As they discussed the evening's game, Mays talked about all the factors he needed to consider: the opposing team, St. Louis; their pitcher, the veteran Curt Simmons, known for his sliders and curves at this point in his career; and the weather conditions, including the ever-important wind. Given all that, Mays said, "I ought to hit it tonight," meaning of course home run number 400.[35] "It'll be before the fifth," he added. "After that, the wind kicks up on a night like this."[36]

Sure enough, in the bottom of the fourth, Mays uncorked his very own called shot, and for his 400th home run to boot. After the game, he collared the filmmaker. "You ought to be happy," he said.

"I'm miserable," was the answer. "Here we have you calling your four hundredth home run in advance . . . and there's no way we can use it."

Mays was incredulous. "Why not?"

"It'll have to look staged," the filmmaker told him. "It'll look like you hit the home run first and we rigged the interview afterward. . . . I'm sorry, Buck, but all we can do is throw it out and forget it." The incident became one of Mays' favorite stories.[37]

As the long season headed into its final month, the Giants were just outside of pennant contention. One good hot streak could vault them past Los Angeles, St. Louis, and Philadelphia into first place. Dark prodded his team harder than ever. Once again, Mays, who had started nearly every game, began to feel the first hints of exhaustion.

In September, as the Giants hosted the Cubs at Candlestick Park, Mays came to bat in the bottom of the fourth with the bases loaded. He fouled off a pitch, then he sank to one knee in the batter's box, overcome with dizziness. "I couldn't believe it was happening again," he said.[38] He had to be helped off the field and was rushed to a local hospital, where doctors ran all the tests they'd done the year before. The diagnosis was the same—fatigue.

Mays spent three days in bed.[39] When he returned to the field, the Giants had fallen out of the pennant race for good. The defending World Series champions ended the season in a disappointing third place, 11 games behind the pennant-winning Dodgers. They'd hit more home runs than any other team in the National League, now that Willie McCovey had come into his own as a slugger, but the homers weren't enough.

It was something of an off-year for Mays personally, too. For the first time since his return from the army, he did not lead the league in any of the major offensive categories, although he was second in slugging average and runs scored and third in home runs.

When the 1964 season began, Mays played like a man possessed. After a month of play, he was batting .497 with a slugging average over 1.000—in other words, he had more total bases than at-bats.[40] From late April into early May, he had a 20-game hitting streak.[41] His performance was driving the Giants, but the whole team was doing well. They led the National League standings through May.

Then word of Jackie Robinson's new book began to trickle out. After a decade and a half of integrated baseball, Robinson had combined a memoir with interviews of other baseball men to produce *Baseball Has Done It*, an overview of the state of the game in a new era.

One of those interviewed was Alvin Dark. After three years of managing one of the most thoroughly integrated teams in major-league baseball, his words seemed to come from another man. The Louisianan let loose every patronizing stereotype of the traditional white South. Dark opined that "people in the South . . . have well and truly liked the colored people. As for socializing with them . . . there is a line drawn in the South, and . . . it may never be corrected." On integration: "I'd rather stay away from it as much as possible . . . I feel that right now it's being handled a bit too fast." On black ballplayers: "There has never been any trouble between colored boys and other players on this club. . . . Colored boys have never given me any trouble as manager." On relations between blacks and whites: "The older people in the South have taken care of the Negroes. They feel they have a responsibility to take care of them."[42] And so on, for three solid pages.

When Dark's comments were made public, there was an uproar in the San Francisco press. Horace Stoneham was furious. Mays, however, reacted with equanimity. "I knew what Dark was saying," he said later. "I was from the South, and so was he. I understood what he was talking about."[43]

What Robinson had to say about Mays, though, stung. Robinson noted that Mays had been asked to contribute his thoughts on race to *Baseball Has Done It*, and that Mays had declined, saying that he didn't know what to say. "No doubt [he] did not wish to stir things up," Robinson concluded. "But there's no escape, not even for Willie . . . from being a Negro, which is more than enough to stir things up when bigots are around. . . . I hope Willie hasn't forgotten his shotgun house in Birmingham's slums, wind whistling through its clapboards, as he sits in his $85,000 mansion in San Francisco's fashionable Forest Hills."[44]

Typically, Mays did not respond to Robinson directly or immediately. Two years later, in his own memoir, he would say, "My being a Negro is a part of this story—more than you might suspect, but probably less than some people would like. . . . Maybe—all things considered—[I was] the first [black major leaguer] you could point to and say, 'Look what he did,' instead of saying, 'Look, he's colored.'

"No question about what Jackie Robinson started. But maybe I started something too."[45]

It was in this atmosphere of on-field success and outside criticism that Dark asked Mays to be the first black team captain in major-league history. Only four years before, national newsmagazines had been saying that white players' inability to accept a black player as clubhouse leader was "understandable." Only weeks before, Dark himself had been quoted making what many had seen as pro-segregationist remarks. So Mays was rendered temporarily speechless at Dark's offer.

Dark said, "You deserve it. You should have had it long before now."

"They'll kill you," Mays warned him, meaning the press. "They'll tear you apart." But he accepted the job. It was an honor, certainly, and Mays took it as such. Apart from that, it was an eminently practical move. Both Mays and Dark were motivated by one thing: victory. The controversy over the Robinson book would not improve Dark's relationships within the clubhouse. "If it was true that Dark was losing communication with his players, then of course making me captain was a sound thing for him to do," Mays noted.[46]

Dark announced Mays' new appointment in a pregame clubhouse meeting on May 21, and Mays promptly hit two homers, as if in celebration.[47] His teammates seemed pleased with his new job. They respected Mays' on-field skills as much as they ever had, and now they were beginning to appreciate the other ways he could help them. The players' committee Dark had instituted the season before established Mays as the go-to clubhouse veteran, and players were comfortable now coming to him with personal problems.[48] Giving him the title of captain seemed to them a natural progression.

Mays had been right, though: the appointment meant even more criticism for Dark in the press. Just days after news of Mays' new title broke, a San Francisco columnist disparaged player, manager, and the entire concept of team captaincy all at once: "Willie Mays has as much reason to be captain of the Giants, even if in name only, as I have to be placed in charge of our space program. His naming to the fictitious job was, apparently, a public relations gimmick to becalm the Negroes of this area, many of whom are rightly enraged by Mr. Dark's odd views of the race question."[49] As the criticism mounted, Mays assured Dark that he didn't believe the notion that the captain's position was nothing but a sham, and he took the job seriously.

The Giants went through a slump that knocked them out of first place, but they regained some confidence with a double-header in the Mets new ballpark, Shea Stadium, on May 31. Cepeda won the first game for Juan Marichal with a steal of home. But the second game seemed endless. It went on for 23 innings and took more than seven hours to play. All told, the 32-inning extravaganza was the longest day in baseball history, lasting 10 hours and 23 minutes from first pitch to final out.

"At first, it was sort of fun," Mays said.[50] Many of the loyal Mets fans stayed for the duration. Then the concession stands ran out of food. The players began to wilt. Cepeda lined into a triple play that caught Mays and Jesus Alou off base in the fourteenth inning. Dark lost his temper arguing a call in the fifteenth and was thrown out of the game. Players were shuffled and reshuffled so many times that Mays was forced to play shortstop for three innings. In the end, thanks in large part to Gaylord Perry's 10 scoreless innings of relief, the Giants won the game 8–6 on a triple, a double, and an infield grounder.[51] The games were exhausting, but exhilarating, too. They launched the Giants on a winning road trip that by mid-June settled them back into first place.

Mays was selected for the All-Star team and was lauded as its "star of stars," even though he was hitless in the National League's victory at Shea Stadium. When he worked a walk in the ninth inning, the entire ballpark knew he was going to go for a stolen base—yet steal second he did. With that, Mays controlled the pace of play, throwing off the timing of Boston's Dick Radatz and the fielding positions of the other American Leaguers. Within moments, he had drawn a bad pickoff throw and had taken home to tie the game and set off a four-run National League rally.[52]

Back with the Giants, though, the season had become another battle as the club experienced streaks and slumps, and as five National League teams stayed in the running for the pennant. For the Giants, "backstage bickering," as Mays called it, made it that much harder to focus on the game. "We weren't a happy crew," Mays said later.[53] The new team captain had his hands full.

It was nothing to what happened late in July. The club was on a road trip, staying at a Pittsburgh hotel, when several players received a newspaper clipping in the mail. It was a column that had appeared in Newsday, a suburban New York daily. Once again, Alvin Dark was talking about race relations. "We have trouble because we have so many Spanish-speaking and Negro players on the team," Dark said in the interview. "They are just not able to compete with the white ball player when it comes to mental alertness." Cepeda and McCovey came in for particular criticism for not "sacrificing" themselves and not having "pride in their team."[54] (Dark did not mention the fact that both of them had been forced to switch positions constantly over the previous four seasons, which had affected their play for the worse.)

One by one, the black and Latino players came to their captain to talk the column over. Mays asked them all to gather in his Pittsburgh hotel room to discuss it as a group. When they did, their anger rose. The mood was downright mutinous. Mays had to shout them down to achieve some order as Cepeda and others threatened to refuse to take the field for Dark.

Once he had their attention, Mays laid out a case for the players to remain calm. It was cool-headed and practical: the Giants had a chance to win the pennant with Dark as manager, but not if there was turmoil at the top; forcing him out would make him a racial martyr, and "ain't one of us going to have a moment's peace" from the press in that event; finally, whatever Dark might say in an interview, he had never fielded a team based on the players' races. "He helped me," Mays said. "And he's helped everybody here . . . because he wants to win, and he wants the money that goes with winning. Ain't nothing wrong with that."[55]

Mays' speech held the team together, but when Dark gave a press conference in New York, their next stop on the road trip, Mays almost wished he had remained silent. After all Dark had said about Mays deserving the team captaincy, now the manager really was using it for public relations purposes. "I thought I proved my feelings when I named Willie Mays captain," Dark told the reporters. "If I thought Negroes were inferior, would I have done that?"[56]

"I was actively sick" on hearing this defense, Mays said later. He never lay down on Dark, but Mays did not speak to his manager for the rest of the season.[57]

Mays had been right about the pennant race, though. In spite of all their problems the Giants were in the thick of the tough five-way fight until the very end. Mays was hitting home runs at a league-leading pace, followed closely by teammates Cepeda and Jim Ray Hart. In the field, Mays remained superlative. He tried to stay conscious of his body's 33 years and not risk injury unless it was necessary. But in a pennant race, he felt that every play deserved his all-out effort.

One catch stood out. In a game at Philadelphia, Mays was playing close in on Ruben Amaro, a utilityman who rarely hit the ball out of the infield. It was the fourth inning with two out in a one-run game. Uncharacteristically, Amaro let loose a long drive that headed all the way out to the 385-foot sign on the right center field wall. Mays whirled and tore after it. He grabbed the ball just before it hit the wall, flipped his legs out before him so that his feet rather than his head would take the impact, and crashed off the wall and onto his back. The ball was still in his glove.[58]

"That made the fans come roaring to their feet," he noted proudly. "You know you've done something, when you hear it from the enemy fans."[59]

In the season's closing days, the Cardinals pulled ahead to snatch the pennant. The Giants finished fourth, but only three games out. With 47 home runs, Mays again took the home-run crown; he led the league in slugging, too.

On the last day of the 1964 season, Stoneham announced that Dark would not return to manage the next year.

NOTES

1. Einstein, *Willie Mays,* 39.
2. Mays, with Sahadi, *Say Hey,* 197.
3. Ibid., 207.
4. Mays, as told to Einstein, *Willie Mays,* 253.
5. Mays, as told to Einstein, *Willie Mays,* 252; Einstein, *Willie's Time,* 128.
6. Mays, with Sahadi, *Say Hey,* 211.
7. Mays, as told to Einstein, *Willie Mays,* 256.
8. Mays, with Sahadi, *Say Hey,* 209–211.
9. Einstein, *Willie Mays,* 185.
10. Einstein, *Willie's Time,* 150.
11. Martin Luther King Jr., "Letter from Birmingham City Jail," cited in Diane Ravitch, *The American Reader* (New York: HarperCollins, 1990.)
12. Einstein, *Willie's Time,* 188.
13. Ibid., 181.
14. Mike DiGiovanna, "Day with Mays Helped O.J. Escape the Ghetto," *Los Angeles Times,* October 30, 1985; Mays, with Sahadi, *Say Hey,* 199–200.
15. Mays, as told to Einstein, *Willie Mays,* 251.

16. Mays' own memoir *Say Hey* (211) repeats this story.

17. Mays, as told to Einstein, *Willie Mays*, 289. This memoir, published in 1966, is closer to the event in question and more probably reflects his thinking at the time.

18. Joan Walsh, "Willie Mays," Salon.com, July 13, 1999.

19. Mays, with Sahadi, *Say Hey*, 212.

20. Einstein, *Willie's Time*, 175.

21. *New York Times*, May 4, 1963.

22. Mays, with Sahadi, *Say Hey*, 212.

23. *New York Times*, May 4, 1963.

24. *New York Times*, June 16, 1963.

25. David Bush, "Candlestick Classics #2: A Fight to the Finish," *San Francisco Chronicle*, September 21, 1999.

26. Mays, as told to Einstein, *Willie Mays*, 257–258.

27. Mays, with Sahadi, *Say Hey*, 214.

28. Ibid., 222.

29. Due to the double-game years of 1959–1962, however, this was Mays' fourteenth All-Star Game overall.

30. Mays, as told to Einstein, *Willie Mays*, 52.

31. Mays, with Sahadi, *Say Hey*, 213.

32. Ibid., 215.

33. Einstein, *Willie's Time*, 199.

34. Mays, as told to Einstein, *Willie Mays*, 257.

35. Einstein, *Willie's Time*, 130.

36. Mays, as told to Einstein, *Willie Mays*, 124.

37. Ibid., 124–125.

38. Mays, with Sahadi, *Say Hey*, 216.

39. Mays, as told to Einstein, *Willie Mays*, 258.

40. Ibid., 188.

41. Mays, with Sahadi, *Say Hey*, 221.

42. Mays, as told to Einstein, *Willie Mays*, 260–262.

43. Mays, with Sahadi, *Say Hey*, 218.

44. Einstein, *Willie's Time*, 287–288.

45. Mays, as told to Einstein, *Willie Mays*, 25.

46. Ibid., 259.

47. Mays, with Sahadi, *Say Hey*, 221–222.

48. Mays, as told to Einstein, *Willie Mays*, 26.

49. Charles McCabe in the *San Francisco Examiner*, May 24, 1964; quoted in Einstein, *Willie's Time*, 204.

50. Mays, with Sahadi, *Say Hey*, 223.

51. *New York Times*, June 1, 1964; Tom FitzGerald, "When the Giants Won the N.Y. Marathon," *San Francisco Chronicle*, May 31, 2001.

52. *New York Times*, July 8, 1964.

53. Mays, as told to Einstein, *Willie Mays*, 266.

54. Einstein, *Willie's Time*, 207.

55. Einstein, *Willie's Time*, 211; the meeting is also described in *Say Hey* (225) and *Willie Mays: My Life In and Out of Baseball*, (267–268).

56. Mays, as told to Einstein, *Willie Mays*, 268.

57. Ibid., 268–269.

58. Hano, *A Day in the Bleachers*, 160.

59. Mays, as told to Einstein, *Willie Mays*, 168.

Mays received his second Most Valuable Player award in 1965—eleven years after his first MVP. *National Baseball Hall of Fame Library, Coopers-town, N.Y.*

THE VETERAN YEARS,
1965–1971

With Alvin Dark finishing out the 1964 season, Horace Stoneham had enough time to make a well-considered decision before naming the next Giants manager. The team's new leader had to be someone who could reach out to the club's disaffected players, unlike Dark. He'd have to be able to get along well with Mays, unlike Rigney. And he had to be someone with whom Stoneham felt personally comfortable.[1] One man fit all these criteria: Herman Franks.

Mays was gratified when Stoneham felt him out about Franks before naming the former Giants coach to the post. He agreed that Franks was a good choice, believing that Franks' knowledge of Spanish would go a long way toward motivating the Latino players.[2]

Franks, a catcher during his playing days, appeared in fewer than 200 games in a six-season major-league career that was interrupted by military service in World War II. He played for Durocher in Brooklyn in 1940 and 1941, and a few years after he left the service Durocher brought him to New York as a Giants coach. Franks had become close to Stoneham in the years since, so the owner felt he could trust him. He had been the manager of the Santurce team in the Puerto Rican League during the one winter-ball season Mays played there, so he and Mays had a long-term relationship as well.

Though schooled in the Durocher management style, Franks was much more relaxed than any of his predecessors had been (with the short-term and inconsistent exception of Sheehan). "You felt the guy would make time for you," Mays said.[3] Franks put more responsibility in the hands of his coaches, and on the shoulders of his team captain. Not only did he encourage the players, especially the younger ones, to talk to Mays, he consulted with Mays on a daily basis to plan line-ups and gauge the team's mood. Mays became, in effect, an assistant manager.

The story of Mays' amped-up captaincy leaked out to the press and was bandied about in print all season long. The reporters were consumed with one question: did this mean Mays could one day become baseball's first black manager?[4] Mays would not discuss the details of his responsibilities for publication, however, until after his playing days had ended. Of course he would "give advice" to teammates while in the field, he would say all through the 1965 season. "Other fielders gave me advice when I when I first came up; now it's my turn. But we use signals and quiet things—I don't like to make a public exhibition out of it."[5] (He did not share the fact that when his "advice" was ignored, he could and did have Franks bench the offending player until the maverick was "ready to play with the team."[6])

When pressed about his role within the clubhouse, Mays had to explain the obvious. "They ain't going to come and talk to me if they think I'm going to brag about it," he would say of his teammates.[7] About the team's internal difficulties, from one player's drinking problem to another's marital woes, the Giants captain remained silent.

Franks, for his part, had no qualms about discussing Mays' role on the team. A reporter asked him if Mays really did have so much influence on line-ups and fielding strategy. Yes, he did, Franks replied. Why, the reporter wanted to know, had the manager given Mays such authority? "Because he knows more about those things than I do," said Franks. "You got any hard questions?"[8]

Mays was also secretive about the injuries he nursed all season. He had torn several shoulder and leg muscles in an early exhibition game. He could tape the leg and get by, but the shoulder pain made it almost impossible for Mays to make his trademark heaves from the outfield. So he did the only thing he could do: he faked the opposition out. Before each game, during fielding practice, "I would cut loose with two or three throws, to third and to home plate. The throws were strong and accurate, and I did this the entire year without any other team knowing that I couldn't make those throws once the game began."[9] It was a favorite trick of aging veterans, including Joe DiMaggio, and at age 34 Mays was fast approaching that category.[10]

There was no concealing the leg injury he suffered in late June, though. Mays pulled a groin muscle and could not hide his pain. Still, he wanted to play, hobbled though he was.[11] Franks tried him in left field and right field for a few games, where he wouldn't have to cover as much ground as in center. He tried to rest Mays entirely, too, but more often than not the center fielder would come in at some point to pinch hit. In any case, as Mays well knew, "when I'm at the park, I never get any real rest because I'm always working myself up about the game."[12]

The muscle strains had no measurable impact on his hitting. He had 22 home runs on the season by the third week of June. The 22nd blast tied him with Stan Musial on the all-time list. The groin injury put a damper on Mays' power, though. For two weeks Mays and Musial remained tied at 475 homers apiece. Finally, on July 8 in Philadelphia, Mays pulled a long, high fly into the left-field seats. Now, with 476 home runs to his credit, Mays was second only to Mel Ott as the greatest slugger in National League history, and seventh on the list over-all.[13]

Two days later Mays was injured again, this time in all too obvious a fashion: he collided with the Phillies catcher in a play at the plate, bruising his hip. First, Mays made sure he was called safe. Then he allowed himself to be taken to the hospital. (The catcher had it worse—he had to be carried off the field on a stretcher.) Phillies manager Gene Mauch paid Mays a backhanded tribute after the game: "The guy comes into home four feet in the air, kicks my catcher in the face, and still manages to touch home plate. He'll limp to the Hall of Fame."[14]

The All-Star break gave Mays a little time to recover—not that he skipped the game, which took place in his old minor-league home town, Minneapolis. In fact, Mays hit in the lead-off spot and smashed the second pitch of the contest into the bleachers in deep left center. He stayed in the game for all nine innings and scored the winning run in the ninth after drawing a walk and heading home on a high-hopping grounder hit by Ron Santo of the Cubs. Mays' homer gave him sole possession of the record for All-Star hits with 21 (the record he broke was, again, Musial's). But to him, it was more important that the National League won the game 6–5.[15]

Even with the injuries, and even with an 0-for-24 stretch in July, Mays' stats for the season were outstanding. His batting average was well over .300 at mid-season, where it would remain. At the end of July he led the league in home runs, with 24.

Better still, the Giants were winning games, vying for first place the whole season. Their success was a surprise. The club had only one reliable starting pitcher, Marichal, and the slugging Orlando Cepeda missed almost all of the season with a knee injury that required surgery to correct.[16] On the other hand, Cepeda's absence gave Willie McCovey his chance to claim the first baseman's slot full-time, and he stepped up with solid fielding and 39 home runs.

August became a month of high drama and extreme emotion. The Giants had an eight-game winning streak, their hottest stretch since 1962, as they traded first place with four other National League teams. Mays had one of the best months of his career, in terms of statistics and in terms of his legend, but it came at a price.

The West Coast rivals were at odds once again; the Dodgers were one of the clubs in pennant contention. For many Californians, the teams' performances were a welcome distraction from the ugly reality of their streets. That month, a week-long race riot destroyed the Watts neighborhood of Los Angeles, killing 34 people, injuring nearly 900 more, and causing millions of dollars in property damage.

Tension and fear were palpable throughout the state in the riot's aftermath. Two days after the violence ended, the Dodgers met the Giants for a four-game series in Candlestick Park. The games were closely fought. Two of them ended in extra-inning Dodger victories after the visitors tied each game in the ninth. The Giants won the third game relatively easily 5–1. Mays had a home run in every game of the series, bringing his total for the month to 13. All the contests included aggressive jockeying at the plate between batters and catchers on both sides.

The fourth and final game of the series pitted Marichal against Koufax. In the first inning, Los Angeles's Maury Wills bunted for a single and came around to score. The Dodgers scored a second run in the top of the second, then Wills came up again. Marichal, who had a reputation as a headhunter, sent Wills sprawling with a high and tight pitch. Koufax, in token retaliation, threw a ball high over Mays' head when he led off the home half of the inning. It was a courtesy pitch, typical of Koufax, who never hit batters intentionally. As far as baseball custom was concerned, the conflict should have ended there.

Instead, in the bottom of the third, it escalated when Marichal came up to bat. Behind the plate, catcher John Roseboro knew that Koufax wouldn't throw at Marichal, but he thought that Marichal deserved to be hit.[17] When Roseboro tossed the ball back to the mound after the second pitch, he threw it so close to Marichal's head that it nicked his batting helmet.

Marichal turned, raised his bat, and clubbed Roseboro over the head with it, opening up a two-inch gash that bled profusely. The benches cleared as the horrified players rushed to separate the combatants and, perhaps, to join the fight. Mays made straight for Roseboro, both out of personal concern—he and Roseboro were friendly off the field—and to prevent him from going after Marichal and worsening the brawl. "He's the one who had his head creased. So he was the first one who had to be held back," Mays explained later.[18]

He didn't see the blood until he reached Roseboro's side. While Dodgers and Giants shouted at one another and several near-fights rose up and were quelled, many in the ballpark watched Mays speak to Roseboro soothingly, walk him back toward the Dodger dugout, and press a towel to his bloody face. Roseboro, still furious, tried to go after Marichal again; Mays restrained him. Then, as one writer described it, he "cupped the enemy's head in his hands and surveyed his wounds with a look of deep anguish on his expressive face. It appeared from a distance that Willie Mays had tears in his eyes."[19]

What Mays did to prevent a full-scale riot impressed baseball. That he did it with such humanity impressed the world. Reporters would refer to him as "Peacemaker Mays" for the rest of the season and beyond.

While Mays genuinely cared about Roseboro's well-being, when the game resumed he just as genuinely cared about winning it. A cautious Koufax, deprived of his inside pitch after the umpires had issued warnings to both sides, walked two batters, then up came Mays. He expected the fastball, and when he got it, he launched it over the center field fence.[20] The Giants won the game 4–3. With that, the Bay Area fans' attitude toward Mays went from admiration to adoration.[21]

If Mays was the hero of the afternoon's drama, Marichal was without doubt its villain. His teammates hustled him off the field before the umpires even had a chance to throw him out, but obviously some kind of league-defined sanction would have to be imposed.

Some on the Dodgers called for Marichal's indefinite suspension from the game. Outraged fans across the country flooded letters-to-the-editor columns with demands that he be banned from baseball altogether. For the league, settling on a punishment was not so simple. National League president Warren Giles understood that a suspension of any length would punish the Giants more than it would punish Marichal. "Shall I penalize Willie Mays?" Giles demanded. "If so, how does such fine and decent conduct deserve a penalty? This man was an example of the best in any of us."[22]

Giles settled on a fine of $1,750 and a nine-day suspension. Behind the scenes, he explained his reasoning. Marichal would miss two scheduled starts in his nine days of punishment, limiting the impact on the pennant race. When he resumed his regular place in the pitching rotation, he would pitch on September 5—and he would not appear in the Dodgers-Giants series scheduled to begin in Dodger Stadium on Labor Day, September 6. In fact, under no circumstances was Marichal to show up in Los Angeles at all for that series, given the fragile state of the city's peace in the wake of Watts. Franks complied with both the letter and the spirit of the order, even though it forced him to pitch Marichal on only two days' rest when a rainout altered the pitching rotation.[23]

Meanwhile, Mays helped ease memories of the brawl with the hottest homer-hitting month of his career, and with another major milestone. His home run off Koufax was his 491st lifetime, putting Lou Gehrig's total of 493 within easy reach. On the road in the week after the Marichal riot, Mays homered in Pittsburgh and again in New York. Now he was tied with Gehrig on the lifetime list. He had also tied Ralph Kiner's National League record for most home runs hit in a single month, with 16. On August 29 at Shea Stadium, one blast surpassed both those marks. Mays was now fifth on the lifetime home run list with 494, and held the NL record for most homers in a month: 17—a record that would stand for more than 30 years.

Kiner, who was now broadcasting for the Mets, was there to see his record broken. Mays was solicitous in a postgame interview. "Are you sore?" he asked Kiner.

"Sure I'm sore," replied Kiner, with refreshing honesty. "Wouldn't you be?"[24]

A few days later, when the Giants went to Los Angeles, Marichal was not with them. His face had even been erased from local billboards advertising a juice he had endorsed, replaced by—what else?—the image of Peacemaker Mays.[25] The entire Giants line-up was fiercely booed by the Dodgers fans. That is, until Willie Mays' first at-bat. For Mays, the crowd roared, came to its feet, and delivered a standing ovation. "Mays had become a sociopolitical figure," one writer concluded.[26] San Franciscans were not the only ones who adored him in the wake of the Marichal brawl.

The Giants won the game. When they won the next day, too, they stood in first place in the National League and were in the early part of a 14-game winning streak.

One of those games, at Houston on September 13, included another milestone for Mays: his 500th career home run. When he powered the ball into the center field seats, tying a game that the Giants would eventually win, yet another enemy crowd gave Mays an ovation.

Warren Spahn was one of the teammates who congratulated Mays on the landmark homer. At 44 and in his final season, the veteran had been acquired by the Giants to shore up their shaky pitching staff. "I threw you the first one," Spahn said, remembering their initial meeting back in 1951, "and now I've seen the five-hundredth. Was it the same feeling?"

"Same feeling, same pitch," Mays replied.[27]

As ever, the milestones were secondary to Mays. Home run number 500 was a thrill, but not so much as number 501 the next night, which came in the ninth inning with two out, two on, and the Giants down by three. "Everyone— even the popcorn sellers—knew that I would be swinging for the big one" in the situation, Mays noted.[28] He swung and missed on the first two pitches, then worked the count to 2–2. As the tension built, the Houston pitcher, Claude Raymond, wouldn't give an inch. Neither would Mays, who fouled off four pitches in a row until at last he drove one into the left-field seats. That tied the score, and the Giants went on to win the game in the tenth.[29]

By this time, the Giants looked like a lock for the pennant. But in the closing weeks of the season, the Dodgers surged. Inspired, perhaps, by Sandy Koufax's perfect game on September 9, Los Angeles rode a 13-game winning streak that edged San Francisco out of first place. Mays was disappointed with the team's second-place finish, though he consoled himself that the Giants had far surpassed anyone's expectations. For that, he credited Franks, whose contract option had already been picked up for the 1966 campaign.

Mays could take some credit too, though. In the season's final game, at home against Cincinnati, he hit his 52nd homer of the year. It would prove to be his career high, and it led the league—both leagues, in fact. Mays' .645 slugging average also led the league. He became the first National Leaguer to hit 40 or more home runs in six seasons. His stats, as well as the leadership he demonstrated in the Marichal brawl, made him a shoo-in for the year's Most Valuable Player award, which was announced in November. The fact that Mays' previous MVP had come in 1954, eleven years earlier, was a testament to his remarkable consistency.

Mays' off-season was almost as busy as his season had been. Michael, now five, came to live with Mays for an extended time, attending kindergarten in San Francisco. Earlier in the year Mays had lent his name to establish an insurance firm, the Willie Mays Agency Inc., and now he began to study the business with the thought that it might provide him a post-baseball career.[30] He also joined Franks, who was already a successful real-estate developer in his native Salt Lake City, in a building management company there.[31] The front office was less than thrilled with the potential conflict of having a manager and a player sharing business interests, but on the other hand it was evidence of the trust the two men felt in one another.

Also, after years of behind-the-scenes volunteer work, Mays decided to take on a public role as a spokesman for the Job Corps, a national work program for youth. His status as baseball's "legend in residence," as he would one day put it, still took him aback; when Vice President Hubert Humphrey invited him to Washington and asked him personally to undertake a nationwide Job Corps tour, Mays was gratified. He accepted quickly, with one proviso: that he would not have to make a set speech, but could just talk to Corpsmen and potential recruits in his own unscripted words.[32]

He did not give much thought to his physical condition, though, and a few weeks into the tour, just before going onstage, Mays once again grew dizzy and passed out. Luckily he was in Salt Lake City at the time, and Franks was with him. The manager brought Mays to his home and had him examined by a physician there. Again, the verdict was exhaustion, and a concerned Franks insisted Mays stay a few days to rest.[33]

He took things a little easier during the weeks until spring training, collaborating on a new memoir and playing golf. Mays was somewhat surprised to find that people were willing to pay him just to play a round of golf with him, and because he enjoyed the game anyway, he didn't mind the extra cash.[34] It was more relaxing than a national speaking tour, at any rate.

The latest collapse worried the Giants management greatly. Franks resolved to rest Mays more frequently during the season, but only a few innings at a time, by removing him from games early whenever possible. Franks' intentions were good, but he had just as hard a time following through on them as Dark had. Mays compiled almost as many at-bats in 1966 as in the season before. He more than earned his $125,000 salary, once again the highest in baseball.[35]

There was another, subtle change in Mays during the 1966 season: he had suddenly become much more conscious of his place in the game's history. The kid who in 1954 hadn't much cared about going after Babe Ruth's home run record had developed into a man who kept careful track of the statistics he was amassing. "By now I was intensely aware of where I stood on the all-time homer list," he would say.[36]

At the opening of the 1966 season Mays' 505 home runs put him fifth on that list, behind Babe Ruth, Jimmie Foxx, Ted Williams, and Mel Ott. Realistically, Mays didn't think he had much chance to surpass Ruth's 714 lifetime home runs. He'd have to have five more 40-homer seasons to get near it; now almost 35, he couldn't be sure his career would last that much longer.

But Mays could be reasonably sure to hit seven more home runs. That would put him ahead of Mel Ott, who had hit 511, making Mays the greatest slugger in Giants history and, more importantly, the top home run hitter in the National League. He set his sights on that goal.

It didn't take long to accomplish it. Mays' 1966 season got off to a roaring start. He racked up six homers in the team's first 13 games, tying Ott's record. He hit number 511 in the Houston Astrodome against Robin Roberts, the veteran former Phillie who had been on the mound for Mays' 51st home run of the 1955 season.

Surpassing Ott was not so easy. The Giants returned to San Francisco for a ten-game home stand the next day, and a horde of reporters and TV crews descended on Candlestick Park to capture the record-breaking 512th home run of Mays' career. Mays was feeling that old performance pressure that dogged him as far back as his rookie days. Pressing and playing with a bruised hand, he did not homer as the Braves and the Cardinals came and went. His batting average dropped below .300 as he went 3 for 23. Franks, concerned, took him out of one game and sent him home to clear his head.

Finally, the Dodgers arrived for the last series of the home stand. On May 4, after striking out twice against the lefty Claude Osteen, Mays hammered a high outside changeup over the right-field fence. It was Number 512 at last, and after Mays left the field for the dugout, the San Francisco fans shouted him out for a curtain call. "I thought to myself, heck, I've got a lot more of these left in me," Mays said later.[37]

The fan who caught the home-run ball came to the clubhouse after the game. Stoneham offered $100 and Giants tickets in exchange for it. The fan wanted more, arguing that the ball could go to the Baseball Hall of Fame someday. Mays, standing nearby, was asked what he thought.

"Keep it," Mays shrugged. He took the ball from the fan's hand, autographed it, and gave it back.[38] (It would be decades before the sports memorabilia craze would make such a conversation unthinkable, but it was hardly the first time Mays was so cavalier about his career's relics. In 1955, he gave his glove to the six-year-old son of teammate Don Liddle when he overheard the child say that he needed a new one. Years later, after countless Little League games and a couple of nights left out in the rain, the glove went to Cooperstown when Craig Liddle realized that it was the one with which Mays had made The Catch in 1954.[39])

All the focus on Mays' hitting didn't mean he was neglecting the other aspects of his game. Though Mays was stealing fewer bases each year, his base-running skills were as sharp as ever. He proved that against the Mets this season when he went from third to home on a wild pitch that stayed about six feet in front of the plate. "I wouldn't've sent anybody from first to second on that play," Franks said afterward, but Mays had been running on the pitch: "I could see from the trajectory of the ball that it was going to be in the dirt," he said.[40] The Mets catcher, Choo Choo Coleman, was so flustered by Mays' break for the plate that he froze. Mays scored standing up.[41]

In a game at Dodger Stadium in the late spring, Mays had a rare defensive achievement: he threw for the cycle—that is, he threw runners out at first, second, third, and home in a single game. The performance was only slightly marred when the Giants Tito Fuentes missed making the tag at second; the throw was true, and Mays' mastery was obvious. "He should play in handcuffs to even things up a bit," one reporter recommended in his coverage of the game.[42]

The games against the Dodgers were all-important because, again, the two California teams were contending for the pennant, this time with Pittsburgh in the hunt as well. Many of the Giants players found it easier to concentrate on the race now that the front office had resolved the festering problem of Orlando Cepeda. The contract controversy of 1963 had made him bitter, and he missed most of the 1965 season to knee surgery. Cepeda returned to the Giants in 1966 to find McCovey ensconced at first base, and his unhappiness was obvious. In

May the Giants finally faced up to the fact that carrying both Cepeda and Mc-Covey made no sense. They traded the "Baby Bull" to the Cardinals, and there, playing as the regular first baseman, Cepeda blossomed. In 1967 he would be the National League's MVP, and in 1968 he led St. Louis to the pennant.[43]

After all the hoopla attending Mays' 512th home run, the baseball world seemed to regard his achievement of the next major milestone, reaching Ted Williams' total of 521, as a foregone conclusion. Mays tied Williams' mark in Chicago on June 23 off Dick Ellsworth, part of a 6–4 Giants win. Four days later in St. Louis, he hit his 522nd off Bob Gibson. It came in the first inning with one man on. "I was just trying to hit the ball off Gibson," Mays said after the game—it was only his second career home run off the overpowering right-hander.[44] "I knew this one was gone when I hit it." It was June 27, and he was now in sole possession of third place on the career home-run list.

Mays returned to St. Louis a few days later for the All-Star Game. The city was in the grip of a heat wave that sent the on-field temperature to 105 degrees. Hundreds of fans in the crowd of 50,000 collapsed with heat prostration as they watched the hottest All-Star Game on record, but that didn't stop Mays from playing all 10 innings of a closely contested game. He was 1 for 4 and scored one of the National League's two runs in their 2–1 victory.

Mays continued to have a solid season at the plate, and in August his home-run total began to approach that of the next slugger on the lifetime list, Jimmie Foxx, who had hit 534 during his career. On August 16 in a game at Candle-stick Park, Mays homered against the Cardinals to tie Foxx's mark. The next day, August 17, he hit another one, surpassing Foxx. The home crowd exploded as Mays powered the ball over the fence in right center, and the Giants surged out to greet him at the plate. But the first man to shake Mays' hand in congratulation, breaking all protocol, was the home-plate umpire, Chris Pelekoudas. The umpire then bent down and took an inordinately long time to dust off the plate, allowing the crowd to cheer Mays out for a curtain call.

With 535 career home runs, Mays was now the top right-handed slugger in baseball history, and second only to Babe Ruth overall—but still 179 home runs behind the great Bambino. "Until I got that 'close' at 535," Mays would later admit, "I don't think I gauged how monumental his record was."[45]

The records were satisfying, but there was still a pennant race to be fought, and Mays paced the team with his hitting and his base running. He won a key extra-innings game against the Dodgers in September when, despite a pulled thigh muscle, he scored from first on a single.[46] For the Giants to get ahead, though, the Dodgers had to stumble, and with Sandy Koufax's 27 wins, they didn't. The Giants played bridesmaid once again, this time finishing just $1\frac{1}{2}$ games behind Los Angeles.

In the last week in September, Mays' peacemaking skills were called on by the mayor of San Francisco. Race riots had broken out in the city. To try to calm them, the police imposed evening curfews in several neighborhoods; to encourage people to stay home, local TV and radio stations agreed to broadcast the Giants game from Atlanta. Mays took to the airwaves in the hours before game time with a taped message to the people of the adopted hometown he had come to love so much. His statement was simple: "Root for your team. I know I'll be out there in center field trying my best."[47]

The Giants won the game, and the people, indeed, stayed home. Mayor John Shelley credited the ballclub, and especially Mays, for helping to keep the peace.[48]

The pressures of the 1966 season had been intense, as Mays surpassed one home-run milestone after another, but he had gotten through it all intact—no collapses, fainting spells, or hospitalizations. When the regular season began the next spring, though, he began to wonder whether he was feeling some delayed effects. In April, for the first time in his career, he struck out four times in one game—against a rookie pitcher, no less, Gary Nolan of Cincinnati.[49]

Mays wasn't the only one feeling sluggish; the Giants had a sub-.500 April to start the 1967 season, and their hitting was weak through the whole first half. Mays' bat warmed up gradually. By the All-Star break he was hitting over .300 again and had 12 home runs. But he certainly wasn't himself, not even in the All-Star Game on July 11, which he attended as a manager's selection and got into as a pinch hitter. He struck out. The fact that Mickey Mantle was also in the game as a pinch hitter, and struck out as well a half-inning before Mays' appearance, was irresistible to sportswriters, who reported the appearances of the two veterans as "the most poignant moments of the game."[50]

After the break, Mays caught another of the "summer colds" that had begun to plague him during baseball season. The chilly Bay Area summers, combined with the climate changes of constant road trips and the recirculated atmosphere of a succession of airplanes, were hard on his body. This cold was worse than most, though; it had Mays feverish and racked with chills before a night game in Candlestick. It was obvious that Mays could not play, but he suited up anyway and took the line-up card out to the umpires. He didn't want to let the opposing manager know that he was unavailable to pinch hit.

When the back-up center fielder pulled a muscle in the first inning, Mays had to take the field after all. Shivering and miserable, he played the game through. Afterward, he checked himself into a local hospital, where he remained for five days. It seemed that only the restrictions of formal medical care would get Mays rest when he needed it. The rest was not enough, though. Mays felt weak for the rest of the season, and his numbers reflected it. For the first time in his career, he was not among the league leaders in any category, offensive or defensive. His batting average was .263, thirty points lower than any season since 1952, and he hit just 22 home runs. He had fewer than 500 plate appearances, and appeared in fewer than 150 games, for the first time in 14 years.

The team's fortunes improved in the second half, and they had a dominant 20–7 record down the stretch. It was good enough for second place in the league yet again, but well behind the pennant-winning St. Louis Cardinals.

Mays felt stronger as the 1968 season approached. He knew, of course, that age would catch up to him one day, but he felt nowhere near ready to retire, or to give up his fielding position. He pointed to the lingering cold, not his 36 years, as the reason for his off-year in 1967; he rationalized that 22 home runs and a .263 average would be great numbers for most ballplayers, even thought they were not up to his standards. Yet he was haunted by the experiences of other center fielders. Joe DiMaggio retired before reaching his 37th birthday. Duke Snider reduced his center field starts after he turned 34. Mantle, five months Mays' junior, had already switched to first base to save his legs.

Mays was shocked and saddened when he heard that Martin Luther King Jr. had been assassinated on April 4. Typically, Mays was publicly silent about the loss. Even with trusted friends, he had a hard time expressing what King, and King's courageous work in Birmingham and in other cities in Mays' home state, had meant to him. "Nixon is your president," he once said to a friend who was white. "But Martin Luther King was *my* president."[51] The opening of the baseball season was delayed for several days in mourning.

When the season began, Mays imbued himself with a positive attitude. He was going to get off to a strong start, by force of will if necessary. He would soon be 37, and he knew what the baseball world would be thinking: "People simply didn't play center field at that age." But center was where he wanted to remain. "I still preferred the open space and freedom of center, where I could run and throw," he said.[52] Mays wanted to prove—perhaps to himself as well as to observers—that he could still perform there. He hit .471 in the first week of the season. In the end, he played all but one of his 143 starts in his beloved center field, posting a .289 average and 23 home runs.

It wasn't a season for offense, though. Throughout baseball, it was "The Year of the Pitcher." Batting averages plummeted and ERAs dropped. Juan Marichal had 26 wins, leading the National League, but that was nothing compared to the 31–6 season Denny McLain had for Detroit. And both those achievements were eclipsed by Bob Gibson of the Cardinals, who posted a 1.12 ERA—the lowest by a starter in modern baseball history—and led St. Louis to an early and insurmountable lead in the NL standings. The trend was capped in September, when the Giants and the Cardinals traded back-to-back no-hitters in Candlestick Park (Gaylord Perry notched one for San Francisco and the next day Ray Washburn, in turn, no-hit the Giants). It was a first in baseball history, but in 1968 it seemed almost routine.

With all the whispers Mays was hearing about the decline in his skills, the All-Star Game in Houston was a sweet vindication for him. This year he hit in the leadoff spot for the National League, and he provided the game's biggest thrills in the first inning. Mays beat out a single off Cleveland's Luis Tiant, took second base on Tiant's attempted pick-off, got to third on a wild pitch, and scored the game's only run as the AL infielders executed a double play.[53] The National League won 1–0, and Mays was named the game's MVP. More than 25 years later, the sequence was still remembered as one of the most exciting in All-Star history.[54]

During the season, a 22-year-old rookie joined the club as Mays' back-up in center. Bobby Bonds entered the league with a splash: he hit a grand slam in his first at-bat, the first player ever to do so.[55] Franks saw in Bonds a great set of skills: speed, power potential, and fearlessness in the field. Reporters began to buzz about the "next Willie Mays." Franks soon installed Bonds in the lead-off spot in the line-up, and Mays, very much aware of the importance of mentors in his own life, became a guide to the young outfielder. When Bonds' wife Pat asked the veteran if he would become godfather to their son, the four-year-old Barry, Mays was touched. He accepted and began a lifelong relationship with the Bonds family.[56]

When the season ended, the Giants were in second place for the fourth straight year, nine games behind pennant-winning St. Louis. In their four years under Franks, San Francisco had been the winningest team in the majors, with a 367–280 record. But they had not taken a pennant in all that time, and their home attendance dropped, though that may have had as much to do with the new Oakland A's franchise across the bay as with any failing on the Giants part. Franks' four-year managerial deal ended with the season, and Stoneham did not renew his contract.

Mays' relationship with Franks had remained close throughout his tenure, and he was unhappy to see the manager go. He was even less happy with Franks' replacement, Clyde King. King had been a pitcher with Brooklyn for most of his seven-year major league career (Mays had homered off him in Ebbets Field in 1951), and had been managing in the minor leagues since. Best known for his work with pitchers and with young players, he greeted Mays with a startling idea: that Mays should become the Giants leadoff hitter.

"Why would you want me to lead off?" Mays asked King. "I'm no kid, you know."[57]

King's logic made a certain kind of sense. The 1968 Giants had been poor first-inning scorers. They needed someone who could get on base and spark the offense. Mays' on-base average was still high, he could draw a walk, and he had some speed. And without his home-run stroke, Mays was less suited for the third spot in the batting order than he used to be.

Mays could see what King was driving at, but for one fact: he was almost 38 years old. The idea struck Mays as ludicrous and insulting all at once. At his age, after a career in center field, his major physical worry was his legs. Having him bat leadoff would give him more at-bats, meaning he would tire earlier in each game or earlier in the season. Injury was another possibility, if he would be expected to steal more bases.

Mays complained about the new assignment within the clubhouse, but outwardly he accepted it. "I had to do it for the team," he said later.[58] King had Mays batting leadoff all through spring training and for the first two weeks of the season before giving up on the plan. Bonds went back to the leadoff spot, and that move paid off: he became the second 30-30 man in baseball history that year, with 32 home runs and 45 stolen bases. The first, of course, had been Willie Mays. Perhaps he really was Mays' heir.

As far as Mays was concerned, though, King's meddling had done damage enough. He began to have knee trouble in the late spring, and started slumping at the plate, too. King and Mays seemed to find it impossible to communicate without misunderstanding one another, and their frustrations came to a head before a game at the Astrodome in late June, when Mays thought King was pulling him on and off the line-up card and King thought Mays was refusing to take the field. Mays exploded in the dugout; McCovey, Gaylord Perry, and pitching coach Larry Jansen had to hold him back to keep him from pummeling the manager.[59]

After the game, King could not leave well enough alone. He told Mays that he was going to be fined for his pregame outburst. "If I'm fined, I quit," Mays retorted.

It took the club's vice president, Chub Feeney, to broker an uncomfortable peace. King did not fine Mays; Mays issued King a formal apology. "But I lost any respect I ever had for King," Mays concluded. "I thought of him as a back stabber, and we didn't talk for the rest of the year."[60]

In a way, they didn't need to. By this time Mays was so confident of his on-field leadership, and his teammates so trusted his judgment, that he could control fine aspects of the game from center field. "He's managing in place of King," Franks noted as he watched a game from the stands that season. Mays had overthrown the cutoff man to allow an opposing runner to take second on a single. "He wanted that hitter to move up to second base so first base will be open. Now they'll walk the next hitter on purpose. Then they'll get the next guy out and have the guy after him having to lead off the next inning. That's the way Willie's got it planned."[61]

Mays' teammate McCovey was the hero of that year's All-Star Game, which was a 9–3 National League rout, but as usual Mays was there too. He got into the game as a pitch hitter in the fifth inning and flied out to right field. He received a standing ovation, despite his lack of production in the game.[62]

In August, Mays bought a spacious 18-room home in the San Francisco suburb of Atherton.[63] It would remain his primary residence for the next three decades. He needed the space for the family members who came and went, including his father, Aunt Ernestine, and Michael, who was almost ten years old now and able to spend longer stretches of time with his father. Mae Allen was spending a good deal of time with Mays also. She had moved to the San Francisco area to be closer to him and was doing social work, with a special concentration on adoption issues.

Meanwhile, there were games to be won in the Giants quest for, not a pennant, but a divisional title. The 1969 season was the first one in which the leagues were split into eastern and western divisions, and once again, the Giants were contending. They were in first place in the National League's new western division on September 22 when Mays hit a pinch two-run homer to win the game 4–2. The home run was significant another way, too: it was the 600th of his career. Mays hit it against a rookie pitcher, Mike Corkins, and against a rookie team, the San Diego Padres, in their new stadium. When the Giants rushed Mays at the plate to congratulate him on the achievement, it was all their opponents could do to keep from rushing him themselves. After all, most of them had been following his career since they were children.

"Why'd it have to be me?" Corkins lamented after the game.

His manager, Preston Gomez, was sympathetic. "Son," he said, "there've been 599 before you."[64]

The home run was satisfying, but it was one of only 13 Mays hit that year, by far his lowest full-season total yet. And even though the Giants led the division late, they stumbled in the closing weeks and finished three games behind Atlanta.

Mays' knees had bothered him all season long, and he'd sat out more games than ever before; he played in only 117 contests. Still, he was unwilling to give up his post in center field. He hoped that a restful off-season, and not hitting in the leadoff spot, would help him regain some power in 1970.

Meanwhile, the end of the decade meant that the press began to look back and review recent history. Mays was overjoyed to be chosen as one of "Baseball's Greatest Living Players" by one publication. "I was finally in the outfield with DiMaggio," he said.[65] In January, *The Sporting News* named him baseball's Player of the Decade for the 1960s, an honor that Ted Williams and Stan Musial had held before him.[66]

At the same time, a court case was beginning that would have far-reaching impact on the game. Curt Flood, a veteran outfielder with the St. Louis Cardinals, was resisting the trade of his contract to Philadelphia. The reserve clause, the long-standing rule that essentially allowed teams to own all rights to the services of the players they signed, gave Flood no say in the course of his own career. Flood refused to accept the trade and planned to sit out the 1970 season, forgoing his $90,000 salary to do so. Now he was suing baseball for damages, and his suit was supported by the Major League Players Association, which at last was beginning to act like a true labor union. It would be more than two years before Flood's suit would be settled, but it was clear that baseball was on the verge of great change.[67]

King managed only the first 42 games of the 1970 season as the team got off to a poor 19–23 start. After all the second-place finishes, Stoneham was losing patience. When the club lost a 17–16 contest to the lowly Padres, he fired King and replaced him with a longtime Giants hand, Charlie Fox, who had been a coach with the club previously. Fox was a familiar figure around the clubhouse, and he knew the players well.

The comfortable atmosphere encouraged some players to bring their children to the clubhouse before games. One little boy came in regularly with his father, but it was Mays he would follow. Barry Bonds, now six, was all over Mays in the Giants clubhouse and, soon, out in the field as well. He was a born athlete—as a toddler, he once batted a Wiffle ball so hard it broke a window.[68] As Mays well knew, natural ability was important, but early guidance was crucial, too. He encouraged Barry to suit up in his own little Giants uniform and shag batting-practice flies with him and the elder Bonds.

Many years later, when Barry Bonds was a major leaguer himself, he remembered these as formative experiences. "Willie was always challenging me as a kid," he said. "I remember when he'd catch the ball and he would just flick it and it would go all the way back into the infield. And I could barely reach the infield as a kid. And he would tease me: 'C'mon, how are you ever going to make the major leagues if you can't throw the ball to second base?' "[69]

Mays continued to make spectacular and reckless plays in the field, whatever the state of his knees. One that often shows up in highlight films today happened in April when Mays in center and Bonds in right converged with one another, and with Candlestick Park's outfield fence, on a line drive by Bobby Tolan of Cincinnati. Mays and Bonds both leaped at the same moment and crashed together, midair. Both fell to earth. Mays lay still. Bonds scrambled up, looked about for the ball, then spotted it—safely gripped in Mays' glove. Bonds grabbed it and held it up for the umpires to see: out.[70]

When the season began, Mays needed just 78 more hits to reach the 3,000 mark. On July 18, in a game at Candlestick Park against the Expos, he did it, on a sharp single between third and short. The game stopped as the fans erupted. Former teammates and rivals, including Monte Irvin, Stan Musial, and Carl Hubbell, were there to celebrate. Mays was the ninth man in baseball history to rack up 3,000 hits. Hank Aaron had done it just a few weeks before. ("I had to wonder if I would ever get out of that man's shadow," Aaron would write after both their careers had ended.[71])

On September 28 Mays hit another landmark, becoming the sixth ballplayer to compile 10,000 official at-bats. The celebration for this achievement was muted; as one writer put it, "the almost dreary force of accumulation was at work, so that he . . . set records through the mere act of little more than showing up."[72] Still, it was one more for the record books.

The team had a winning record for Fox, but it wasn't enough. They finished third in the western division despite a stellar 37–17 record in the last two months. "Overall, I was feeling pretty good," Mays said.[73] He had improved on 1969's numbers across the board, with a slugging average over .500 and 28 home runs. He wasn't ready for retirement—not quite yet.

He was still a target for some fellow ballplayers, though. Curt Flood's year away from the game had given him time to write his own memoir. *The Way It Is*, published in January 1971, slammed Mays for his lack of involvement in social causes. Mays, Flood charged, "reports from the privileged isolation of his huge success that he has absolutely nothing to complain about."[74]

It was accurate, so far as it went. Mays had never seen himself as an activist or an organizer. When he had complaints, he did what he could to work them out privately. This season, for example, for the first time Mays had serious issues with the Giants over his contract. The ballclubs, recognizing that the ongoing Flood case could radically change the way baseball did business, were beginning to negotiate multiyear deals with some players. About to turn 40, with two decades of service to the "Giants family" under his belt, Mays was looking for long-term security. He proposed a ten-year, $750,000 deal, envisioning three more years of playing time and then a coaching or front-office job with the club.

He was hurt when Stoneham turned the proposal down. The owner's counteroffer of five years for $375,000 didn't give Mays the security he was seeking. Instead, the two men worked out a two-year, $360,000 deal that included no post-retirement job promises.[75]

None of that affected his play in the beginning of the 1971 season. Mays started with a bang, hitting four home runs in the first four regular-season games, and just like that the Giants were leading the division. Fox had given

Mays the informal title of player-coach to go with his de facto status on the team, and Mays took the designation seriously enough to schedule early-morning training sessions for "his" outfielders.[76]

It was obvious to Mays that Hank Aaron was likely to pass him on the all-time home run list one day. Aaron was three years his junior, and he had not suffered the kind of productivity drop-off that Mays had seen as he aged. Mays accepted all that. But ever the competitor, he saw to it that Aaron's 600th home run—which came in a game against the Giants on April 27—was part of a Braves loss. Mays' tenth-inning single, his fourth hit of the contest, won the game for San Francisco.[77] He could still cast quite a shadow.

The rivalry was an affectionate one, though; a week later Aaron attended a formal fortieth birthday party the local baseball writers threw for Mays. Joe DiMaggio was there too, and while many speeches were made that night, DiMaggio's words meant the most to Mays: "He is a hitter all right, and one of the best that ever lived. But this man does it all. He fields, he runs, he studies, he hardly ever makes mistakes. He is a very special person."[78]

Now called a "patriarch of the National League," Mays was selected to start in the All-Star Game on July 13.[79] He led off, but only so he could get his at-bats and leave the game quickly. He came up twice and was hitless in the first National League loss since 1962.

The Giants blazing start carried them through the rest of the season as injuries nagged at their veterans. When McCovey hurt his knee in the second half of the season, it was Fox's opportunity to take Mays out of center and install him at first base. Mays did a respectable job there and played 48 games in the position, but he was never really comfortable in the infield.

McCovey's absence from the line-up was more of a problem, though. Without the protection of his bat, opposing pitchers had no reason to give Mays anything he could hit. Consequently, Mays racked up 112 walks during the season—a league-leading total that was, by far, the highest of his career. All those bases on balls contributed to Mays' .425 on-base percentage, which also led the league. And they gave Mays opportunities on the basepaths that he took gleefully: he stole 23 bases, his highest total since 1960.

Still, the point of the exercise was to get into the postseason. "I had yearned for one more World Series," Mays said.[80] The Giants had a terrible run in the final few weeks of the season—they were 7–19 in September—but their great start, and Bonds' bat, pulled them through. They won the division by a single game over Los Angeles. The team ended the season on the road and had to head back to Candlestick Park for their first-ever league championship series.

The Pittsburgh Pirates, led by Willie Stargell and Roberto Clemente, had won the National League's eastern division by a comfortable seven-game margin. The

Giants were ragged and their pitching was thin; Marichal, their one reliable starter, was playing hurt. San Francisco won the first game of the series on a two-run McCovey homer (Mays, having been intentionally walked, was the man on base), but after that, the Giants were spent. They lost the next three games of the playoff in succession. Game 2 featured a two-run home run by Mays, but because it came when the Giants were already down 9–2 it didn't affect the outcome. Marichal pitched well in Game 3, but the Pirates were better; they won it 2–1. Clemente was the star of the final game, which Pittsburgh won at home, 9–5.

It was a huge disappointment to finally get so close to a pennant and to lose it yet again. But Mays's exhaustion was so complete, he found it hard to work up any emotion, one way or the other. He was 40 years old, and he had left it all on the field. He had no way of knowing that his playoff home run would be his last as a Giant.

NOTES

1. Einstein, *Willie's Time*, 219.
2. Mays, with Sahadi, *Say Hey*, 228.
3. Ibid.
4. Mays, as told to Einstein, *Willie Mays*, 286–287; Jack Mann, "They Love Herman and Willie," *Sports Illustrated*, September 27, 1965.
5. Mays, as told to Einstein, *Willie Mays*, 119.
6. Mays, with Sahadi, *Say Hey*, 164.
7. Mann, "They Love Herman and Willie."
8. Einstein, *Willie's Time*, 316.
9. Mays, with Sahadi, *Say Hey*, 227.
10. Mays, as told to Einstein, *Willie Mays*, 74.
11. Ibid., 138–140.
12. Mays, with Sahadi, *Say Hey*, 230.
13. Mays, as told to Einstein, *Willie Mays*, 271.
14. Ibid., 141.
15. *New York Times*, July 14, 1965.
16. Mays, as told to Einstein, *Willie Mays*, 183, 276–277.
17. Steve Delsohn, *True Blue: The Dramatic History of the Los Angeles Dodgers, Told by the Men Who Lived It* (New York: William Morrow, 2001), 68.
18. Mays, as told to Einstein, *Willie Mays*, 281.
19. "The Battle of San Francisco," *Sports Illustrated*, August 30, 1965.
20. Mays, with Sahadi, *Say Hey*, 234.
21. Einstein, *Willie's Time*, 244.
22. Ibid.

23. Mays, as told to Einstein, *Willie Mays*, 282–283; Einstein, *Willie's Time*, 244–245.

24. Mays, with Sahadi, *Say Hey*, 235; Einstein, *Willie's Time*, 226.

25. *Sports Illustrated*, September 13, 1965.

26. Einstein, *Willie's Time*, 245.

27. Mays, with Sahadi, *Say Hey*, 236.

28. Ibid., 236.

29. Einstein, *Willie's Time*, 227–229. This at-bat would expand in future retellings to 7, 11, or 13 consecutive fouls, although the actual four were dramatic enough.

30. Mays, as told to Einstein, *Willie Mays*, 186–187.

31. Einstein, *Willie's Time*, 224.

32. *Sports Illustrated*, November 29, 1965.

33. Mays, with Sahadi, *Say Hey*, 239–240.

34. Ibid., 238.

35. *New York Times*, March 31, 1966; *New York Times*, February 28, 1969.

36. Mays, with Sahadi, *Say Hey*, 240.

37. Ibid., 243.

38. Einstein, *Willie's Time*, 248–249.

39. George Vecsey, "Hazy Sunshine, Vivid Memory," *New York Times*, September 29, 2004.

40. "Baseball's Living Legend," *The Sporting News*, October 26, 1998.

41. Glenn Dickey, "Giants Will Find Trading for Help Difficult," *San Francisco Chronicle*, July 13, 2004.

42. Einstein, *Willie's Time*, 62.

43. Mike Eisenbath, "Colorful Cepeda," *St. Louis Post-Dispatch*, July 12, 1992.

44. Associated Press, June 28, 1966.

45. Mays, with Sahadi, *Say Hey*, 244.

46. Einstein, *Willie's Time*, 250–251.

47. Mays, with Sahadi, *Say Hey*, 244.

48. Einstein, *Willie's Time*, 252–254.

49. Mays, with Sahadi, *Say Hey*, 246–247.

50. *New York Times*, July 1, 1967.

51. Einstein, *Willie's Time*, 292.

52. Mays, with Sahadi, *Say Hey*, 248–249.

53. Ibid., 250.

54. John Donovan, "Few and Far Between," *Sports Illustrated*, July 12, 2004.

55. "San Francisco Giants: History: Timeline" Web site, http://sanfrancisco.giants.mlb.com/NASApp/mlb/sf/history/sf_history_timeline_article.jsp?article=28.

56. Ron Kroichick, "One Size No Longer Fits All," *The Sporting News*, July 5, 1999; "Mays Takes Swing at Small Parks," *New York Post*, October 23, 2002.

57. Mays, with Sahadi, *Say Hey*, 251.

58. Ibid., 250.

59. Einstein, *Willie's Time*, 315.

60. Mays, with Sahadi, *Say Hey*, 252.

61. Einstein, *Willie's Time*, 63.

62. *New York Times*, July 24, 1969.

63. *New York Times*, August 26, 1969.

64. Einstein, *Willie's Time*, 318.

65. Mays, with Sahadi, *Say Hey*, 253.

66. Bill Brown, "Nobody Did It Better," *The Sporting News*, January 29, 1990.

67. *New York Times*, June 20, 1972.

68. Hank Hersch, "30/30 Vision," *Sports Illustrated*, June 25, 1990.

69. "Major League Baseball: Generations of Heroes," video, Major League Baseball Productions, 1999.

70. Hano, *A Day In the Bleachers*, 159–160.

71. John Shea, "How Does Bonds Rate Historically?" Scripps-Howard News Service, October 13, 2002.

72. Einstein, *Willie's Time*, 262.

73. Mays, with Sahadi, *Say Hey*, 255.

74. Einstein, *Willie's Time*, 286.

75. Mays, with Sahadi, *Say Hey*, 256–257.

76. Einstein, *Willie's Time*, 320.

77. John Shea, "How Does Bonds Rate Historically?" Scripps-Howard News Service, October 13, 2002.

78. Mays, with Sahadi, *Say Hey*, 258.

79. *New York Times*, July 14, 1971.

80. Mays, with Sahadi, *Say Hey*, 259.

Though shocked and hurt by his 1972 trade to the Mets, the New York fans' adulation buoyed Mays in his final seasons on the field. *National Baseball Hall of Fame Library, Cooperstown, N.Y.*

BACK TO NEW YORK,
1972–1973

After a few weeks of sleep and the occasional golf game, Mays was able to put the long 1971 season behind him. He turned his attention to an issue he had long delayed: marrying Mae.

The two had dated, on and off, for the previous decade, and during the 1971 season Mae had become a fixture at Giants home games. "Finally, one day, I decided it was time for me to grow up a little," Mays said later. "I decided to ask her to marry me."[1] He surprised her with a diamond ring, and they planned a small, private wedding in Mexico City over the Thanksgiving holiday. On November 29, they were married there in a civil ceremony.[2]

Spring training began, but not quite as usual. The Players Association, now headed by labor lawyer Marvin Miller, was flexing its muscles with new pension-fund demands. The Curt Flood case had made it all the way to the U.S. Supreme Court, and the owners, fearing the verdict, were doing all they could to limit the players' power. At the end of March, the Players Association declared a strike.

For Mays, the prospect of a strike was unsettling. He had always been personally close to his team's ownership, and he thought he could understand the owners' point of view. After all, "they were the ones who were saddled with the expenses when the team was lousy and the fans stayed home."[3] But he also understood that his experience was substantially different from that of many other ballplayers. Small gestures he made to share the wealth in his own clubhouse, like spreading around the token payments he received for radio appearances, could only go so far. In solidarity with them, he supported the Players Association action. He served as the Giants player representative, and he was firm on one point: "Whatever we do, we've got to stick together."[4] Due in part to his influence, the players, from veterans to rookies, did present a consistent united front to management.

Mays was so eager to get back to work, though, that he led a contingent of Giants in a Candlestick Park workout session when it was rumored that the strike was about to be settled after 13 days. In the interim, he had had to be rebuffed from the stadium when he tried to collect some workout equipment for use at home.[5] This was one 41-year-old who did not want to lose any ground.

Once the season finally got underway, it was clear that Mays had been thrown by the change in his 25-year spring routine. He was 19-for-49 with no home runs and just three RBIs in the first month. He was also perplexed by a trickle of rumors being reported in the papers—rumors that he was about to be traded. Stoneham had told him nothing of the sort, and May refused to believe that such a thing could happen unless the owner gave him fair warning.

But it did. On May 11, a reporter reached Mays in his hotel room in Philadelphia, the latest stop on a Giants road trip. How did Mays feel, the writer asked, about being traded to the Mets?

Blindsided, Mays couldn't give an honest answer. First, of course, he had to know who he'd been traded for. The reporter said that word was Mays would go to the Mets for a minor-league pitcher and some cash, rumored to be somewhere between $50,000 and $500,000.

Now Mays felt hurt, betrayed, and abandoned. "After all those years. . . . What happened to that family atmosphere [Stoneham] had always spoken of?" he wanted to know.[6]

Stoneham maintained silence about the matter, so the newspapers resorted to printing the rumors. Over time, the full story came out. The Giants were struggling financially. Stoneham was looking to sell the franchise. Before he did, in his paternalistic way, he wanted to secure Mays' future. But the club could not afford to give him a multiyear deal, and perhaps could not be sold with one on the books.

The New York Mets could afford such a deal, though. Three years after their "miracle" World Series win, they still attracted more than two million fans to Shea Stadium each year, and their media revenues were huge. Even more importantly, the Mets ownership knew and loved Mays, and had wanted him on their roster since they hosted Willie Mays Appreciation Day way back in 1963. Joan Payson, the Mets principal owner, would guarantee a $165,000 annual salary for as long as Mays wanted to play, and a ten-year post-retirement deal that would pay him $50,000 annually to work for the club, perhaps as a coach.

Crowning the agreement, it would give Mays the chance to end his playing days in New York, where his career had begun and where the fans still adored him. It is now generally accepted that the Mets paid the Giants a token $50,000 for the contract, although according to Stoneham, the minor leaguer was included merely to keep the rosters even, and no money was exchanged between the clubs at all.[7]

Mays' teammates were unhappy to lose him; Bonds in particular was said to be devastated.[8] Stoneham was so upset and embarrassed about having to let his favorite player go, he could not bring himself to tell Mays the news personally. It would be years before the two men could talk about the trade.[9]

Within hours, Mays had left the team in Philadelphia to go to New York. There was no time for a proper farewell to the club with which he had spent half his life. In years to come, the trade would be lamented by Giants fans as one in a long line of Stoneham's exasperating personnel decisions.

Mays remained hurt at the way Stoneham had handled the matter, but felt better once he understood how much the Mets and their fans wanted him. The quote he finally gave reporters was politic, but also heartfelt: "When you come back to New York, it's like coming back to paradise."[10]

It was also like coming back to a firm-handed management style. The Mets new manager, Yogi Berra, had taken the job after the beloved Gil Hodges had died suddenly in April, and he was still establishing himself in the position. He made it clear that he had no need of an assistant manager, and that Mays would not be writing himself on and off his line-up cards. Mays held his peace, but the adjustment wasn't easy, and the two men would have several disagreements over the next two seasons.

However, Mays' new teammates were thrilled to have him join them. Jim Beauchamp, a part-time first baseman, immediately made him feel welcome by giving up his uniform number to Mays, who would remain number 24 for good. The Mets were mostly young—almost all the starters were under 30—but experienced ballplayers. Mays had been a star for most of their lives, and they were awed to have him with them. They were also charmed by his upbeat clubhouse manner. Two days before Berra planned to start him in his first game as a Met, Mays was in the clubhouse having his arm rubbed by the team trainer. Five Mets surrounded him and began some good-natured ribbing. "Hey, old man," pitcher Tom Seaver joked, "you mean it takes you this long to get ready for one game? *This* long?"

Mays answered, laughing, in his trademark tenor, "Now how can you say that? You ain't even made it through your first ten years in the big leagues yet."[11]

Mays appeared in a Mets uniform for the first time on May 14, a damp and drizzly Sunday afternoon at Shea Stadium. The visiting team was none other than the San Francisco Giants. "At first it seemed strange—maybe awful is a better word—for me to put on a uniform with '24'on it that wasn't a Giants uniform," Mays admitted later. But his new teammates made it easier, and so did the screaming, shouting New Yorkers in the stands. "The crowd of more than forty thousand fans at Shea was cheering so wildly for me I got goose bumps," Mays said.[12]

Berra had him batting lead-off. In the first inning, Mays drew a walk from his former teammate Sam McDowell. Two more batters walked, loading the bases for Rusty Staub. He launched the ball over the right-field wall for a grand slam and a 4–0 Mets lead. The Giants tied things up in the fourth, making the score 4–4 when Mays stepped into the batter's box to lead off the bottom of the inning. His flair for the dramatic as great as ever, he worked the count to 3–2 and then drove McDowell's next pitch into the Giants bullpen. "It was one of those marvelous moments in sport when a man does not merely rise to the occasion but soars above it,"[13] one reporter noted. The home run was the game's winning hit, in the best fairy-tale fashion.

"I could feel the crowd on its feet and jumping up and down like we had just won the pennant," Mays said later.[14] Those who weren't cheering were crying for joy.[15] It was the fans' reaction, more than anything else, that made Mays feel finally at home again in New York.

It also helped when Mae joined him there for the season. They took an apartment overlooking the Hudson River in the Riverdale section of the Bronx, and after every game Mae cared for her husband's aching joints and strained muscles.[16]

The Mets were plagued with hard-luck injuries all season long, and Mays stepped up to fill in the gaps as best he could. In his first few games with the team, he had three more game-winning hits—two home runs and a fourteenth-inning RBI single. But it was more playing time than anyone had anticipated, and it wore Mays down. His left knee was especially bothersome.[17]

When the season began, Mays and Hank Aaron were neck-and-neck on the all-time home-run list, Mays with 646, Aaron with 639. During the season, inevitably, Aaron pulled ahead. It happened on June 1, as Aaron was putting together another solid season and Mays had his least productive year at the plate. When asked about Aaron's continuing assault on Babe Ruth's total, Mays often took a fatalistic note. "I knew Hank was going to pass me—it was just a matter of time," he would say.[18] Some observers, meanwhile, felt that Mays was relieved to have given up the burden of chasing Ruth.[19]

Mays was chosen by the fans to start in the 1972 All-Star Game in Atlanta. He played center field for the first half of the game, but didn't get on base. The National League won in extra innings 4–3, on a single by Joe Morgan.[20]

The Mets weren't scheduled to play in Candlestick Park until late in July. "There was some funny feeling in my stomach when I went into the visitors' clubhouse for the first time," Mays said.[21] But the San Francisco fans were still fans of his, and they were cheering for Mays when he came up to bat. He grounded out twice as the Mets took a 1–0 lead. Mays came up again with two out and one on in the fifth. He lofted the first pitch he saw over the fence in left-center for the 650th home run of his career. The crowd went crazy, stomping and hollering, even though it meant the ballgame went to the Mets.

They were magical moments, but there were fewer of them than ever before. Mays played in only 69 games for the Mets in 1972, with eight home runs and a .267 batting average. He had serious doubts about whether he should take the field at all in 1973. "I didn't want to hang on. I had too much pride for that," he said later.[22] He decided to get an impartial second opinion from his old friend Herman Franks.

Franks traveled to the Mets 1973 spring training camp in Florida to watch Mays work out. He concluded, "You can still hit, and if you don't get hurt, you can make it through another season."[23] That, of course, would be the trick. A 42-year-old body does not heal the way a younger one can. Early on, Mays strained his already painful left knee to the point that it needed cortisone shots; then, favoring the right knee, he strained that one too. Less than a month into the season, fluid had to be drained from both joints. A few months later, Mays crashed into the outfield wall when he misjudged a fly ball and cracked several ribs. By the middle of the season, Mays had privately decided that this one would be his last.

Even with all the injuries, Mays' canniness and professionalism made a huge impact on his teammates. Years later they would recall how his quick thinking and knowledge of the game gave the team an edge. "One time I saw him at bat," pitcher Tug McGraw remembered, "and we had a man on second. A curveball went in the dirt and ricocheted off the catcher. The catcher throws his mask off and he's not sure where the ball is. The ball had rolled over by the third base dugout and Willie started pointing toward the first base dugout." Confused, the catcher went the wrong way after the errant ball, "and our guy scored from second."[24]

Mays made it into one last All-Star Game, his 24th, in Kansas City. It was another National League victory, by a score of 7–1. The crowning touch was a two-run homer by Bobby Bonds in the fifth inning. Mays stood by proudly as Bonds was named the game's MVP.

At that point, the Mets were dead last in the National League's eastern division. The entire division was playing sub-.500 ball, however, so as late as August 31 the standings showed them only 5½ games behind the leading team.

Numerically, anyone could win it. Berra had been telling his players for weeks that every other team had had their hot streak, so the Mets were due. In September, it happened—the Mets started to win. Led by Seaver, McGraw, and the rest of the pitching staff, the club and their fans united under the optimistic slogan "Ya Gotta Believe!"

In the midst of their drive for the division lead, Mays made his retirement decision public. September 25 was declared Willie Mays Night. Fan excitement was such that local ticket scalpers would fondly remember it as their "best night ever" for the next 25 years.[25] Mays was showered with gifts and accolades for nearly an hour before the evening's Mets-Expos game began. Mae stood at his side, as did his father and the 14-year-old Michael, in the full dress uniform of the military school he attended. Fans displayed homemade signs, from the simple "We Love You Willie" to the gladiator-style "We who are about to cry salute you."[26] Finally, in a long, unscripted, somewhat rambling speech, Mays bid an emotional goodbye to baseball, thanking the 54,000 fans in attendance, his teammates, and New York. He said, in part: "In my heart, I'm a sad man. Just to hear you cheer like this for me and not be able to do anything about it makes me a very sad man. . . . But, as you know, there always come a time for someone to get out. And I look at the kids over there, the way they are playing and the way they are fighting for themselves, and it tells me one thing . . . Willie, say good-bye to America."[27] As he closed, tears coursed down his face. The Mets won that night 2–1, keeping their hopes for the season alive.

In the dugout afterward, Berra ambled past Mays and said casually, "I may need you to play tomorrow. Okay?"[28]

It was very much okay with Mays, who didn't have to say goodbye quite yet after all. When Joan Payson called him at home that night and said, "You can't go home now, Willie," that sealed it. Mays would ride out the season with the Mets for the next five days—or as long as it lasted.[29]

The team kept going. They won 18 of their last 23 games, pulled their winning percentage all the way up to .509, and won the division by a game and a half when they defeated the Cubs on the last day of a season that had to be extended a day when rain canceled the deciding games.

Mays rode the bench in the season's final push, lending the team his moral support and vocal encouragement. Four days after the raucous celebration of their divisional championship, the Mets met the Cincinnati Reds in a five-game playoff to decide the National League pennant.

The Big Red Machine, featuring Pete Rose, Johnny Bench, and Joe Morgan, were the league champions in 1972 and had the best record in baseball in 1973. They were battlers, but the Mets still believed. The Reds took the first game

2–1 in Cincinnati; the Mets won Game 2 on a two-hit shutout by the 23-year-old Jon Matlack.

The 1–1 series moved to New York, where 54,000 fans rocked Shea Stadium when their team put up a five-run second inning. The score was 9–2 in the fifth when the burly Rose slid hard into the small but scrappy shortstop Bud Harrelson at second base. The two men traded pushes, then punches, as the crowd roared and both benches emptied. Order was restored, the game resumed, and the top of the inning ended, but the fans were not done. When the hated Rose took his position in left field in the bottom of the fifth, a near-riot broke out in the stands. The spectators pelted Rose with beer cans, half-eaten food, and other debris. The irascible Rose threw some of the garbage back. When a whisky bottle whizzed dangerously close to his head, however, he and the rest of the Reds left the field. League officials warned the Mets that they would forfeit the game if the fans could not be controlled.

Berra called on Mays, the peacemaker of 1965, to lead a group of the most recognizable Mets into left field to settle the unruly crowd. Mays stretched out his arms and made an emotional appeal for calm. Apparently unwilling to defy the National League's patriarch, the still-angry fans took their seats again, and the game resumed. The Mets won it with no further scoring on either side.[30]

New York needed one more win to take the pennant, but Cincinnati came back to win the next day 2–1 on a Pete Rose home run. It all came down to Game 5. It was tied 2–2 in the bottom of the fifth when the Mets rallied to load the bases. Berra sent Mays up to pinch-hit. It was obvious that Mays wanted to do something spectacular for his adopted home team. He over-swung and hit a high chopper down the third base line—so high that the man on third had time to score before it came back down. It was far from spectacular, but it got the job done: Mays had batted in the go-ahead, game-winning run. Improbably, the Mets won the pennant. The fans took the victory as a license to riot once again. At least 15,000 rushed the field at game's end and tore it apart.[31]

For one last time in his career, Mays was part of a playoff series so dramatic that the World Series that followed paled in comparison. New York was pitted against the Oakland A's, a team that had taken full advantage of the American League's new designated hitter rule with sluggers like Reggie Jackson and Sal Bando. The first two games were set for Oakland.

Mays got to start in Game 1, but he looked tired and slow in the field and on the basepaths. In the first inning he lined a single to left field, then stumbled as he rounded first base. "It's got so you pray they won't hit a fly ball to him," TV announcer Joe Garagiola said—but privately, off the air.[32] The Mets lost the game 2–1.

The Mets were up 6–4 in the ninth inning of Game 2 when Berra sent Mays out to center field for defensive purposes. It was the most difficult time of day for outfielders—late afternoon—and Mays did something he had never done in his entire baseball career: he lost a fly ball in the glare. Oakland began a rally on his misplay, tied the score, and the game went into extra innings. Mays played his heart out, as if he felt the need to redeem himself. In the tenth, he got down on his knees and begged the umpire to change his mind when Harrelson was called out at the plate.

In the twelfth, Mays came up with two men on. The A's great reliever, Rollie Fingers, was on the mound. Mays decided to use the only advantages he still had: knowledge of the game, and guile. "As I stepped into the batter's box I called time. I said to the catcher, Ray Fosse, 'Gee, you know, Ray, it's tough to see the ball with that background. I hope he doesn't throw me any fastballs. I don't want to get hurt."[33] Fingers fired in a terrific outside slider. Mays seemed not even to see the pitch. He stepped out of the batter's box again and cried out, "I can't *see!*" Whereupon Fosse signaled for a fastball.[34]

It was exactly what Mays had set him up to do, and he chopped the ball over Fingers' head and through the middle, scoring the winning run. "I just felt I couldn't let the kids down," Mays said later.[35]

The Series went to New York for the next three games, and the Mets won two of them. Mays got into one of the games as a pinch hitter and grounded out. They were up 3–2 when the Series went back to Oakland. All they needed was one more game.

They didn't get it. Oakland won both remaining contests, and the championship, with Mays still on the bench. Only later would he admit how disappointed he was that he didn't get just one more chance.[36]

NOTES

1. Mays, with Sahadi, *Say Hey*, 260.
2. *New York Times*, November 30, 1971.
3. Mays, with Sahadi, *Say Hey*, 286.
4. John Shea, "On Baseball," *San Francisco Chronicle*, April 8, 2001.
5. Ron Fimrite, "The Week That Wasn't," *Sports Illustrated*, April 17, 1972; *New York Times*, April 14, 1972.
6. Mays, with Sahadi, *Say Hey*, 262–263.
7. Einstein, *Willie's Time*, 329–331. Given the secrecy of the negotiations and the rumors surrounding the deal, press reports of the time vary.
8. John Shea, "Passing the HR Torch," *San Francisco Chronicle*, September 27, 2003.
9. United Press International, February 12, 1986.

10. Mays, with Sahadi, *Say Hey*, 265.

11. William Leggett, "How Sweet It Is!" *Sports Illustrated*, May 22, 1972.

12. Mays, with Sahadi, *Say Hey*, 265.

13. William Leggett, "How Sweet It Is!" *Sports Illustrated*, May 22, 1972.

14. Mays, with Sahadi, *Say Hey*, 265.

15. "Letter from the Publisher," *Sports Illustrated*, March 1, 1982.

16. Einstein, *Willie's Time*, 333.

17. Duncan Bock and John Jordan, *The Complete Year-by-Year N.Y. Mets Fan's Almanac* (New York: Crown, 1992), 96.

18. John Shea, "How Does Bonds Rate Historically?" Scripps-Howard News Service, August 13, 2002.

19. Einstein, *Willie's Time*, 332.

20. *New York Times*, July 25, 1972.

21. Mays, with Sahadi, *Say Hey*, 266.

22. Ibid., 267.

23. Ibid., 267–268.

24. Paul Post and Ed Lucas, "Turn Back the Clock," *Baseball Digest*, March 2003.

25. Tim Layden, "The Hustle," *Sports Illustrated*, April 7, 1997.

26. Mark Emmons, "In These Days of Bloated Stats, Mays' Greatness Still Stands Out," *San Jose Mercury News*, September 18, 2003.

27. Mays, with Sahadi, *Say Hey*, 268; Einstein, *Willie's Time*, 336.

28. Einstein, *Willie's Time*, 336.

29. Mays, with Sahadi, *Say Hey*, 269.

30. *New York Times*, October 9, 1973.

31. Jack Lang and Peter Simon, *The New York Mets: Twenty-five Years of Baseball Magic* (New York: Henry Holt, 1986, 1987), 133–136.

32. Einstein, *Willie's Time*, 338.

33. Mays, with Sahadi, *Say Hey*, 269.

34. Einstein, *Willie's Time*, 339.

35. Mays, with Sahadi, *Say Hey*, 270.

36. Ibid.

FULL CIRCLE

Retirement, Mays felt, was the hardest thing he'd ever had to do. He was so accustomed to the regimentation of baseball life that he found himself a little lost when all the choices of everyday living were up to him. To Mays, it had been comforting to have the club tell him "when spring training started, when to get on the bus, when to come to play."[1] Even a simple thing like figuring out when to wake up in the morning without a club-arranged wake-up call was unexpectedly stressful for him.

The trade agreement that Stoneham and Payson had made included the expectation that Mays would work for the Mets in some capacity after he chose to retire from the playing field. His actual job, however, had not been specified. Mays' greatest desire, now that he was no longer playing, was to be the kind of mentor he had had throughout his own career. His father, Piper Davis, Leo Durocher, Herman Franks, and other baseball men had given him guidance, encouragement, and instruction. During his playing days, Mays had taken a similar role with certain individual ballplayers, like Cepeda and Bonds, on a short-term, part-time basis. Now that he could devote his full attention to the task, he imagined that coaching would be the perfect job for him.

But when he reported for spring training, Mays found that suiting up in the team uniform, as coaches do, and then remaining on the bench as the game went on was unbearably painful to him. Sitting there, unable to contribute, "was as if I was in a bad dream trying to walk and something was holding me back."[2] Eventually, Mays spoke with Payson and defined his duties to his own unusual specifications. He would come to Shea Stadium before each of the Mets home games, hang around the clubhouse, watch batting practice and fielding practice, and talk to "the kids." Then, when the game began, he would head home and watch the action on TV. Payson, a fan of Mays' for two decades, was happy to have him associated with her ballclub in any capacity.

During spring training, Mays returned to New York to be inducted into the Black Athletes' Hall of Fame. Satchel Paige, Jesse Owens, and Muhammad Ali, along with the late Jackie Robinson and Josh Gibson, were also among the group's first class of inductees. At the celebratory induction dinner, Mays made a rare statement about the effect of racism in his life. He recalled his days in the Interstate League, when his appearance in Hagerstown, Maryland broke the league's color line. "I was at it by myself, and I had a lot of hardship that no one knows about," he said. "I don't like to speak about it because I was very ashamed of it. I've been told, 'Willie, you don't care about your people.' But that's a lie. The suffering that I received in the last, I would say, 23 years, I couldn't talk about because it was inside of me. I had to hold it. But this award here again tells me that the young blacks have a hell of a chance. This award here tells me again that we are getting together. As one man said, it may take a little while, but we're coming."[3]

In the first few days of the 1974 season, Hank Aaron tied and then surpassed Babe Ruth's lifetime home run record of 714. When Aaron hit his 715th homer on April 8, he also broke Mays' National League record for runs scored, with 2,063.

Mays was comfortable in the job duties he and Joan Payson had agreed to, but she was not the sole owner of the ballclub. The rest of the team's owner-ship and management structure was not so sentimental about Mays' presence. When he showed up for spring training in 1975, he found that a formal bat-ting instructor had been hired. "Now, I really felt like a spare part," he said later.[4] After Payson died on October 4 of that year, Mets chairman M. Donald Grant altered Mays' duties with the club. Now he was to spend more time on corpo-rate matters and public relations—attending booster-club dinners, making ap-pearances for the farm teams—than on mentoring young players. He continued to attend spring training as a "roving instructor," but he was not a factor in the dugout.

That left him time for other employment. Throughout the 1970s, Mays worked as a public-relations ambassador for several companies, including Colgate-Palmolive. His duties for these firms extended the discovery Mays had made a few years before: that people were willing to pay him to play a round of golf with him. Now, large corporations were willing to pay Mays to play golf and eat meals with their officers and clients.

Charity work also drew his attention. Mays had established the Say Hey Foundation in the final years of his playing career. It was dedicated to helping needy kids get a college education—something that Mays had never had, and now regretted. The foundation identified students in need and gave them funds and guidance as they prepared for and worked through college. Mays organized an annual golf tournament and other events on the foundation's behalf, and he was tremendously proud of the achievements of "his kids."[5] Mays also participated in baseball clinics for children and co-authored a children's book on baseball techniques.[6] If he couldn't mentor major leaguers, perhaps he could be a role model for even younger players.

On January 23, 1979, to no one's surprise, the Baseball Hall of Fame announced that Mays had been elected in his first year of eligibility. He had received 94.6 percent of the electors' votes—the highest percentage in 43 years, since the very first induction class that included such immortals as Babe Ruth and Ty Cobb. Still, there were some squawks from Mays supporters who felt that his selection should have been unanimous. Columnist Dick Young, for one, disparaged the non-Mays voters: "If Jesus Christ were to show up with his old baseball glove, some guys wouldn't vote for him. He dropped the cross three times, didn't he?"[7]

To celebrate the news, Mays appeared at a press conference, flanked by the Mets top officers and baseball commissioner Bowie Kuhn. Inevitably, the questions he was asked, as he and the reporters looked back over his 22 years in the game, centered on his inimitable style as a fielder. What had been his greatest catch, his favorite play? "I didn't have a best play," Mays maintained. "If the ball went up, I knew I must catch it. This was for the enjoyment of the people who came out to see me play."[8]

Just as inevitably, one reporter asked Mays, "Who was the greatest player you ever saw?" Mays answered with a smile, "I thought I was." Then he paused. "I hope I didn't say that wrong."[9]

The Hall of Fame induction ceremony took place in Cooperstown, New York on August 5. There was a somber pall to the proceedings; Thurman Munson, the New York Yankees catcher, had died in a plane crash three days before. As always, a number of the living Hall-of-Famers attended the ceremony, including Monte Irvin, Warren Spahn, Stan Musial, and Satchel Paige.

Mays was the only player elected to the Hall that year by the baseball writers. His fellow inductees in the Class of 1979 were Hack Wilson and Warren Giles, both Veterans' Committee selections. Wilson, long deceased, and Giles, the former National League president, were the decided sidelights of the day. Mays was the star attraction. He sent two busloads of friends to the ceremony, and he accepted the honor with a short speech. In it, he said that to him, baseball meant one thing: love. "It means dedication. You have to sacrifice a great many things to play baseball. I sacrificed a bad marriage and I sacrificed a good marriage. But I'm here today because baseball is my number one love."[10]

Just a few months later, the baseball commissioner, Bowie Kuhn, threw Mays out of the game he loved so much. That's how Mays saw it, at any rate. The reality was a little more complicated. Mays' public relations work was now his primary source of income. In 1979, he was offered a PR job with Bally's, a casino in Atlantic City, New Jersey. Like the other large firms that had employed him, Bally's wanted to hire Mays as a goodwill ambassador, a famous name to play golf or share a meal with its high-rolling clients. He would also visit schools and community centers as a guest speaker. The job did not involve the promotion of gambling per se; Mays would not appear in casino advertising, for example. He himself was barred from all casino gaming by the terms of his contract, under which he would be paid a handsome $100,000 a year for ten years.

Mays was all set to take the job when Kuhn stepped in. Baseball commissioners going all the way back to the Black Sox scandal of 1919 have been sensitive to the notion of ballplayers associating themselves with gambling in any way. It didn't matter that in this case the ballplayer in question was retired, or that no actual gambling was involved in the job. It didn't matter that several baseball-team owners bred and raced thoroughbred horses, another facet of the gambling industry. Flatly, Kuhn told Mays that he could not work for any baseball team and also for Bally's.

Mays chose the casino. It was, he said later, "one of the hardest things I've ever had to do," and it affected him deeply.[11] News accounts of Mays' activities in the 1980s almost universally refer to his bitterness, impatience, or surliness, in sharp contrast to previous portrayals of his personality.

A few months later, Mickey Mantle joined Mays in baseball limbo when he, too, accepted a casino public relations job. Kuhn had to prohibit two of the game's most beloved stars from working with ballclubs.

Both men took the sentence as an outright ban from baseball. They stopped attending Old-Timers' Days, Hall of Fame induction ceremonies, and other special events, much to the chagrin of the commissioner's office, which had only meant the sanction to apply to paid baseball employment. As one Kuhn assistant said in exasperation, "They can go to any Old Timers Game they want. They're just using Kuhn as an excuse so they don't have to show up."[12]

In the long run, the ban had unexpected benefits for Mays. It forced him to consider his life outside of the game. Deprived of the annual routines of the baseball season and the daily demands of the baseball schedule, he had to learn to meet the expectations and needs of the business world. If it was somewhat humbling to have to do so at the age of 49, he found it freeing as well.[13]

Mays quickly saw that his image had not been deeply damaged by the casino flap. With his primary home still in the Bay Area, he had become a San Francisco icon, right alongside his childhood idol Joe DiMaggio. During his time away from baseball, Mays was in demand for all of the city's great events, such as the glittering formal dinner that President Ronald Reagan gave to honor Queen Elizabeth II's state visit to California in 1983.[14] He and Mae attended, along with DiMaggio and hundreds of San Francisco's leading lights.

Later that year, the Giants retired Mays' uniform number, 24, in a ceremony preceding a game against the Mets. This was one baseball event that Mays attended, ban or no ban. Leo Durocher was there too, as was Willie McCovey. Mays' was only the fifth uniform number the Giants had retired in their long history, after those of Carl Hubbell, Mel Ott, McCovey, and Juan Marichal. "San Francisco is number one in my heart," Mays told the Candlestick Park crowd.[15]

And of course, the ban had no effect on his ability to give out private baseball advice. Mays' godson, Barry Bonds, had continued to play ball in Little League and high school, and his talent was apparent—so much so that the Giants had chosen him in the second round of the amateur draft in 1982. But Mays and Bobby Bonds encouraged the teenager to go to college instead. With all the success stories he had seen up close in his ongoing Say Hey Foundation work, Mays was firmly convinced of the benefits of higher education. "I wish I had that opportunity to go to college and play ball," he said, "but in the south, you didn't have those options."[16] (Some cynical observers would later maintain that the real reason Bonds chose college was that the Giants $70,000 signing offer had been too low.[17]) The younger Bonds went to Arizona State.

The baseball world soon came to believe that the ban of two of the sport's most famous veterans had been a foolish move, but Kuhn felt he could not back down from the stand he had taken. The arrival of a new baseball commissioner opened the door for a change. Peter Ueberroth took Kuhn's job in March 1985, and one of his first actions as commissioner was the reinstatement of Mickey Mantle and Willie Mays. "They are two of the most beloved and admired athletes in the country today," Ueberroth said, "and they belong in baseball."[18]

Now out of the game for five years, Mays could choose to return to baseball on his own terms. He would no longer be bound by the plans of a paternalistic club owner. He knew that a full-time job on the field was not what he wanted. He also knew there was one thing he missed above all else: spring training. And now that the passage of time had eased his hard feelings over Stoneham's trade, Mays' sentiments turned him back toward San Francisco. In his first lengthy interview after the ban was lifted, Mays returned again and again to the notion of attending the Giants spring training camp. He had clearly been following the team's fortunes under their manager, Mays' old teammate Jim Davenport. "He's got kids on that team . . . who know how to play the game, but they don't know the *art* of the game," Mays explained. "What I really miss is spring training. Davvy would understand I'm not out there trying to get his job." He was almost plaintive as he noted, "You know, even though I'm busy, I've left March open every year just for this reason."[19]

Meanwhile, Mays had taken an apartment in Birmingham (one of four he kept in various cities), the first home he'd had in the area since he'd left it in 1950, in hopes of becoming involved in youth programs there. In August, he attended a "Back to Fairfield" celebration for his old hometown's 75th anniversary. Cap Brown, Mays' first sports hero, was there as a park was dedicated in Mays' honor.[20]

In 1986, Mays finally filled his March schedule with spring training workouts, as he'd been longing to do for years. The Giants had a new general manager, Al Rosen, and a new manager, Roger Craig. Both were former opponents of Mays'—Rosen with Cleveland, Craig with Brooklyn, L.A., and the Mets—and knew very well what his energy and enthusiasm could do for the team's young players. They invited Mays and Willie McCovey to come to Scottsdale, Arizona for the team's preseason work. "I want my players to have fun playing the game, the way those two did," Craig said.[21] Both attended, donning the Giants uniform once again and shouting advice and encouragement. The Giants new owner Bob Lurie quickly hired Mays as a "special assistant" to Rosen, so that he could make public appearances for the club.[22]

From a greater distance, Mays was watching another young ballplayer, too. Barry Bonds had been drafted by the Pirates after college, spent one year in the minor leagues, and in 1986 began his first season in the majors. With 36 stolen bases on the year, it looked like the young outfielder might develop both speed and power, as his father and godfather had before him.

The Giants went from last place in the western division in 1985 to third place in 1986, and in 1987 they were the division champs. Mays thought that his motivational work had helped, and he was one of the team's biggest boosters. "I know I got more excited watching the Giants' pennant race in 1987 than I did at any time while I was playing," he said.[23] They lost the league championship series to the Cardinals, though. For the first time since his own induction in 1979, Mays was among the 24 Hall-of-Famers who returned to Cooperstown for the 1987 ceremonies. He was there to honor Ray Dandridge, his Minneapolis Millers roommate. Dandridge had never made it to the major leagues, despite a .340 lifetime batting average, but his 15-year career as one of the Negro Leagues' greatest third basemen had won him entry to the Hall.

Two years later, with Mays cheering them on, the Giants made it to the 1989 World Series against their cross-bay rivals, the Oakland A's. Their contest was almost made irrelevant when the region was shaken by a deadly earthquake just before the start of Game 3. Mays and the rest of the crowd made it out of Candlestick Park safely, but the Series had to be delayed for more than a week as the Bay Area worked to pick up the pieces. When the Series resumed, the Giants were swept in two more games.

Leo Durocher's death in the fall of 1991 hit Mays hard. Mays not only attended the funeral, he gave a eulogy—a rare tribute from a man who had been too overcome with emotion to make it through his mother's or Aunt Sarah's funeral services. "I can't stress the feeling that I have for this man," Mays said. His voice broke as he tried, and failed, to hold back tears. "All I can say is I lost a dear father. All the things you heard about Leo, how evil he was . . . he never treated me any way but perfect."[24]

Across the country in Pittsburgh, Barry Bonds had been steadily improving his game. In 1990, his breakout year, he hit 33 home runs for a league-leading slugging average of .565 and drove in 114 runs. He was the league MVP that season and led the Pirates to the first of three successive eastern division championships, but each time they were defeated in the National League championship series. Frustrated, Bonds was looking to leave the Pirates as soon as he became a free agent after the 1992 season. Sentimentally, there was one place he wanted to be: San Francisco. He signed with the Giants in December.

"Growing up as a kid, my only dream was to play with my dad and Willie," Bonds remembered. "I said, 'I want to play in the same outfield.' And Willie said, 'I'll be in my grave by the time you get to the major leagues!'" Bonds' return to the Bay Area gave him a chance to play in the same Candlestick Park outfield where his father and Mays had taught him how to throw. When he took his position as the Giants left fielder, Bonds could look to his left and almost see Mays in center and his father in right field. "So I really do have that dream come true," he concluded.[25]

Sweeter still was the fact that Mays himself was often at Candlestick Park, too. He had signed a lifetime contract as a special assistant to the Giants new owner, Peter Magowan. Godfather and godson grew closer, now that they saw each other so frequently. Bonds earned another MVP in his first year with the Giants, when he led the National League in home runs; the next year he led the league in stolen bases. The comparisons to his speedy-yet-powerful father and godfather were unavoidable.

"That's the one thing I never want, comparisons," Mays would say. "Compare me to anybody else, fine. . . . But I don't want to hear comparisons with Barry, and I want him to understand that . . . I did my thing when I played, and now he's doing his thing."[26]

Joe DiMaggio's death in 1999 triggered a cascade of news stories on baseball history. The Yankee Clipper had been widely hailed as "America's greatest living baseball player" in the final years of his life; now, in poll after poll, fans had little hesitation in agreeing that the title belonged indisputably to Mays. As far as many baseball men were concerned, they were all a little late to the party. "You're assuming DiMaggio *was* the greatest living player," said Hall of Famer Bob Gibson, when asked if he agreed with the poll results.[27]

Later that year, Orlando Cepeda was inducted into the Baseball Hall of Fame. Mays attended the ceremony, as he would do for the next several years, and Cepeda saluted him in his speech. "I learned so much from him," Cepeda said.[28]

Only a few weeks later, on August 27, William Howard "Cat" Mays died at a hospital near his home in Redwood City, California. His health had been failing for some time, and he had been blinded by glaucoma.[29] Cat's son and his grandson Michael led the mourners at a memorial service a few days after his death. Michael, now 40, had gone through some difficult times of his own; in 1987, in the midst of a battle with Hodgkin's disease, he had been arrested on drug and gun-possession charges.[30] With his father's support, Michael was now healthy and working in film and stage production. He was also becoming involved in outreach programs in his home neighborhood of Harlem, New York, encouraging the city to invest in its parks and teaching a new generation of kids the old street games, like his father's favorite, stickball. Some of Michael's programs took place on the very streets where Willie Mays had hit his five-sewer balls almost fifty years before.[31]

More good-byes were to be said on September 30, when the Giants played their final game in much-maligned Candlestick Park. They would play the 2000 season in a brand-new ballpark, but not before a ceremonious farewell witnessed by 62,000 in brilliant, windless 82-degree weather. Four former Giants managers—Bill Rigney, Charlie Fox, Herman Franks, and Roger Craig—joined the team's current skipper, Dusty Baker, in the pregame line-up card exchange. After the game (which was, of course, with the Dodgers; the visitors won it), dozens of former Giants were introduced as, one by one, they jogged out to their old field positions. Last of all was Willie Mays, who walked past the assembled center fielders and headed to the mound. Mays threw the final pitch of Candlestick Park's baseball history to his godson, Barry Bonds, in an actual and symbolic intergenerational exchange. Finally, Mays led all the ballplayers in one last circuit of the stadium.[32]

In the spring of 2000, when the Giants inaugurated their new field, Pacific Bell Park, reminders of their great star were everywhere. The stadium's official address was 24 Willie Mays Plaza. Most fans entered it through the Willie Mays Gate. Inside, they might dine at the "24" Restaurant, or grab a Say Hey Sausage from a vendor. Topping it all was a larger-than-life bronze statue near the main entrance. It was a representation of Mays in his prime, following through on a home-run swing. Mays was there for the unveiling on March 30, as were Franks and Fox, Bobby Thomson, and Barry Bonds, who called the new ballpark "the house they built for Willie."[33]

But in 2000, the house belonged to Barry, who at the age of 35 was on the brink of a remarkable run of five career-defining seasons. Up to that point he had hit 445 home runs over 14 seasons of play. In 2000 he set a personal home-run record with 49, and in 2001 he set a new all-time record with an incredible 73 homers. The unprecedented late-career explosion of 258 home runs in five years raised suspicions that Bonds had taken illegal performance-enhancing drugs, such as steroids. Bonds vehemently denied this.

Mays, as he so often had done in controversial situations, was publicly silent on the rumors. Instead, in 2001 he credited Bonds' achievements to an unexpected source: suits. "He's the type of kid who needs motivation, and I know what motivates him," Mays said—competition. Mays bought 12 suits, one for each of his Giants batting records, and he gave his godson one suit for every record he seized. Bonds got one on August 16, 2001 when he hit his 53rd home run of the season, breaking May's 1965 record. But, as Mays pointed out, "One year I got 20 triples; he's got to get that. I got 3,187 hits [as a Giant]; he's got to get that. . . . So, I'll put the suits in the closet and tell him, 'The next time you do something, you come pick one up.' "[34]

In 2002, the United States Congress honored the Negro Leaguers in a Washington, DC ceremony, and Mays was a featured speaker. Piper Davis and Ray Dandridge were not there; they, like many others who played segregated ball, had already died by the time the nation got around to saluting them. Of those who had survived, more than 80 attended the celebration, including Buck O'Neil and "Double Duty" Radcliffe. Mays' speech paid tribute to the men who had taught him how to be a pro, and who had believed in his chances to go beyond the Negro Leagues. "I was 16 years old, 17, 18," he remembered. "My friends made me a great ballplayer. They said, 'We're too old. We can't make it. You can make it.' I've never forgotten that. They may think I did, but I didn't." Tears streamed down Mays' face as he closed: "This is why I'm here. So guys, thank you. Thank you very much."[35]

Bonds was having another outstanding season, during which he would rack up 46 home runs, win another MVP award, and at last lead his team to the World Series. Mays was with the club for every game, making a point of wearing his 1954 World Series ring so it could inspire his godson. He told reporters that he planned to leave the ring to Bonds in his will, though he fully expected him to win one of his own soon.[36] The Giants lost the Series to the Anaheim Angels in seven games, however.

Bobby Bonds had been diagnosed with lung cancer midway through the 2002 season. In 2003, his condition worsening, he was able to see his son play one last time three days before his death on August 23. Mays supported the family in their grief, but encouraged Barry to return to baseball sooner rather than later. "I want him to get back on the field. He needs that," Mays said. "We know how sad he is. He needs to get back on the field and take it out on baseball."[37]

Bonds did get back on the field. The 45 home runs he hit that season brought him within three of Mays' mark on the lifetime list.

Mays traveled with the team as the 2004 season opened and Bonds chased his 660th career home run to join Mays at third on the all-time leader list. Mays took a diamond-studded torch along, the same one he had used to carry the Olympic flame through San Francisco's streets in 1996, intending to pass it to his godson after he reached the milestone. But in every game on the six-day road trip, Bonds fell short. He was, he admitted, struggling with the notion of surpassing his childhood idol. "I love him so much," Bonds said. "It's a hard subject to talk about."[38]

Mays didn't seem to mind the delay. He was relaxed and at ease, perhaps more than at any other time since his retirement two decades before. He passed the time playing cards with the sportswriters and generating quotable quips. A favorite of the traveling entourage came when a reporter asked what Mays thought he would earn if he were playing today. "Oh, about $45,000," was the answer. Willie, came the astonished reaction, why so little? "Well, I'm 72 years old!" he said.[39]

Finally, in the fifth inning of the Giants home opener, Bonds did it, sending a fastball over the wall and into San Francisco Bay. Mays presented the torch to him as he crossed home plate, genuinely glad that third place on the lifetime homer list was staying within the Giants family. Despite a record number of intentional walks, Bonds hit 45 home runs during the 2004 season. He hit his 700th at Pac Bell Park on September 17.

After season's end, the steroids controversy intensified when grand jury testimony of Bonds and other players was leaked to the press. They had been subpoenaed in late 2003 in an investigation of BALCO, a company accused of distributing illegal steroids to athletes. According to the report, Bonds had testified that he had once, and unknowingly, taken steroids.

Mays' reaction was continued support of his godson. "It seems like it doesn't want to go away," Mays said of the scandal. He would not accept the suggestion that the steroid revelation diminished Bonds' career achievements even as Bonds sat out the beginning of the 2005 season.[40]

Mays preferred instead to focus on 2004's other events, like his return visit to Hagerstown, Maryland, in August. The town that had given him such a harsh introduction to the minor leagues was now embarrassed about its racist past. Its mayor invited Mays to come back, 54 years later, so that the town could apologize and demonstrate that Hagerstown had become "a compassionate community that promoted racial unity."[41]

Hundreds of applauding locals crowded into a hotel ballroom to greet Mays on his return. "There is no excuse for what happened to you here," the mayor declared, and he renamed a major thoroughfare Willie Mays Way. The town's minor-league ballclub, now a Giants affiliate, retired uniform number 24.

The room hushed when Mays got up to speak. He dabbed at his eyes with a handkerchief. "This is just a wonderful, wonderful feeling," he said. "To come here again and for people to greet me with hugs. . . . What happened here so long ago was a sad moment, but I can say now that I am proud to be back."[42]

The people of Hagerstown, black and white, rose to their feet and cheered him out into the night.

NOTES

1. Mays, with Sahadi, *Say Hey*, 272.
2. Ibid.
3. Einstein, *Willie's Time*, 73–74, 349.
4. Mays, with Sahadi, *Say Hey*, 273.
5. Ibid., 279–280.
6. Larry Stewart, "Say, Hey, He's Coaching Children's Baseball," *Los Angeles Times*, July 30, 1990; Willie Mays, with Maxine Berger, *Willie Mays, Play Ball!* (New York: Simon and Schuster, 1980).
7. Einstein, *Willie's Time*, 346.
8. Ibid., 347.
9. Ibid., 346.
10. Mays, with Sahadi, *Say Hey*, 274.
11. Ibid., 276.
12. Einstein, *Willie's Time*, 4.
13. Mays, with Sahadi, *Say Hey*, 275–277.
14. Donnie Radcliffe, "Reigning on Her Parade; The Reagan's Glittering Dinner After the Queen's Day on the Town," *Washington Post*, March 4, 1983.
15. United Press International, August 20, 1983.
16. John Shea, "Passing the HR Torch," *San Francisco Chronicle*, September 27, 2003.
17. Richard Hoffer, "The Importance of Being Barry," *Sports Illustrated*, May 24, 1993.
18. Ron Fimrite, "Mantle and Mays," *Sports Illustrated*, March 25, 1985.
19. Ibid.
20. Associated Press, August 13, 1985.

21. *Sports Illustrated*, April 14, 1986.

22. United Press International, February 12, 1986.

23. Mays, with Sahadi, *Say Hey*, 288.

24. Associated Press, October 11, 1991.

25. "Major League Baseball: Generations of Heroes," video, Major League Baseball Productions, 1999.

26. John Shea, "Passing the HR Torch," *San Francisco Chronicle*, September 27, 2003.

27. Mark Emmons, "In These Days of Bloated Stats, Mays' Greatness Still Stands Out," *San Jose Mercury News*, September 18, 2003.

28. "Induction Speeches: Orlando Cepeda," Baseball Hall of Fame Web site, http://www.baseballhalloffame.org/hof_weekend/1999/speeches/cepeda_orlando.htm.

29. "Willie Mays Sr.," *San Francisco Chronicle*, September 1, 1999.

30. Associated Press, August 13, 1987.

31. Yusef Salaam, "Parks 2001 Campaign," *New York Amsterdam News*, September 19, 2001; Bill Gallo, "A Week for the Ages at Ballparks," *New York Daily News*, September 2, 2001.

32. Mark Purdy, "Despite Its Faults, Candlestick Park Still Produced Its Share of Electricity," *San Jose Mercury News*, October 1, 1999.

33. *New York Times*, April 1, 2000.

34. Stephen Canella, "Suiting Up for the Giants," *Sports Illustrated*, September 3, 2001.

35. Dave Sheinin, "Repaying a National Debt; Negro Leaguers' Trail-Blazing Achievements Are Recognized," *Washington Post*, September 19, 2002; "Mays, Congress Fete Negro Leaguers," *Miami Herald*, September 19, 2002.

36. Gwen Knapp, "'Say Hey!' Has the Ring of Truth for Bonds," *San Francisco Chronicle*, October 21, 2002.

37. John Shea, "Mays Provides Support to Godson," *San Francisco Chronicle*, August 24, 2003.

38. William C. Rhoden, "Chasing History and His Godfather, All at Once," *New York Times*, April 10, 2004.

39. Phil Taylor, "A Shot to the Heart," *Sports Illustrated*, April 19, 2004.

40. Ron Kroichick, "Players Support Move Toward Stronger Drug-Testing Policy," *San Francisco Chronicle*, December 8, 2004.

41. Mark Kram, "Mays Enjoys Sunset Serenade," *Philadelphia Daily News*, August 10, 2004.

42. Ibid.

THE LEGEND OF WILLIE MAYS

"There have been only two geniuses in the world. Willie Mays and Willie Shake-speare," actress Tallulah Bankhead said in 1962. "But, darling, I think you'd better put Shakespeare first."[1]

In 1998, when *The Sporting News* ranked baseball's 100 greatest all-time players, Willie Mays came in second. He was behind the immortal Babe Ruth, who had done one thing in his major-league career that even Mays had not—he was an excellent pitcher before it became obvious that his powerful bat should be in the line-up more often than once every four days. Apart from that, Mays' all-around skills were simply awesome. "Sometimes," he said, "the things I did amazed even me."[2]

Mays hit for average, and he also hit for power. He hit home runs to left field, right field, and center. He led the National League in homers four times. He won the batting crown once and led the league in slugging five times. His line drives could tear the glove off a fielder's hand. His histrionics at the plate could fool a pitcher into serving up a ball that Mays could drive out of the park. His knowledge of field conditions and opposing hurlers allowed him to call shots hours in advance.

Mays ran. He led the league in stolen bases four years in a row—the first man to be a league-leading slugger *and* a league-leading runner. He'd beat out a chopper for a single, or go from first to third on a single to left, or race home from third on a wild pitch. He was unstoppable when a game was on the line.

Mays threw. Writers likened his arm to a howitzer. He threw from the deepest reaches of the ballpark to just the right spot in the infield with uncanny accuracy. Teammates would say that his throws came in humming, like a pitcher's off the mound—but from 400 feet away.

Mays fielded. His most celebrated moment, in a lifetime of celebrated moments, came in the Polo Grounds' center field, when an over-the-shoulder catch saved a World Series game, but he never thought much of that play. How about the times he was knocked out by an impact with the outfield wall, but held on to the ball for an out? Or when he caught flyballs barehanded? Or when he plucked a pop-up from the air above a teammate's head so neatly that no one in the ballpark knew where it had gone? The impossible became routine with Mays in the field.

These are the five tools baseball scouts look for and ballclubs love to tout. Mays had them all, and he used them to become perhaps the most complete ballplayer the game has ever seen. He holds a range of records across the spectrum of baseball skills: most extra-inning home runs (22); most consecutive years playing 150 games or more (13); most consecutive years of 300 or more total bases (13); most consecutive years with over 100 RBIs (8); most Gold Gloves of any outfielder (12); most lifetime put-outs for an outfielder (7,095); most All-Star Game at-bats (75); most All-Star hits (23) and runs scored (20). (As Ted Williams is said to have observed, they invented the All-Star Game for Mays.) He reached the 100 home run mark in his second full season of play—one of the quickest such rises in baseball history. He is the only man to hit at least one home run in every inning up to and including the sixteenth. He is one of only two players to be a member of the so-called 500 home run club, the 3,000 hit club, and the 30-30 club.

But as he always said, winning, not stats, drove him. The Giants and the Mets were both involved in exciting pennant races in almost every season Mays played. Yet he made it to the World Series only four times in his 22 seasons, and in the end he had a single championship ring on his hand. Forty years later, he was still waiting for his beloved Giants to win it all again.

Championships or no, Mays himself may have been baseball's greatest box-office draw ever. In the mid-1960s, Mays and a writer friend attempted to calculate his value to the Giants—his monetary value, that is. Thee years after their last pennant win and a decade after the franchise last won the World Series, the San Francisco Giants were the league's top draw on the road. In 1963, for example, they attracted close to 1.7 million fans to ballparks when they were the visiting team. The next club on the list of road-game attendance that year, the St. Louis Cardinals, drew about 350,000 fewer fans to their away games. Figuring an average $2.50 ticket price and a per-fan average of $1 spent at the concession stands, Mays calculated that the Giants earned more than $1.2 million each year just for being the Giants.[3]

Or really, just for being Willie Mays' Giants. With his crowd-pleasing theatrics at the plate and in the field, it was Mays who the fans were coming to see. Whether or not they were contending, for 14 straight years, from 1958 through 1971, the Giants led the National League—and often both major leagues—in attendance on the road. Then, in 1972 and 1973, the New York Mets took the lead in road attendance. In those two years, Willie Mays played in the Mets orange and blue. In the business of baseball, those stats alone would put Mays in the Hall of Fame.

The numbers are silent on the question of affection, but most fans agree that Mays had to be among the game's most beloved figures. One of the few things that Presidents Bill Clinton and George W. Bush have in common is their favorite ballplayer. Bush, a onetime owner of the Texas Rangers, idolized Mays from the first time he saw him at the Polo Grounds as a kid "because of his speed, his power. He was such a charismatic ballplayer."[4] Clinton has attended fundraisers for Mays' Say Hey Foundation and cites his Mays-signed baseballs as some of his most treasured presidential souvenirs.

Major league pitchers, of course, did not love Mays quite so much. Warren Spahn, who was on the mound for Mays' first home run in 1951 and in the dugout to witness Number 500, was only partly joking when he lamented of that first homer, "I'll never forgive myself. We might have gotten rid of Willie forever if I'd only struck him out."[5]

Mays also had a prickly relationship with many of the sportswriters who covered the Giants, although in his day such things were rarely discussed in print. He was never a source of pithy post-game quotes, and he grew more suspicious of the press as time went by. "You saw it—you say it!" he'd often tell reporters after a game. A few writers gained his trust, Charles Einstein chief among them. Einstein wrote two memoirs with Mays and a separate brief biography during the ballplayer's career. Later, Einstein's overview of the man and his era, *Willie's Time*, was a Pulitzer Prize and National Book Award finalist. Much information in this book was gleaned from Einstein's work, as well as from Mays' post-career autobiography, *Say Hey*, written with Lou Sahadi. Contemporary sources, such as newspapers and magazines, confirmed these accounts.

"I don't speak out," Mays was still saying late in his life, when an interviewer pressed him for yet more words. "I don't do things for the notoriety . . . I played my 22 years, and I'm proud of it."[6] He left his legacy there, out on the field.

NOTES

1. "Baseball Almanac" Web site, http://baseball-almanac.com/quotes/quomays.shtml.
2. Glenn Dickey, "Baseball's Living Legend," *The Sporting News*, October 26, 1998.

3. Mays, as told to Einstein, *Willie Mays*, 79–80.

4. Don Yaeger, "Q&A: George Bush," *Sports Illustrated*, September 29, 2003.

5. John Shea, "Warren Spahn 1921–2003," San Francisco Chronicle, November 25, 2003.

6. Joan Walsh, "Willie Mays," Salon.com, July 13, 1999.

APPENDIX: WILLIE MAYS CAREER AND POSTSEASON STATISTICS

CAREER STATISTICS

Year	Club	League	G	AB	R	H	2B	3B	HR	RBI	BA	PO	A	E	FA
1951	N.Y. Giants	National	121	464	59	127	22	5	20	68	.274	353	12	9	.976
1952	N.Y. Giants	National	34	127	17	30	2	4	4	23	.236	109	6	1	.991
1953	In Military Service														
1954	N.Y. Giants	National	151	565	119	195	33	13	41	110	.345	448	139	7	.985
1955	N.Y. Giants	National	152	580	123	185	18	13	51	127	.319	407	23	8	.982
1956	N.Y. Giants	National	152	578	101	171	27	8	36	84	.296	415	14	9	.979
1957	N.Y. Giants	National	152	585	112	195	26	20	35	97	.333	422	14	9	.980
1958	S.F. Giants	National	152	600	121	208	33	11	29	96	.347	429	17	9	.980
1959	S.F. Giants	National	151	575	125	180	43	5	34	104	.313	353	6	6	.984
1960	S.F. Giants	National	153	595	107	190	29	12	29	103	.319	392	12	8	.981
1961	S.F. Giants	National	154	572	129	176	32	3	40	123	.308	385	7	8	.980
1962	S.F. Giants	National	162	621	130	189	36	5	49	141	.304	429	6	4	.991
1963	S.F. Giants	National	157	596	115	187	32	7	38	103	.314	397	7	8	.981
1964	S.F. Giants	National	157	578	121	171	21	9	47	111	.296	376	12	6	.984
1965	S.F. Giants	National	157	558	118	177	21	3	52	112	.317	337	13	6	.983
1966	S.F. Giants	National	152	552	99	159	29	4	37	103	.288	370	8	7	.982
1967	S.F. Giants	National	141	486	83	128	22	2	22	70	.263	277	3	7	.976
1968	S.F. Giants	National	148	498	84	144	20	5	23	79	.289	310	7	7	.978
1969	S.F. Giants	National	117	403	64	114	17	3	13	58	.283	205	4	5	.976
1970	S.F. Giants	National	139	478	94	139	15	2	28	83	.291	303	9	7	.975
1971	S.F. Giants	National	136	417	82	113	24	5	18	61	.271	576	29	17	.972
1972	S.F. Giants	National	19	49	8	9	2	0	0	3	.184	29	0	0	1.000
	N.Y. Mets	National	69	195	27	52	9	1	8	19	.267	184	5	4	.981
1972	Totals		88	244	35	61	11	1	8	22	.250	213	5	4	.990
1973	N.Y. Mets	National	66	209	24	44	10	0	6	25	.211	246	6	4	.965
Major League Totals		22 years	2992	10,881	2062	3283	523	140	660	1903	.302	7752	233	156	.981

POST-SEASON RECORD

Year	Round	Club	G	AB	R	H	2B	3B	HR	RBI	BA
1951	World Series	N.Y. Giants	6	22	1	4	0	0	0	1	.182
1954	World Series	N.Y. Giants	4	14	4	4	1	0	0	3	.286
1962	World Series	S.F. Giants	7	28	3	7	2	0	0	1	.250
1971	NLCS	S.F. Giants	4	15	2	4	2	0	1	3	.267
1973	NLCS	N.Y. Mets	1	3	1	1	0	0	0	1	.333
	World Series	N.Y. Mets	3	7	1	2	0	0	0	1	.286
Totals			25	89	12	22	5	0	1	10	.247

A = assists; AB = at-bats; BA = batting average; E = errors; FA = fielding average; G = games; H = hits; HR = home runs; PO = put-outs; R = runs; RBI = runs batted in; 2B = doubles; 3B-triples

AWARDS AND RECORDS

1951 NL Rookie of the Year
1954 NL MVP; NL Highest Batting Average .345
1965 NL MVP

SELECTED BIBLIOGRAPHY

MEMOIRS AND BIOGRAPHIES OF WILLIE MAYS

Einstein, Charles. *Willie Mays: Coast to Coast Giant.* New York: Putnam, 1963.

Einstein, Charles. *Willie's Time: Baseball's Golden Age.* With a new preface by the author. Carbondale: Southern Illinois University Press, 2004 (originally published 1979).

Mays, Willie, as told to Charles Einstein. *Willie Mays: My Life In and Out of Baseball.* New York: E.P. Dutton and Co., 1966.

Mays, Willie, with Lou Sahadi. *Say Hey: The Autobiography of Willie Mays.* New York: Simon and Schuster, 1988.

OTHER BOOKS OF INTEREST

Dorinson, Joseph, and Joram Warmund, eds. *Jackie Robinson: Race, Sports, and the American Dream.* Armonk, NY: M.E. Sharpe, 1998.

Durocher, Leo, with Ed Linn. *Nice Guys Finish Last.* New York: Simon and Schuster, 1975.

Getz, Mike. *Brooklyn Dodgers and Their Rivals, 1950–1952.* Brooklyn, NY: Montauk Press, 1999.

Hano, Arnold. *A Day In the Bleachers.* Cambridge, MA: Da Capo, 1995 (originally published 1955).

Honig, Donald. *Mays, Mantle, Snider: A Celebration.* New York: Macmillan, 1987.

Kelley, Brent. *"I Will Never Forget": Interviews with 39 Former Negro League Players.* Jefferson, NC: McFarland and Company, 2003.

Mays, Willie, with Maxine Berger. *Willie Mays, Play Ball!* New York: Simon and Schuster, 1980.

Ribowsky, Mark. *A Complete History of the Negro Leagues.* New York: Birch Lane Press, 1995.

Riley, James A. *The Negro Leagues.* New York: Chelsea House, 1997.

ARTICLES

Brown, Joe David. "The Onliest Way I Know." *Sports Illustrated*, April 13, 1959.

Cannon, Jimmy. "If Only Mays Knew How Great He Really Is. . . ." *New York Post*, June 27, 1958.

Dickey, Glenn. "Baseball's Living Legend." *The Sporting News*, October 26, 1998.

Fimrite, Ron. "Mantle and Mays." *Sports Illustrated*, March 25, 1985.

Kahn, Roger. "For the Record." *Los Angeles Times*, October 25, 2002.

Mann, Jack. "They Love Herman and Willie." *Sports Illustrated*, September 27, 1965.

Millstein, Gilbert. " 'Natural Boy' of the Giants." *New York Times Magazine*, July 11, 1954.

WEB SITES

Academy of Achievement, Interview: "Willie Mays": www.achievement.org/autodoc/page/may0int-1.

Brilliant Careers: "Willie Mays," by Joan Walsh: www.salon.com/people/bc/1999/07/13/mays/.

"San Francisco Giants History": http://sanfrancisco.giants.mlb.com/NASApp/mlb/sf/history/index.jsp.

Western Neighborhoods Project: "Willie Mays on Miraloma Drive," by Steve W. LaBounty: www.outsidelands.org/sw5.html.

NEWSPAPERS AND MAGAZINES CONSULTED

American Heritage
Associated Press
Baseball Digest
Birmingham World
Los Angeles Times
Miami Herald
New York Amsterdam News
New York Daily News
New York Post

Selected Bibliography

New York Times
New York Times Magazine
Philadelphia Daily News
Pittsburgh Post-Gazette
San Francisco Chronicle
San Jose Mercury News
Scripps-Howard News Service
Sports Illustrated
St. Louis Post-Dispatch
Staten Island Advance
The Sporting News
Washington Post

INDEX

Index

192

About the Author

MARY KAY LINGE is a freelance writer and editor who specializes in popular reference and nonfiction. This is her first biographical work. She lives in Staten Island, New York and is a longtime baseball fan.

DATE DUE			